Spreadsheets for Agriculture

David Noble and Charles Course

Longman
Scientific &
Technical

Longman Scientific & Technical,
Longman Group UK Limited,
Longman House, Burnt Mill, Harlow,
Essex, CM20 2JE, England
and Associated Companies throughout the world.

Copublished in the United States with
John Wiley & Sons, Inc., 605 Third Avenue, New York, NY 10158

© Longman Group UK Limited 1993

First published 1993

ISBN 0 582 05389 7

British Library Cataloguing in Publication Data
A CIP record for this book is available from the British Library

Library of Congress Cataloging-in-Publication Data
A CIP record for this book is available from the Library of Congress

Printed in Malaysia

Contents

Ioan Ap Dewi, Lecturer in Animal Production, School of Agricultural and Forest Sciences, University College of North Wales, Bangor, Gwynedd.

Graham Bunn, Jonathan Bunn, Farmers, Salhouse, Norwich, Norfolk.

Nigel Chapman, Computer Officer, Department of Economics and Agricultural Economics, University College of Wales, Aberystwyth, Dyfed.

Charles Course, Farm Management Consultant, Bidwells, Trumpington Rd, Cambridge.

Dylan Gorvy, Graduate, Department of Agriculture, University of Edinburgh.

Tim Hess, Lecturer in Agricultural Water Management, Silsoe College, Cranfield Institute of Technology, Beds.

Ian Howie, Agricultural Consultant, Wormbridge, Hereford

Nicolas Lampkin, Lecturer in Agricultural Economics, Department of Economics and Agricultural Economics, University College of Wales, Aberystwyth, Dyfed.

Andrew Landers, Senior Lecturer in Agricultural Mechanization, Royal Agricultural College, Cirencester, Glos.

Joe Morris, Reader in Rural Resource Economics, Silsoe College, Cranfield Institute of Technology, Beds.

David Noble, Senior Lecturer in Operations Research, Department of Mathematics, Swinburne University of Technology, Hawthorn, Victoria, Australia.

William Stephens, Lecturer in Irrigation Agronomy, Silsoe College, Cranfield Institute of Technology, Beds.

Alistair Stott, Lecturer, Department of Agriculture, University of Edinburgh.

Roy Sutherland, Senior Agricultural Economist, Scottish Agriculture College, Aberdeen.

Nigel Williams, Senior Lecturer in Agricultural Economics and Management, Department of Agricultural Economics, Wye College, University of London, Kent.

INTRODUCTION

Aims and objectives

This book is primarily aimed at anyone who has access to a PC in the rural sector. The book is a compilation of pre-prepared spreadsheets for a wide range of applications. The majority of people who use PCs and spreadsheets in their work are busy and appreciate the benefits of getting the widest possible use out of their machines. However, there is usually a trade-off between the time that will be saved by automating any particular set of calculations and the time that must be invested in developing the routines to do so. For an activity which is regularly repeated it is often worth devoting the time to develop a blank spreadsheet overlay which can be frequently reused. Invariably, when such spreadsheets are developed, significant amounts of time are spent developing the spreadsheet and subsequently refining it. During this time the user limits the amount of time he is able to devote to actually obtaining answers from the spreadsheet.

It became apparent during recent years that many spreadsheet users were regularly developing spreadsheets for the same or very similar applications. It did not appear particularly efficient for ten different users to each devote significant amounts of time to developing wheels in parallel; some of which would turn very slowly, others which would not turn at all. The worst situation arose where spreadsheets were developed which worked successfully for a period of time, after which major flaws or errors were identified.

Consequently, it was felt that there was significant scope to save many people a lot of time as well as improve their efficiency by bringing together a collection of the best spreadsheets which have been developed and used in the Rural Sector. This would have the further benefit of enabling a much wider number of people to use the spreadsheets, for many applications, without having to invest the time in their development.

It is our belief, that it is not necessary for someone wishing for instance to schedule irrigation applications to a crop to fully understand the physics and arithmetic relationships necessary in making such calculations. Previously if a farmer had wished to develop a spreadsheet to assist him with scheduling his irrigation, he would have needed a thorough understanding of some quite complicated and confusing relationships. By referring to the appropriate spreadsheet in this book, it is now possible for farmers who normally use their PCs for other purposes, to, for example, schedule their irrigation as well.

How to use the book

The aim of this book is to enable anyone with a PC and spreadsheet programme to use their spreadsheet very quickly for specific applications, without having to devote large amounts of time to developing spreadsheets that they are confident are correct. The book has been so prepared that anyone can take a specific application spreadsheet from the book and set it up on their own PC. The spreadsheets are all written in such a way that they can be continuously re-used. It is therefore suggested that whenever a spreadsheet from the book is set up for the first time, a blank version with no data is saved on a separate disk file for future use.

Users may wish to modify and amend the spreadsheets as presented; in these instances it is suggested that the spreadsheet is first set up as per the book, and is used with a set of trial data. This will enable a correct set of output to be generated, which can be subsequently used to test updated or modified spreadsheets.

Spreadsheet software

Throughout the book the aim has been to make the spreadsheets as universal as possible. Consequently, certain features which are specific to individual spreadsheet programmes have been avoided wherever possible. However a choice had to be made from a number of speadsheet software packages as to which to use for this book. The one chosen by the authors to illustrate the spreadsheets is Supercalc4 v1.1, primarily because of its ability to print out the cell formulas in tabular form along with the spreadsheet borders, ie. the column letters and row numbers. Most of these formulas will be immediately understandable to users of other spreadsheet software since the vast majority of software uses similar syntax. However, one or two Supercalc4 functions may need to be explained. The principal differences in syntax between Supercalc4 and Lotus123 are explained at the end of this introduction.

A number of the spreadsheets have been developed further by their authors with the use of macros to ease operation. As these macros are software specific they have not been included in this book. Should readers wish to consider the use of a specific spreadsheet with its macros, they should contact the individual authors.

Alternatively this book can be used as a means of selecting a spreadsheet for a specific application which can then be purchased rather than set up by the individual user. Any readers interested in purchasing copies of specific spreadsheets as a ready to use disk file, should contact the individual spreadsheet authors.

Spreadsheet authors

The spreadsheets in this book have been prepared by a number of authors. Many have been extensively edited and improved by the editors in an attempt to encourage "good practice" amongst those who read this book and subsequently attempt to write their own spreadsheets. One feature which the editors have encouraged throughout is good spreadsheet layout, in order to ease understanding and use. In particular, wherever possible, all data input has been concentrated in one section of the spreadsheet, usually in the opening screen. Another feature which the editors have encouraged is efficient use of formulas in order to reduce formula complexity and computation time. The editors have tried, wherever possible, to verify the technical aspects of all the spreadsheets included in the book, but no liability whatsoever can be accepted by the authors or the editors for losses resulting from the use of the spreadsheets.

Format and layout of the book

The book is a collection of individual spreadsheets. Each specific spreadsheet is effectively a single chapter of the book. Most chapters of the book follow a similar format. They all begin with details of the authors and purpose of the spreadsheet. This is followed by an explanation regarding the use of the spreadsheet, and then by a detailed explanation of the formulas and layout used within the spreadsheet.

Each chapter then contains a print-out of an example of the use of the spreadsheet followed, where appropriate, by a print-out of the formulas used to perform the calculations. There are two exceptions to this (Spreadsheets 3 and 24). Both these chapters describe larger spreadsheets than most of the rest of the book. Consequently in Spreadsheet 3, the rapid whole farm budget, only the main calculations are described in detail, and in Spreadsheet 24, the suckler herd embryo model, only the structure of the spreadsheet is described.

This layout should enable readers to quickly and easily select a spreadsheet suitable for their needs, to understand how the spreadsheet is used and to then set up the spreadsheet on their own computer. Wherever possible realistic examples have been used to assist in understanding the spreadsheets.

SUPERCALC4 vs LOTUS 123

Most of the formulas used by Supercalc4 v1.1 will be immediately understandable to users of other spreadsheet software. What follows is an explanation of those features which are different to Lotus 123 v2.0.

Cell references

In Lotus, if the formula being used starts with the reference to a value in another cell then a numerical symbol such as + or - must precede the cell reference,

eg. B3 = + B1 * B2

In Supercalc4, the initial + sign is not necessary, so the formula becomes

B3 = B1 * B2

Functions

In Lotus 123, all functions are preceded by @. In Supercalc4, this is not necessary.

Ranges

The standard symbol used to denote a range in Supercalc4 is the colon (:). Thus, for instance, in Spreadsheet 13.2.2 the range of cells from B21 to B39 is denoted by B21:B39.

In Lotus 123 this is denoted by B21..C39.

Textual values

It is often necessary to examine the contents of a cell which contains text (as opposed to some numerical value) and depending on what the text is to do one thing or another. An example of this is in Spreadsheet 13.2.3 where the cell entry at F46 is

IF(B46=("DELETE"), 0, G8)

This means that, if the text DELETE appears in cell B46, then 0 is displayed in cell F46, otherwise the value displayed in F46 will be the value currently displayed in G8.

In Supercalc4 ("DELETE") is known as a textual value, ie. the text is first of all enclosed in "......" and then in brackets, (......).

In Lotus 123 the corresponding formula would be

@IF(B46="DELETE", 0, G8)

ie. there is no need to enclose the text in brackets.

Supercalc4 also has the limitation that textual values cannot contain more than 9 characters. This is a limitation that Lotus 123 does not have and means that more than 1 column will need to be used if the amount of text to be displayed exceeds 9 characters (eg. in Spreadsheet 16).

Testing for multiple conditions (AND, OR and NOT)

It is possible in most spreadsheet software to test to see if more than one condition at a time is true by using the logical operators AND, OR and NOT within the IF function.

Thus in Spreadsheet 13.3.1 the formula at cell B46 is

IF(AND(H8>0,H8<B3), ("DELETE"), ("OK")).

This has the effect that if the value of cell H8 is both greater than zero and less than the value of cell B3, then the word DELETE appears in cell B46, otherwise the word OK appears.

The Lotus 123 form of this formula would be

@IF(H8>0#AND#H8<B3, "DELETE", "OK").

Similar transformations have to be performed to convert Supercalc4 logical operators OR and NOT into Lotus 123 #OR# and #NOT#.

The DATE function

The DATE function in Supercalc4 works in exactly the same way as that in Lotus 123. The only difference is that the order of the arguments is different. The Supercalc4 DATE function requires the arguments to be in the order (month,day,year) whereas in Lotus 123 the order is (year,month,day).

Thus in Spreadsheet 20.5.2 the formula at cell B28 is

DATE(B5, B4, B6) -DATE (12, 31, B6 - 1)

This has the effect of calculating the day number (in the B6th year) of the B4th day of the B5th month.

The corresponding function in Lotus 123 would be

@DATE(B6, B5, B4) - @DATE(B6 - 1, 12, 31)

Summary

	Supercalc4	Lotus 123
Cell references	No initial + sign required	Initial + sign required
Functions	No initial @ sign required	Initial @ sign required
Ranges	Denoted by a colon (:) eg. B21:B39	Denoted by two dots (..) eg. B21..B39
Textual values	Require enclosing in both double quotes and brackets eg. ("DELETE")	Require enclosing in quotes eg. "DELETE"
Testing for multiple conditions	AND, OR and NOT operators eg. AND(H8>0,H8<B3)	#AND#, #OR# and #NOT# operators eg. H8>0 #AND# H8<B3
DATE function	DATE(month,day,year)	@DATE(year,month,day)

Yield-price calculator for cropping enterprises

Purpose: To calculate either the crop yield or the output price required to maintain a specified profit margin, and to produce a table of the results for a range of production costs and at various levels of either output prices or yields.

Author: Ioan Ap Dewi

Spreadsheet Name: CROP-Y

1.1 Possible uses

The spreadsheet has two broad areas of application:-

(a) Assessing the effects on enterprise profitability of changes in input cost, output price and crop yield. The spreadsheet can simulate changes over specified ranges of grain prices or yields. For example, the effect of changes in product price or yields required to maintain a profit margin can be examined. Conversely, the effect of product price required to maintain margins at given levels of yield and production cost can be investigated.

(b) Assessing the viability of new enterprises. Specific data on farm fixed costs and the required profit margin can be entered. The yields required to meet these specifications can then be calculated for a range of likely product prices and variable costs. Conversely, the required grain/seed price could be calculated and compared with likely values.

1.2 Application

An example table of results is given in rows 21 to 37 of Fig 1.1. The fixed costs are specified by the user as are the range of variable costs considered in the table. The desired margin over production costs is entered or can be set to zero to calculate break-even yields or output prices. If yields are to be calculated, the user specifies the range of output prices to be considered in the table and vice-versa.

Data can be entered in either Imperial or Metric units. The spreadsheet will alter its prompts accordingly.

1.3 Input data

The input data required by the spreadsheet are listed below:-

D4   0 or 1 to select Imperial or Metric units

D5   0 or 1 to specify that either prices or yields are to be calculated in the results table.

D8   Desired margin over total production costs. Zero can be entered to calculate break-even values of prices or yields.

D10   Fixed costs.

D13   Minimum variable costs required - this specifies the lowest value of variable costs used in the output table.

D14   Maximum variable costs required - this specifies the highest value of variable costs used in the output table.

D17   Minimum prices or yields required - this specifies the lowest value of prices or yields used in the output table.

D18   Maximum prices or yields required - this specifies the highest value of prices or yields used in the output table.

1.4 Output table calculations

The main body of the table (B26:L36) consists of calculations of the required prices or yields. These are all calculated in the same way, ie.

$$\text{Price (or yield)} = \frac{\text{margin over production costs} + \text{fixed costs} + \text{variable costs}}{\text{yield (or price)}}$$

eg. B26 = (D8 + D10 + B24) / A26

1.5 Hidden cells

Hidden cells are cells whose contents are hidden by using a formatting statement. They are a valuable and useful way of simplifying the appearance of the spreadsheet by hiding information that is not directly required.

In the CROP-Y spreadsheet there are 5 hidden cells:

E4   used to produce the correct units (Imperial or Metric) in cells C8, C10, C12 and H23).

E5   used to produce the correct prompt at cell B16

E6   used to produce the correct prompt at cell C21

E14   used to set up the increment in variable costs in cells C24:L24.

E18   used to set up the increment in yields or prices in cells A27:A36.

The contents of the hidden cells are shown in Fig 1.2.

1.6 Other calculations

The only other cells containing calculations are:

A16	to produce the required prompt
B21	to produce the required title for the output table
A23:A24	to produce the required title for the first column of the output table
B24:L24	to produce the range of values of variable costs required
A26:A36	to produce the range of values of either yields or prices required

Fig 1.2 shows all the formulas used in the spreadsheet with the exception of those in columns D to L of the main body of the output table. These are the same as those in column C but with the reference to C24 changed to D24, E24, F24 etc. These formulas can be generated with the copying facility but care is needed to ensure that references to some cells, eg. D8 and D10, remain unchanged.

1.7 Example

The example illustrates the calculation of winter wheat grain prices at various production costs and grain yields. Data is entered in Metric units. The required margin over production costs has been entered as zero so that the calculated values are the break-even grain prices. It can be seen, for example, that at grain prices of £100/tonne, yields of at least 7.0t/ha are required to break-even at variable costs greater than about £250/ha.

	A	B	C	D	E	F	G	H	I	J	K	L
1												
2	ARABLE CROPS - YIELDS, PRICES AND PRODUCTION COSTS - I. Ap Dewi											
3												
4	Imperial (0) or Metric (1)	1										
5	Prices (0) or Yields (1)	0										
6												
7	Desired margin over total											
8	production costs (£/ha)	.00										
9												
10	Fixed costs ......(£/ha)	450.00										
11												
12	Variable costs ...(£/ha)											
13	Minimum	200.00										
14	Maximum	500.00										
15												
16	Yields (t/ha)											
17	Minimum	4.00										
18	Maximum	10.00										
19												
20												
21	Required Prices (£/t)											
22												
23	Yields						Variable costs ....(£/ha)					
24	(t/ha)	200.00	230.00	260.00	290.00	320.00	350.00	380.00	410.00	440.00	470.00	500.00
25												
26	4.00	162.50	170.00	177.50	185.00	192.50	200.00	207.50	215.00	222.50	230.00	237.50
27	4.60	141.30	147.83	154.35	160.87	167.39	173.91	180.43	186.96	193.48	200.00	206.52
28	5.20	125.00	130.77	136.54	142.31	148.08	153.85	159.62	165.38	171.15	176.92	182.69
29	5.80	112.07	117.24	122.41	127.59	132.76	137.93	143.10	148.28	153.45	158.62	163.79
30	6.40	101.56	106.25	110.94	115.63	120.31	125.00	129.69	134.38	139.06	143.75	148.44
31	7.00	92.86	97.14	101.43	105.71	110.00	114.29	118.57	122.86	127.14	131.43	135.71
32	7.60	85.53	89.47	93.42	97.37	101.32	105.26	109.21	113.16	117.11	121.05	125.00
33	8.20	79.27	82.93	86.59	90.24	93.90	97.56	101.22	104.88	108.54	112.20	115.85
34	8.80	73.86	77.27	80.68	84.09	87.50	90.91	94.32	97.73	101.14	104.55	107.95
35	9.40	69.15	72.34	75.53	78.72	81.91	85.11	88.30	91.49	94.68	97.87	101.06
36	10.00	65.00	68.00	71.00	74.00	77.00	80.00	83.00	86.00	89.00	92.00	95.00
37												

Fig. 1.1 Crop yield — price spreadsheet.

	A	B	C	D	E	F	G	H	I
2	ARABLE CROPS - YIELDS, PRICES AND PRODUCTION COSTS -	I. Ap Dewi							
4	Imperial (0) or Metric (1)			1		IF(D4=0,"(£/acre)","(£/ha)")			
5	Prices (0) or Yields (1)			0		IF(D5=1,"(£/t)",IF(D4=0,"(t/ac)","(t/ha)"))			
6						IF(D5=0,"(£/t)",IF(D4=0,"(t/ac)","(t/ha)"))			
7	Desired margin over total								
8	production costs		E4	0					
10	Fixed costs		E4	450					
12	Variable costs ...		E4						
13			Minimum	200					
14			Maximum	500	(D14-D13)/10				
16	IF(D5=0,"Yields","Prices") E5								
17			Minimum	4					
18			Maximum	10	(D18-D17)/10				
21	Required	IF(D5=1,"Yields","Prices") E6				Variable costs ... E4			
23	A16								
24	B16	D13	B24+E14	C24+E14	D24+E14	E24+E14	F24+E14	G24+E14	H24+E14
25	---	---	---						
26	D17	(D8+D10+B24)/A26	(D8+D10+C24)/A26						
27	A26+E18	(D8+D10+B24)/A27	(D8+D10+C24)/A27						
28	A27+E18	(D8+D10+B24)/A28	(D8+D10+C24)/A28						
29	A28+E18	(D8+D10+B24)/A29	(D8+D10+C24)/A29						
30	A29+E18	(D8+D10+B24)/A30	(D8+D10+C24)/A30						
31	A30+E18	(D8+D10+B24)/A31	(D8+D10+C24)/A31						
32	A31+E18	(D8+D10+B24)/A32	(D8+D10+C24)/A32						
33	A32+E18	(D8+D10+B24)/A33	(D8+D10+C24)/A33						
34	A33+E18	(D8+D10+B24)/A34	(D8+D10+C24)/A34						
35	A34+E18	(D8+D10+B24)/A35	(D8+D10+C24)/A35						
36	A35+E18	(D8+D10+B24)/A36	(D8+D10+C24)/A36						
37	---	---	---						

Fig. 1.2 Formulas for crop yield — price spreadsheet.

Crop cash flow forecast

Purpose: To enable crop costs to be calculated and summarised into a monthly cash flow forecast.

Author: Graham Bunn

Spreadsheet Name: WHEAT

2.1 Introduction

Meticulous monitoring of the cash flows relative to a crop, enterprise and whole business is today an essential part of farm management. The task can be somewhat eased by the use of spreadsheet programs. At a first glance, this one (Figs 2.1 to 2.4) appears daunting but close inspection reveals many of the formulas with the same pattern. One useful feature is that any month can be used to start the cash flow. The following twelve months are then automatically calculated. Some crops obviously span over more than one year and costs which fall outside of the selected window are shown in two columns, one for costs allocated before the start month and one for later than the twelfth month.

Headings for the month columns are generated by a "Look up" facility and to avoid tedious, repetitive typing the costs are entered into the correct column by liberal use of the "IF" argument. Totals are collated by the standard "SUM" instruction.

Although the example demonstrates the growing costs of a crop of Winter Wheat there is no reason why this spreadsheet could not be used in conjuction with other crops to build a Whole Farm Cash Flow. Extra rows are easily inserted to cater for more entries as long as care is taken in copying the formulas as some of the reference cells, eg. F3 and G4, must not be adjusted.

Hidden from the main sheet is a list of numbers and corresponding months that is required by the look up function, this can be found in cells A48:B73.

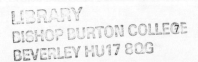

The overall layout is shown in Fig. 2.5.

2.2 Input Data

This is entered in columns A to L and is in two parts:

(a)   the start month, year, crop name and area

Location	Input Item	Example value
F3	Number of the first month in the cash flow (1=Jan, 12=Dec)	2
L3	Year into which the first month falls	1990
E4	Crop name	Winter Wheat
G4	Crop area in hectares (acres may be used providing unit prices are also in acres)	39.95

(b)   Projected costs divided into the headings:

Seeds	rows		12:13
Fertilizer	rows		17:20
Chemicals	rows		24:31
Miscellaneous	rows		35:38

All have the same input requirements. Row 17 can be used as an example.

Location	Input Item	Example value
A17	Amount of units applied per hectare (Kgs, Lts, Grms, or as in cultivations 1 Hectare unit)	200
C17	Description of unit	Kgs
E17	Description of commodity	0-27-30
G17	Unit price - this **MUST** be the same as the application unit, eg. /kg	0.112
J17	Month Number of payment	9

The spreadsheet is capable of looking into a "window" of twelve months in twenty four. Month number 1 equals January. Month number 13 equals January in the next calendar year (here 1991).

The month number has to be selected carefully. If, however, a crop requires an input cost further into the future than two years it can be accommodated into the final growing cost total by being included in a special column (LATER-->). Designating the month number as 25 will ensure its inclusion there. A note to this effect is included on the sheet at row 46.

When crop costs have been entered it is still possible to return to cell F3 to change the month or to G4 to change the area, and to observe its effect. Any change in area will, after recalculation, amend the total cost of the crop (cell L44). This is the classic "what if?" that makes spreadsheets so useful.

2.3 Output

Because of the size of the spreadsheet, and because so much is repetition only a sample of the cell formulas are described below. It must be stressed that when copying these across to other cells that some references are held constant, whilst others are adjusted to the new position.

2.3.1   Month Headings (rows 8 and 10)

(a)   The value in F3, the number of the start month, is checked and a match is selected from the list provided from A50 to A73. When a match is found, cell P8 will display the contents of the cell immediately to the right of the correct value found in the table. The list of months are required by this program to be expressed as textual values thus: ("Jan") using a maximum of nine characters including spaces.

ie. P8 = VLU(F3, A50:B73, 1)

(b)   As above but 1 is added to the value of F3 before the "look up" is performed. Thus the next month to that of column P is displayed. This is repeated by adding one to each of the twelve month columns.

ie. R8 = VLU(F3+1, A50:B73, 1)

(c)   If the start month is in the first year, ie. number 1 to 12, the year displayed will be the same as the input year at L3. If it is greater than 12, ie. into the following year, it will add a value of one to that of the year in L3. This formula, with adjustment for each month column, is the same across the headings.

eg. P10 = IF(F3>12, L3+1, L3)

2.3.2   Costs per hectare (column L)

(a)   The number of units of the commodity applied per hectare is multiplied by the price per unit expressed in £'s.

eg. L12 = G12*A12

(b)   Totals are found at Rows 15, 22, 33 and 40. For example, the one in row 15 adds L12 and L13 (also any new rows inserted at a later date). In this particular cell the total seed cost per hectare is displayed.

ie. L15 = SUM(L12:L13)

Similar totals are found for each month in columns N to AN.

(c)   The total cost of seeds, fertilizer, chemicals and miscellaneous per hectare is displayed at cell L42.

ie. L42 =L13+L22+L33+L40

2.3.3   Monthly costs (columns N to AN)

This consists of a series of formulas that selects which monthly column the commodity application cost is placed in.

(a)   Column N is reserved for any cost that is incurred before the start month displayed in F3. It first checks to see if the month in column J is less than F3. If it is, then it will multiply the cost per hectare (L12) by the total number of hectares (G4), otherwise it will leave it blank.

eg. N12 = IF(J12<F3, L12*G4, (""))

Formulas in columns P, R etc. are almost identical,

ie. P12 = IF(J12=F3, L12*G4, ("")),
    R12 = IF(J12=F3+1, L12*G4, (""))

and so on until column AN where the formula is
    AN12 = IF(J12>F3+11, L12*G4, (""))

All the results in these columns are printed out in integer format.

(b)   Each month's seed, fertilizer, chemical and miscellaneous cost is collated into a total cost of commodities for that particular month.

eg. N44 = N15+N22+N33+N40

2.3.4   Total Projected Cost for Crop

The total projected growing cost for the crop over the area displayed in G4 is the sum of the monthly totals displayed in row 44.

ie. L44 = SUM(N44:AN44)

An alternative formula (G4*L42) would give the same result.

Fig. 2.6 shows the formulas used in columns L to R.

2.4 Final remarks

When the spreadsheet has been completed the author advises that all cells, with the exception of the input cells, be protected to avoid any tearful disasters, as the writing of the formulas can be time consuming.

Whilst inputting data, considerable time can be saved by setting the program to only recalculate the sheet when requested.

If it is required to see the total along the bottom rows (42 and 44) changing as differing areas or commodities are included, then a window screen can be set up.

```
     |  A  |  | C| |           E          || F|| G  | |J||K||     L     |
 1   ===========================================================================
 2
 3            FIRST MONTH..............[  2  ]        YEAR...[      1990  ]
 4            Crop.. Winter Wheat                39.95  Hectares
 5
 6   ---------------------------------------------------------------------------
 7                                               |   *   | COSTS     ||
 8                                               |  Mth  | Per       ||
 9            Amount/                      Unit  |  25=  | HECTARE   ||
10            Hectare                      Price |  EOY  |  (£)      ||
11   ----------------------------------------------------------------------
12                                     @ #       |       |
13        160   Kgs. Basic Seed        @ #  .890 |   9   |    142.40
14                                               |       |   ----------
15                     Total Seeds.........................£    142.40
16   ----------------------------------------------------------------------
17        200   Kgs. 0-27-30           @ #  .112 |   9   |     22.40
18        100   Kgs. Urea              @ #  .116 |   1   |     11.60
19        350   Lts. Nuram             @ #  .110 |   3   |     38.50
20        120   Lts. Nufol             @ #  .075 |   6   |      9.00
21                                               |       |   ----------
22                     Total Fertilizer.....................£     81.50
23   ----------------------------------------------------------------------
24          3   Lts. Hytane            @ #  5.750|  10   |     17.25
25       22.5   Kgs. Avadex Granules   @ #  .972 |  10   |     21.87
26          3   Lts. C.M.P.P. + M.C.P.A.@ #  3.000|   5   |      9.00
27          1   Lts. Sportak           @ # 18.000|   5   |     18.00
28        .75   Lts. Corbel            @ # 17.850|   6   |     13.39
29        2.5   Lts. Growth Regulator  @ #  1.520|   5   |      3.80
30        4.5   Lts. Bolda Fungicide   @ #  2.000|   7   |      9.00
31          1   Ha.  Aphox             @ #  8.710|   7   |      8.71
32                                               |       |   ----------
33                     Total Chemicals.....................£    101.02
34   ----------------------------------------------------------------------
35          1   Ha.  Fertilizer Spreading@ #  7.150|  9   |      7.15
36        8.2   Tns. Marketing & Haulage @ # 12.350| 25   |    101.27
37          1   Ha.  Contract (combining)@ # 65.000| 13   |     65.00
38                                     @ #       |       |
39                                               |       |   ----------
40                     Total Miscellaneous.................£    173.42
41   ----------------------------------------------------------------------
42                     Total Variable Costs per Hectare.....£    498.34
43   ----------------------------------------------------------------------
44                     Total Projected Cost for Crop........£    19909||
45   ----------------------------------------------------------------------
46            * If a cost is anticipated more than one year in advance
47              enter the value 25 in this column
```

Fig. 2.1 Crop cash flow spreadsheet (Columns A to M).

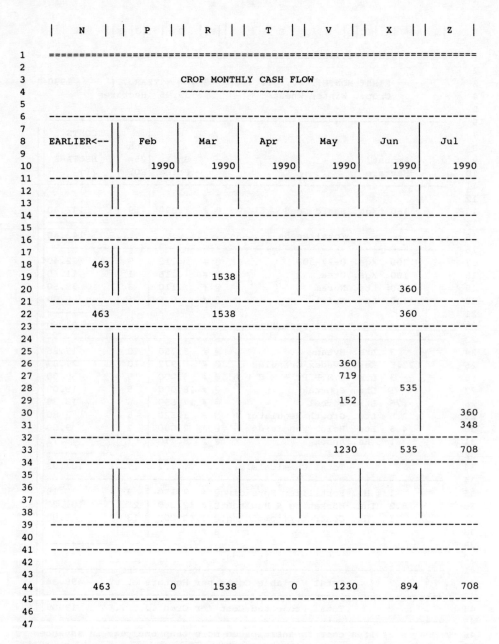

Fig. 2.2 Crop cash flow spreadsheet (Columns N to Z).

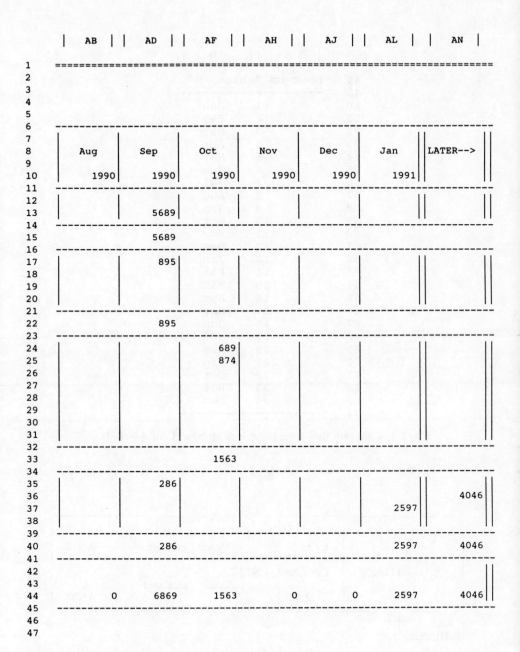

Fig. 2.3 Crop cash flow spreadsheet (Columns AA to AO).

	A		B
48	Look up Tables		
49	-------------------		
50	1		Jan
51	2		Feb
52	3		Mar
53	4		Apr
54	5		May
55	6		Jun
56	7		Jul
57	8		Aug
58	9		Sep
59	10		Oct
60	11		Nov
61	12		Dec
62	13		Jan
63	14		Feb
64	15		Mar
65	16		Apr
66	17		May
67	18		Jun
68	19		Jul
69	20		Aug
70	21		Sep
71	22		Oct
72	23		Nov
73	24		Dec
74	-------------------		

Fig. 2.4 Crop cash flow spreadsheet look up table (Cells A48:B74).

A1	L12	N1 Month Headings	AN10
Input Data	Costs/ha	N12 Totals Calculated	
J38	L44		AN44

A48 Hidden Look Up Table B73

Fig. 2.5 Layout of crop cash flow forecast

	L	N	P	R
6				
7	COSTS			
8	Per	EARLIER<--		
9	HECTARE			
10	(£)		VLU(F3,A50:B73,1)	VLU(F3+1,A50:B73,1)
11			IF(F3>12,L3+1,L3)	IF(F3+1>12,L3+1,L3)
12	G12*A12	IF(J12<F3,L12*G4,(""))	IF(J12=F3,L12*G4,(""))	IF(J12=F3+1,L12*G4,(""))
13	G13*A13	IF(J13<F3,L13*G4,(""))	IF(J13=F3,L13*G4,(""))	IF(J13=F3+1,L13*G4,(""))
14				
15	SUM(L12:L13)	SUM(N12:N13)	SUM(P12:P13)	SUM(R12:R13)
16				
17	G17*A17	IF(J17<F3,L17*G4,(""))	IF(J17=F3,L17*G4,(""))	IF(J17=F3+1,L17*G4,(""))
18	G18*A18	IF(J18<F3,L18*G4,(""))	IF(J18=F3,L18*G4,(""))	IF(J18=F3+1,L18*G4,(""))
19	G19*A19	IF(J19<F3,L19*G4,(""))	IF(J19=F3,L19*G4,(""))	IF(J19=F3+1,L19*G4,(""))
20	G20*A20	IF(J20<F3,L20*G4,(""))	IF(J20=F3,L20*G4,(""))	IF(J20=F3+1,L20*G4,(""))
21				
22	SUM(L17:L20)	SUM(N17:N20)	SUM(P17:P20)	SUM(R17:R20)
23				
24	G24*A24	IF(J24<F3,L24*G4,(""))	IF(J24=F3,L24*G4,(""))	IF(J24=F3+1,L24*G4,(""))
25	G25*A25	IF(J25<F3,L25*G4,(""))	IF(J25=F3,L25*G4,(""))	IF(J25=F3+1,L25*G4,(""))
26	G26*A26	IF(J26<F3,L26*G4,(""))	IF(J26=F3,L26*G4,(""))	IF(J26=F3+1,L26*G4,(""))
27	G27*A27	IF(J27<F3,L27*G4,(""))	IF(J27=F3,L27*G4,(""))	IF(J27=F3+1,L27*G4,(""))
28	G28*A28	IF(J28<F3,L28*G4,(""))	IF(J28=F3,L28*G4,(""))	IF(J28=F3+1,L28*G4,(""))
29	G29*A29	IF(J29<F3,L29*G4,(""))	IF(J29=F3,L29*G4,(""))	IF(J29=F3+1,L29*G4,(""))
30	G30*A30	IF(J30<F3,L30*G4,(""))	IF(J30=F3,L30*G4,(""))	IF(J30=F3+1,L30*G4,(""))
31	G31*A31	IF(J31<F3,L31*G4,(""))	IF(J31=F3,L31*G4,(""))	IF(J31=F3+1,L31*G4,(""))
32				
33	SUM(L24:L31)	SUM(N24:N31)	SUM(P24:P31)	SUM(R24:R31)
34				
35	G35*A35	IF(J35<F3,L35*G4,(""))	IF(J35=F3,L35*G4,(""))	IF(J35=F3+1,L35*G4,(""))
36	G36*A36	IF(J36<F3,L36*G4,(""))	IF(J36=F3,L36*G4,(""))	IF(J36=F3+1,L36*G4,(""))
37	G37*A37	IF(J37<F3,L37*G4,(""))	IF(J37=F3,L37*G4,(""))	IF(J37=F3+1,L37*G4,(""))
38		IF(J38<F3,L38*G4,(""))	IF(J38=F3,L38*G4,(""))	IF(J38=F3+1,L38*G4,(""))
39				
40	SUM(L35:L38)	SUM(N35:N38)	SUM(P35:P38)	SUM(R35:R38)
41				
42	L13+L22+L33+L40			
43				
44	SUM(N44:AN44)	N15+N22+N33+N40	P15+P22+P33+P40	R15+R22+R33+R40
45				

Fig. 2.6 Formulas in cells L6:R45 in crop cash flow spreadsheet.

Rapid whole farm budget

Purpose: To enable the quick and easy production of a gross margin plan and profit budget for a farm by drawing on a built-in data-base from the SAC Farm Management Handbook.

Author: Roy Sutherland

Spreadsheet Name: EASYPLAN

3.1 Background and uses

EASYPLAN (Figs. 3.2 to 3.16) is a program for farm system planning using enterprise gross margins, and for producing a budgeted profit and loss account. It incorporates standard gross margin data for 48 enterprises and also standard fixed costs data, both taken from the SAC Farm Management Handbook (1989). It enables the user to produce a farm budget very rapidly using the standard data simply by specifying the farm system in terms of crop areas and livestock numbers, plus some data on rent, interest, value of land owned and net worth of the farmer. However, the user can also make adjustments to any of the standard data in order to produce a budget which fits the circumstances of the particular farm in more detail - eg. in terms of yields, product prices, variable inputs, labour costs and other overheads.

The main purposes for which it can be used are:

a) **Rapid preliminary budgeting:**
   To assess the potential profit for a given farm system, and also the capital position - eg. a potential farm purchase or rental, or a major change in farm system. In the first instance the budget can be quickly run using the standard data, but the details can be adjusted and refined as a second stage if the result looks promising.

b) **Devising the most profitable farm system:**
   The enterprise gross margins and fixed costs can be adjusted to represent the performance and circumstances of a specific farm. Then alternative systems can be budgeted to try to identify potentially more profitable alternatives.

c) **Comparison of actual performance with standards:**
   Budget the farm system using the standard data and compare the budget results with the actual farm performance to reveal where there may be scope for improvement.

d) **As a financial model of a farm**:
The program can show the effects of changes in yields, or prices, or costs on the profitability and capital requirements of a given farm system.

It may be used by farmers or their advisers for farm planning, and by students for exercises or farm case studies involving farm planning and budgeting. Lecturers can use it directly or through student exercises to demonstrate financial aspects of different farm systems and their sensitivity to variations in yields, prices and costs.

3.2 Program structure

Apart from a short set of user instructions located in the cell range A1:H36, EASYPLAN is made up of three main sections, as shown in Fig. 3.1. First there are the ENTERPRISE GROSS MARGIN BUDGETS located in the range A38:P238. They are set out in groups of up to six enterprises of a given category, whose gross margin budgets can be viewed together within the limits of a single screen - eg. Combine Crops at A40:H56. Thus the user can view the enterprise gross margin data and adjust it if necessary with a minimum of moving around the spreadsheet.

Details of physical inputs and their prices, upon which the budgets are based (eg. seed rates and prices), are not generally included because the user can refer to these in the SAC Farm Management Handbook from which the budgets are derived.

The enterprise gross margin budgets include a set of variable costs for grazing, at varying levels of fertiliser input, located at A200:H210 and for forage crops at I200:P210. The forage for any grazing enterprise is then specified in its gross margin budget in terms of hectares of these grass and forage crops and the forage variable costs are automatically incorporated in the livestock gross margin by referencing the costs for the relevant grass and forage.

The second section of the spreadsheet, in the range R1:Y97, is where the FARM SYSTEM PLAN is entered by the user. The enterprises are listed together with their gross margins and the plan is entered in terms of hectares of the arable enterprises and numbers of livestock. The areas of the grass and forage crops are calculated by the program and shown at the foot of the plan, together with the total farm area and the total farm gross margin.

The third section in the range AA1:AH139 is what forms the standard printout from the program, including the FARM BUDGET (Profit and Loss Account), the ESTIMATED AVERAGE CAPITAL REQUIREMENTS (Balance Sheet) and an ABBREVIATED FARM PLAN which shows the cropping, stocking and main performance assumptions, together with entries for the user's name and a budget title.

3.3 Input data   Location

3.3.1 Essential entries

1) Less Favoured Area (LFA) Status:	'1' for LFA (default non-LFA)	A12
2) Areas of arable crops	(ha)	V13:V21
3) Numbers of livestock for each livestock enterprise		W27:W76
4) Area of rough grazing	(ha)	V89
5) Grass equivalent of rough grazing	(ha)	V93

6) Value of heritable property	(£)	AG61
and/or farm rent	(£)	AE50
and value of tenant's improvements	(£)	AG63
7) Own capital (Net Worth)	(£)	AG74
8) User's name		AD91
9) Budget title		AC93

A1:H36 **USER INSTRUCTIONS**	R1:Y97 **FARM SYSTEM PLAN** (Farm Gross Margin Budget)	AA1:AH56 **FARM BUDGET** (Profit and Loss Account)
A38:P238 **ENTERPISE GROSS MARGIN BUDGETS**	Crop areas and livestock numbers to be entered. Enterprise gross margins, forage areas, total farm area and total farm gross margin are displayed	Rent to be entered if applicable.
A40:H56 Combine Crops I40:P56 Potatoes & Other Crops		AA58:AH77 **ESTIMATED AVERAGE CAPITAL REQUIREMENTS** (Balance Sheet)
A60:H87 Dairy Cows I60:P:83 Rearing Heifers		
A90:H113 Suckler Cows I90:P110 Overwintering Suckled Calves		Values of Heritable Property, Tenant's Improvements and Net Worth to be entered.
A115:H136 Winter Finishing Cattle I115:P135 Summer Finishing Cattle		
A140:H164 Dairy Beef Feeding Cattle		AA84:AH139 **ABBREVIATED FARM SYSTEM PLAN**
A165:H188 Breeding Ewes I165:P188 Feeding Lambs		Plus Main Performance Assumptions, for printing as output. User name and Budget to be entered.
A200:H210 Grazing Variable Costs I200:P210 Forage Crop Variable Costs		
A220:H238 Breeding Sows I220:P238 Feeding Pigs		

Note: Some fixed costs data, intermediate calculations and macros are located in the range AK2:AP119, but these do not normally need to be accessed by the user.

Fig. 3.1 Layout of main sections of EASYPLAN with cell references.

3.3.2 *Optional entries/adjustments from default data*   **Location**

1)   Fixed Costs Adjustments -   Labour   AE38
                                      Machinery   AD40:AD42
                                      Property Repairs   AE44
                                      Miscellaneous   AE45

2)   Adjustment of rate of interest charged on borrowed capital   AC52

3)   Adjustment of breeding livestock valuations   AD67,AF56
                                                                      AC68,AF68

4)   Adjustment of Enterprise Gross Margin Data -

All the data in the enterprise gross margin budgets may be altered if appropriate,

eg. for Wheat -

Yield	(Tonnes/ha)	C42
Price	(£/tonne)	C44
Seed Costs	(£/ha)	C49
Fertiliser and Lime Costs	(£/ha)	C50
Contract and Casual Labour Costs	(£/ha)	C51
Sundry Variable Costs	(£/ha)	C52

There is also one blank arable crop budget titled 'Other Crop' in which the user can enter yield, price, and variable costs for another crop in the locations M42, M44 and M49:M52.

With livestock enterprises there can be a wider range of items which may be adjusted -

eg. for Spring Calving Dairy Cows -

Yield	(litres/cow)	E63
Milk Price	(p/litre)	E64
Concentrates Fed	(kg/litre	E65
Calf Sales	(£/cow)	E68
Herd Replacement Cost	(£/cow)	E69
Barley and Minerals Cost	(£/cow)	E73
Concentrate Price	(£/tonne)	F74
Vet, Med and Other Costs	(£/cow)	E75
Forage Areas required	(ha/cow)	E82:E87

Also the costs of the forage crops utilised by the livestock enterprise can be adjusted.

eg. Grazing 250N   (£/ha)   F205:F208

3.4 Values calculated in the spreadsheet

Because of the size of this spreadsheet not all the calculations will be explained in the same detail as in the other spreadsheets in this book.

3.4.1 *Enterprise gross margin budgets*

These include many items which are calculated by formulas in the appropriate cells.   They are almost all straightforward additions, subtractions, products and divisions, which need no explanation.   Calculations which may not be immediately obvious are as follows:

Forage costs in the livestock budgets are calculated as the sum of the products of the forage crop requirements set out at the foot of the livestock budget and their relevant variable costs as set out in the forage variable costs

eg. for Spring-Calving Dairy Cows,
E76 = (E82*E210) + (E83*F210) + (E84*K210) + (E85*L210) + (E86*M210) + (E87*N210).

The cost of 16% cake in the Dairy Cow budgets (C74:E74) is calculated from the yield and concentrates fed per cow, less allowance for barley fed, times the price of the cake,

eg. for Spring Calving Dairy Cows, E74 = ((E63*E65) - (E73/0.11)) * (F74/1000).

3.4.2 Farm system plan and farm gross margin budget

The list of enterprise gross margins per hectare and per head of livestock displayed in columns T and U are derived from the enterprise gross margin budgets by referencing the appropriate cells,

eg. the Winter Wheat gross margin, T13 = C56.

The hectares used by each livestock enterprise which are displayed in column V are obtained as the product of the number of head entered in column W and the total forage area required per head as calculated in the appropriate enterprise gross margin budget,

eg. for Autumn Calving Dairy Cows, V27 = W27 * C81.

The total areas of the different forage crops are displayed at V79:V86.   These are calculated as the sum of the products of the number of head of each livestock enterprise and the area of the particular forage crop required per head, as indicated at the foot of the enterprise gross margin budget,

eg. the area of Swedes,
V86 = (W27*C87) + (W28*D87) + (W29*E87) + (W31*K83) + (W32*L83) etc, etc.

Because the total formula is too long for one cell it is divided into three parts located in cells S86, T86 and U86 and the formula in V86 is simply the sum of these three.   A 'hide' format is applied to the cells containing intermediate calculations so that they are not displayed. The figures shown at V79 and V80 which are the areas of low intensity grazing (75N and 125N), are calculated as above but also allow for any grazing provided by unfertilised rough (V93).

The total gross margin for each enterprise, which is displayed in column X, is calculated as the product of the gross margin per unit and the number of units entered in the plan, ie. (gross margin per hectare * number of hectares) in the case of arable crops and (gross margin per head * number of head) in the case of livestock enterprises.   The figure produced at X93 is the variable costs of the low intensity grazing which would be required were it not for the rough grazing utilised instead.   This cost saving provided by rough grazing is added to the sum of the enterprise gross margins to give the Total Farm Gross Margin at X96.

3.4.3 Farm budget

The farm type number displayed at AB5 is calculated using IF functions.   These define the farm type according to the descriptions set out on page 339 of the SAC Farm Management Handbook 1989/90, based on

(a)   less favoured area status,
(b)   proportions of farm gross output derived from crops or pigs,
(c)   proportions of farm gross margin derived from sheep, cattle, crops, or dairy cows.

Intermediate calculations in this process are located in the range AK11:AP16.

The figures for total gross output from milk, cattle, sheep, and pigs, which are displayed at AF18:AF21 are calculated as the sums of the products of the number of units of each enterprise in the relevant category and the gross output per unit as shown in the enterprise gross margin budget. However, the crop gross output at AF17 incorporates a calculation by which the barley requirements of the livestock enterprises are deducted from the quantity of barley grown on the farm, so that the crop gross output does not include the value of home-grown barley fed to livestock.

The variable cost totals displayed at AE26:AE31 are calculated as the sums of the products of the number of units of each enterprise and the amount of the variable cost item per unit of that enterprise, including forage cost items. However, the figure for Feed at AE30 includes a calculation deducting the value of home-grown barley which is assumed fed to livestock.

Estimates of fixed costs are calculated for labour, machinery, property repairs and miscellaneous costs at AE38, AD40:42, AE44 and AE45. These calculations utilise data derived from the SAC Farm Management Handbook setting out the average levels of these fixed costs for each of 10 farm types, expressed per adjusted hectare of farm area (except for the LFA Farms-Mainly Sheep and the LFA Farms-Sheep and Cattle, where costs are expressed per ewe). That data is incorporated in the spreadsheet at AK2:AV9. The data for the appropriate farm type is referenced by means of a series of IF functions and the cost estimates derived simply as the products of the standard costs per adjusted hectare for the relevant farm type and the size of the farm in adjusted hectares (or else the standard costs per ewe and the number of ewes).

Interest charges at AE52 are calculated as the product of the Estimated Average Borrowing Requirement, displayed at AC51 by reference to AG76, and the annual interest rate displayed at AC52.

3.4.4 Estimated average capital requirements

The average value of machinery and equipment is calculated at AG65 as the annual average depreciation (AD41) * 4.5. This equates with a 20% depreciation rate (eg. opening value £100,000, depreciation £20,000, closing value £80,000, average of opening and closing values £90,000).

The capital invested in breeding livestock is calculated at AG67 as the sum of the products of the numbers of breeding females included in the farm plan and estimated values for those females (including a share of the value of breeding males to service them) as displayed at AD67, AF67, AC68 and AF68.

An estimate of the average working capital requirement is displayed at AG69. Intermediate calculations of the working capital requirements for each enterprise are located at AK20:AR83. The requirement per unit of an enterprise is calculated as:

(initial outlay on variable costs and trading livestock purchase + final value of sales) / 2 * production period as a fraction of a year.

A first estimate of total capital requirement is then the sum of products of the requirement per unit of each enterprise and the number of units in the farm plan. However that is an overestimate in that it includes the profit element. In AG69 an adjustment is included to correct for this, by applying a measure of the cost/output ratio drawn from the data in the Farm Budget. It may be noted that, when the calculation process is initiated, more than one iteration occurs before the final values are reached in all parts of the spreadsheet. This is because of this adjustment process.

3.4.5 Abbreviated farm system plan

Most of the values displayed in this part of the spreadsheet are simply provided by means of referencing the relevant cells in other parts of the spreadsheet. However, in order to provide a more compact indication of livestock numbers, livestock enterprises of essentially similar character have been brought together as single categories - eg. Dairy Cows. Thus the numbers at AD121:AD139 are summations of the relevant cell references. Similarly the performance figures at AF12:AH139 are averages calculated across groups of individual enterprises.

3.5 Macros

3.5.1 Adjustment of the format of the farm budget

In the Farm Budget the estimate of labour costs which is calculated by the program has to be total labour cost including the value of farmer and family labour, because the amount of labour input which may be contributed by unpaid work by the farmer and family depends on individual circumstances. Thus the profit measure at the end of the budget is titled 'NET SURPLUS (Net Profit less charge for farmer and family labour)' and it is noted against the labour cost that it includes farmer and family labour. However, if the user wishes to adjust the labour cost to paid labour only and thus present a budget showing a Net Profit, he may do so, and there is a macro in the program which can be invoked to delete the notes about farmer and family labour and to convert the NET SURPLUS title to NET PROFIT. This macro is located in the range AO110:AP117 and is invoked by typing N whilst the ALT key is depressed (ALT + N).

3.5.2 Automatic standard printout

A macro is located in the range AK100:AM119 which contains the necessary instructions to produce a standard 3-page printout consisting of the budget title and users name, abbreviated Farm System Plan plus main performance assumptions, Farm Budget and Estimated Average Capital Requirements.

The macro is invoked by typing 'ALT' + P and includes a menu in which the user indicates whether the print is to be on paper of 70 lines page length (ie. A4) or 66 lines.

Reference

Scottish Agriculture Colleges (1989). *Farm Management Handbook, 1989/90.*

	A		B		C		D		E		F		G		H	

1 EASYPLAN EASYPLAN EASYPLAN EASYPLAN EASYPLAN EASYPLAN EASYPLAN EASYPLAN
2
3 A WHOLE FARM PLANNING MODEL ---- Prepared by Roy Sutherland
4   North of Scotland College of Agriculture ---Economics Division
5
6   The model uses data from the Scottish Farm Management Handbook
7   to produce a wholefarm budget in both enterprise gross margin
8   form and gross output/variable costs form.
9 USER INSTRUCTIONS
10   (1)If the farm is eligible for Less Favoured Area subsidies,
11   enter a number 1 in cell A12 in place of the 0 :
12   0
13   Based on this information, together with the enterprise combination
14   which is entered in the FARM SYSTEM BUDGET, the FARM TYPE is
15   identified and the FIXED COSTS are estimated from Scottish Farm
16   Accounts data (p.339-351 in the Handbook) updated to 1989/90.
17   (2)The Handbook ENTERPRISE OUTPUTS & VARIABLE COSTS are
18   located as follows, and may be adjusted if desired
19   COMBINE CROPS -- A40   POTATOES & OTHER CROP -- I40
20   DAIRY COWS -- A60   HEIFER REARING -- I60
21   BEEF COWS -- A90   WINTERING CALVES -- I90
22   FINISHING CATTLE (WINTER) -- A115 FINISHING CATTLE (SUMMER) -- I115
23   DAIRY-BEEF FEEDING -- A140
24   BREEDING EWES -- A165   FEEDING LAMBS -- I165
25   GRAZING -- A200   FORAGE CROPS -- I200
26   BREEDING SOWS -- A220   FINISHING PIGS -- I220
27   (3)To enter CROP AREAS & LIVESTOCK NUMBERS go to R1.
28   (4)The FARM BUDGET is at AA1, showing GROSS OUTPUTS at AA15,VARIABLE
29   COSTS at AA24, & FIXED COSTS at AA36. Enter the RENT & RATES cost
30   at AE50. CAPITAL REQUIREMENTS are estimated at AA58 but entries
31   should be made for HERITABLE PROPERTY VALUE at AG61 or for TENANT'S
32   IMPROVEMENTS at AG63 and the amount of OWN CAPITAL at AG74.
33   Enter the INTEREST RATE on borrowed capital at AC52.
34   (5)To enter your name and a title for your budget go to AA91
35   (6)To print the FARM BUDGET & CAPITAL REQUIREMENTS plus a SUMMARY of
36   your PLAN type P while also pressing the ALT key.
37
38   ENTERPRISE GROSS MARGIN BUDGETS
39   =================================
40 COMBINE CROPS   WINTER   SPRING   WINTER   SPRING   WINTER   PROTEIN
41 =============   WHEAT   BARLEY   BARLEY   OATS   O S RAPE   PEAS
42 YIELD tonnes /ha   7   5.5   6.5   5.5   3.5   4
43
44 PRICE £ per tonne 100   95   95   100   280   182
45   £ per hectare --
46 OUTPUT   700.0   522.5   617.5   550.0   980.0   728.0
47 (excl. straw)
48 VARIABLE COSTS
49 Seed   50.0   48.0   42.0   49.0   24.0   100.0
50 Fertiliser & Lime 106.0   77.0   99.0   65.0   133.0   41.0
51 Contract & Casual   .0   .0   .0   .0   35.0   37.0
52 Sundry   60.0   34.0   55.0   16.0   103.0   33.0
53   ----   ----   ----   ----   ----   ----
54 TOTAL   216.0   159.0   196.0   130.0   295.0   211.0
55   ----   ----   ----   ----   ----   ----
56 GROSS MARGIN   484.0   363.5   421.5   420.0   685.0   517.0
57 --

Fig. 3.2 Rapid whole farm budget spreadsheet (Cells A1:H57).

| I || J || K || L || M || N || O || P |

1   EASYPLAN EASYPLAN EASYPLAN EASYPLAN EASYPLAN EASYPLAN EASYPLAN EASYPLAN
2
3
4
5
6
7
8
9
10
11
12
13
14
15
16
17
18
19
20
21
22
23
24
25
26
27
28
29
30
31
32
33
34
35
36
37
38
39

40	POTATOES ETC	POTATOES	POTATOES	OTHER
41	============	WARE(MH)	SEED(HL)	CROP
42	YIELD tonnes/ha	35	36	.0
43				
44	AV PRICE	66.1	105.1	.0
45	£ per hectare	---------	----------	------
46	OUTPUT	2,313.5	3,783.6	.0
47				
48	VARIABLE COSTS			
49	Seed	420	600	0
50	Fertiliser	141	141	0
51	Contract & Casual	304	805	0
52	Sundry	226	210	0
53		----	----	----
54	TOTAL	1,091.0	1,756.0	.0
55		----	----	----
56	GROSS MARGIN	1,222.5	2,027.6	.0
57				

Fig. 3.3 Rapid whole farm budget spreadsheet (Cells I1:P57).

	A	B	C	D	E	F	G	H
58								
59								
60	DAIRY COWS		AUTUMN	ALL YEAR	SPRING			
61	==========		CALVING	CALVING	CALVING			
62	Winter Milk		60%	50%	40%			
63	Yield litres/cow		5500	5500	5500			
64	Milk Price p/litre		18.7	18.5	18.3			
65	Concs Fed kg/litre		.3	.27	.24			
66	£ per cow -------------------------------------							
67	Milk		1029	1018	1007			
68	Calves		85	85	85			
69	- Herd Replmt		54	54	54			
70			----	----	----			
71	OUTPUT		1060	1049	1038			
72	VARIABLE COSTS							
73	Barley + Mins		60	69	78			
74	16% Cake		177	137	98	160 £/tonne		
75	Vet Med & Other		51	51	51			
76	Forage		90	92	94			
77								
78	GROSS MARGIN /COW		682	700	717			
79	GROSS MARGIN /HA		1364	1372	1379			
80								
81	FORAGE (ha/cow)		.5	.51	.52			
82	Grazing (175N)		0	0	0			
83	Grazing (250N)		.3	.3	.3			
84	Silage (220N)		0	0	0			
85	Silage (275N)		.2	.21	.22			
86	Hay		0	0	0			
87	Swedes		0	0	0			
88	===							
89								
90	SUCKLER COWS			UPLAND SUCKLER COWS				
91	============		Winter	Spring	Summer	Autumn		
92	£ per cow		Calving	Calving	Calving	Calving		
93	Sales		365	293	442	428		
94	Subsidies		103	103	103	103		
95	- Herd Replmt		61	61	61	61		
96			----	----	----	----		
97	OUTPUT		407	335	484	470		
98	VARIABLE COSTS							
99	Barley + Mins		22	11	33	22		
100	Other Feed		18	5	18	32		
101	Vet Med & Other		27	23	31	29		
102	Forage		79	72	92	91		
103								
104	GROSS MARGIN /COW		261	224	310	296		
105	GROSS MARGIN /HA		427	407	449	422		
106								
107	FORAGE (ha/cow)		.61	.55	.69	.7		
108	Grazing (75N)		0	0	0	0		
109	Grazing (125N)		.39	.34	.4	.44		
110	Grazing (175N)		0	0	0	0		
111	Silage (220N)		.22	.21	.29	.26		
112	Hay		0	0	0	0		
113	Swedes		0	0	0	0		
114	===							

Fig. 3.4 Rapid whole farm budget spreadsheet (Cells A58:H114).

```
      |  I  ||  J  ||  K  ||  L  ||  M  ||  N  ||  O  ||  P  |
58
59
60  REARING HEIFERS       Autumn   Spring   Autumn
61  ================      Calving  Calving  Calving
62      £ per head        26 mths  30 mths  30 mths
63  Sales                   570      570      570
64  Purchases               110      110      110
65                         ----     ----     ----
66  OUTPUT                  460      460      460
67  VARIABLE COSTS
68  Barley + Mins            58       58       63
69  Other Feed               94       71       57
70  Vet Med & Other          42       42       42
71  Forage                   87      103      100
72
73  GROSS MARGIN /HEAD      179      186      198
74  GROSS MARGIN /HA        284      270      283
75
76  FORAGE (ha/hd)          .63      .69       .7
77  Grazing (125N)            0        0        0
78  Grazing (175N)          .47      .34      .44
79  Grazing (250N)            0        0        0
80  Silage (220N)           .12      .33      .23
81  Silage (275N)             0        0        0
82  Hay                     .04      .02      .03
83  Swedes                    0       .0       .0
84  =================================================
85
86
87
88
89
90  OVERWINTERING SUCKLED CALVES
91  ===================   Spring   Spring   Winter   Winter
92      £ per head        Steer    Heifer   Steer    Heifer
93  Sales                   515      422      583      496
94  Purchases               351      278      430      350
95                         ----     ----     ----     ----
96  OUTPUT                  164      144      153      146
97  VARIABLE COSTS
98  Barley + Mins            36       30       41       34
99  Other Feed
100 Vet Med & Other          20       18       21       19
101 Forage                   20       20       22       22
102
103 GROSS MARGIN /HEAD       88       76       69       71
104 GROSS MARGIN /HA        731      631      531      546
105
106 FORAGE (ha/hd)          .12      .12      .13      .13
107 Silage (220N)           .12      .12      .13      .13
108 Silage (275N)             0        0        0        0
109 Hay                       0        0        0        0
110 Swedes                    0        0        0        0
111 =================================================
112
113
114
```

Fig. 3.5 Rapid whole farm budget spreadsheet (Cells I58:P114).

	A	C	D	E	F
115	FINISHING CATTLE		WINTER FEEDING		
116	=================	Continen-	Medium	S. Calf	S. Calf
117	£ per head	tal Steer	Steer	Steer	Heifer
118	Sales	695	584	644	545
119	Spec Beef Premium	29	29	29	
120	Purchases	539	444	503	411
121		-----	-----	-----	-----
122	OUTPUT	185	169	170	134
123	VARIABLE COSTS				
124	Barley + Mins	50	45	45	28
125	Other Feed				
126	Vet Med & Other	22	20	20	18
127	Forage	24	22	22	19
128					
129	GROSS MARGIN /HEAD	89	82	83	69
130	GROSS MARGIN /HA	638	631	639	631
131					
132	FORAGE (ha/hd)	.14	.13	.13	.11
133	Silage (220N)	.14	.13	.13	.11
134	Silage (275N)	0	0	0	0
135	Hay	0	0	0	0
136	Swedes	0	0	0	0
137	==				

	A	C	D	E	F	G	H
138							
139							
140	DAIRY-BEEF FEEDING	BULL BEEF		18-20	22-24	YEARLING	STORES
141	===================	Cereal	Silage	Month	Month	Spring	Autumn
142	£ per head	Fed	Fed	Beef	Beef	Born	Born
143	Sales	525	569	583	615	473	443
144	Spec Beef Premium	29	29	29	29		
145	Purchases	179	221	219	177	214	219
146		-----	-----	-----	-----	-----	-----
147	OUTPUT	375	377	393	467	259	224
148	VARIABLE COSTS						
149	Barley + Mins	165	83	57	74	36	
150	Other Feed	108	67	88	70	92	99
151	Vet Med & Other	28	28	43	46	35	36
152	Forage		33	44	64	22	24
153							
154	GROSS MARGIN /HEAD	74	166	161	213	74	65
155	GROSS MARGIN /HA	n/a	1040	554	507	569	384
156							
157	FORAGE (ha/hd)		.16	.29	.42	.13	.17
158	Grazing (125N)		0	0	0	0	0
159	Grazing (175N)		0	.12	.15	0	.13
160	Grazing (250N)		0	0	0	0	0
161	Silage (220N)		0	.17	.24	.13	.04
162	Silage (275N)		.16	0	0	0	0
163	Hay		0	0	.03	0	0
164	Swedes		0	0	0	0	0
165	==						

Fig. 3.6 Rapid whole farm budget spreadsheet (Cells A115:H165).

```
        |  I  ||  J   ||  K  ||  L  ||  M  ||  N  ||  O  ||  P  |
115  FINISHING CATTLE          SUMMER FEEDING
116  ================   Continen-  Medium  S. Calf  S. Calf
117    £ per head       tal Steer  Steer   Steer    Heifer
118  Sales                  708      553     599      522
119  Spec Beef Premium       29       29      29
120  Purchases              609      474     516      424
121                        -----    -----   -----    -----
122  OUTPUT                 128      108     112       98
123  VARIABLE COSTS
124  Barley                   8        5       5
125  Other Feed
126  Vet Med & Other         21       18      18       16
127  Forage                  31       28      28       26
128
129  GROSS MARGIN /HEAD      68       57      61       56
130  GROSS MARGIN /HA       282      274     293      279
131
132  FORAGE (ha/hd)         .24      .21     .21       .2
133  Grazing (125N)          0        0       0        0
134  Grazing (175N)        .24      .21     .21       .2
135  Grazing (250N)          0        0       0        0
136  ========================================================
137
138
139
140
141
142
143
144
145
146
147
148
149
150
151
152
153
154
155
156
157
158
159
160
161
162
163
164
165
```

Fig. 3.7 Rapid whole farm budget spreadsheet (Cells I115:P165).

	A	B	C	D	E	F	G	H
166	BREEDING EWES		Upland	Upland	Loground	Loground		
167	==============		B'Face	F & St	F & St	Early		
168	Lambs Reared /100		130	140	158	140		
169	Av Price £/lamb		30.9	38	39.4	43.7		
170	£ per ewe	-------	------	------	------	------	---	
171	Lamb Sales		40.2	53.2	62.3	61.2		
172	Subsidies & Wool		13.3	13.6	9.1	9.1		
173	- Flock Replmt		5.6	14.0	14.0	13.4		
174			----	----	----	----		
175	OUTPUT		47.9	52.8	57.4	56.9		
176	VARIABLE COSTS							
177	Barley + Mins			7.0	7.0	8.3		
178	Other Feed		6.0	1.3	1.3	7.8		
179	Vet Med & Other		5.7	6.7	6.7	7.4		
180	Forage		9.6	11.1	11.1	8.3		
181								
182	GROSS MARGIN /EWE		26.6	26.7	31.2	25.1		
183	GROSS MARGIN /HA		253	264	309	339		
184								
185	FORAGE (ha/ewe)		.105	.101	.101	.074		
186	Grazing (75N)		.1	0	0	0		
187	Grazing (125N)		.0	.085	.085	.056		
188	Grazing (175N)		0	0	0	0		
189	Silage (220N)		.0	.0	.0	.0		
190	Hay		.005	.008	.008	.018		
191	Swedes		0	.008	.008	0		
192	==							
193								
194								
195								
196								
197								
198								
199								
200	GRAZING							
201	=======							
202	NITROGEN - kg/ha		75N	125N	175N	250N		
203	£ per ha	-------	------	------	------	------	---	
204	VARIABLE COSTS							
205	Seed		18	18	18	18		
206	Fertiliser & Lime		58	76	99	131		
207	Contract		0	0	0	0		
208	Sundry		14	14	14	14		
209			----	----	----	----		
210	TOTAL		90	108	131	163		
211	==							
212								

Fig. 3.8 Rapid whole farm budget spreadsheet (Cells A166:H212).

```
    |   I   ||   J   ||   K   ||   L   ||   M   ||   N   ||   O   ||   P   |

166   FEEDING  LAMBS        Short      Long
167   ==============        . Keep     Keep
168     £ per head ----------------------
169   Sales                 47.8       49.0
170   Purchases             35.0       33.0
171                         ----       ----
172   OUTPUT                12.8       16.0
173   VARIABLE COSTS
174   Barley + Mins          1.7        1.7
175   Other Feed              .0         .0
176   Vet Med & Other        2.6        3.2
177   Forage                 1.2        2.7
178
179   GROSS MARGIN /HEAD     7.3        8.4
180   GROSS MARGIN /HA       729        367
181
182   FORAGE (ha/hd)         .01        .023
183   Grazing (125N)           0        .01
184   Grazing (175N)           0        .0
185   Silage (220N)            0        .0
186   Silage (275N)            0         0
187   Hay                   .002       .003
188   Swedes                .008        .01
189   =====================================
190
191
192
193
194
195
196
197
198
199
200   FORAGE CROPS         SILAGE -- 2 CUT    HAY    SWEDES
201   ============
202   NITROGEN - kg/ha       220N       275N       125N
203     £ per ha ---------------------------------------------
204   VARIABLE COSTS
205   Seed                     18         18         18         10
206   Fertiliser              137        172         85         94
207   Contract                  0          0          0          0
208   Sundry                   14         14         21         16
209                          ----       ----       ----       ----
210   TOTAL                   169        204        124        120
211   ==================================================================
212   Yield - tonnes/ha      29.0       34.0        7.0       75.0
```

Fig. 3.9 Rapid whole farm budget spreadsheet (Cells I166:P212).

```
      |   A   ||    B   ||   C   ||    D   ||   E   ||   F   ||   G   ||   H   |
213
214
215
216
217
218
219
220   BREEDING SOWS                     3 Week            4 Week
221   =============                     Weaning           Weaning
222   Litters /sow /annum                 2.30              2.25
223   Pigs Reared /litter                 9.5               9.6
224   Weaners /sow /annum                21.9              21.4
225   Av Price £/weaner        34.0      34.0             34.0
226      £ per sow ------------------------------------------
227   Weaner Sales                        743               728
228   - Herd Replmt                        39                38
229                                      ----              ----
230   OUTPUT                              704               690
231   VARIABLE COSTS
232   Sow Meal                            174               190        158.0 £/tonne
233   Starter                              49                29        450.0 £/tonne
234   Follow-On                            62                61        220.0 £/tonne
235   Rearing Meal                         89                88        195.0 £/tonne
236   Vet Med & Other                      35                34
237                                      ----              ----
238   GROSS MARGIN /SOW                   294               288
239   ===========================================================
240
```

Fig. 3.10 Rapid whole farm budget spreadsheet (Cells A213:H240).

```
         | I  || J  || K  || L  || M  || N  || O  || P  |
213
214
215
216
217
218
219
220  FINISHING PIGS
221  ===============    Pork   Cutter  Bacon   Heavy
222  Deadweight kg       53.0    64.0   70.0    80.0
223  Price p/kg dw      118.0   114.0  112.0   109.0
224  Weaner Weight kg    27.0    27.0   27.0    27.0
225  Feed Conversion      2.5     2.6    2.7     2.9
226  £ per pig --------------------------------------------
227  Sales               62.5    73.0   78.4    87.2
228  Purchases           34.7    34.7   34.7    34.7
229                      ----    ----   ----    ----
230  OUTPUT              27.9    38.3   43.7    52.5
231  VARIABLE COSTS                                          Feed Price
232  Rearing Meal         7.8     7.8    7.8     7.8         195.0£/tonne
233  Growing Meal        14.2    21.2   25.1    25.7         185.0£/tonne
234  Finishing Meal        .0      .0     .0     7.0         175.0£/tonne
235  Vet Med & Other      2.9     3.2    3.8     3.3
236                      ----    ----   ----    ----
237  GROSS MARGIN /PIG    3.0     6.1    7.0     8.7
238  ==========================================================
239
240
```

Fig. 3.11 Rapid whole farm budget spreadsheet (Cells I213:P240).

```
   |  R   ||   S   ||   T   ||   U   ||   V   ||   W   ||   X   ||   Y   |
```

1   EASYPLAN EASYPLAN EASYPLAN EASYPLAN EASYPLAN EASYPLAN EASYPLAN EASYPLAN
2   (1)Enter arable crop areas in column V & livestock numbers in column W.
3   (2)Forage areas ,total farm area & farm gross margin are shown at R78.
4   (3)Enter rough grazing at V89 and the area of fertilised grass to which
5   it would be equivalent at V93.
6   (4)A summary of your FARM SYSTEM PLAN is shown at AA96.
7
8   FARM SYSTEM PLAN   --- FARM GROSS MARGIN BUDGET
9   ===

	ENTERPRISE	GROSS MARGIN	AREA	£
10	ENTERPRISE	GROSS MARGIN	AREA	£
11	---------	£ per hectare	hectares	
12	ARABLE CROPS (A40)			
13	Winter Wheat	484.0	20.0	9680
14	Spring Barley	363.5	20.0	7270
15	Winter Barley	421.5	10.0	4215
16	Spring Oats	420.0	.0	0
17	Winter O S Rape	685.0	10.0	6850
18	Protein Peas	517.0	.0	0
19	Potatoes Ware(MH)	1,222.5	.0	0
20	Potatoes Seed(HL)	2,027.6	.0	0
21	Other Crop	.0	.0	0
22	-----		-----	
23	TOTAL ARABLE		60.0	
24			-----	

	LIVESTOCK	£ per ha	£ per hd	ha	number	
25	LIVESTOCK	£ per ha	£ per hd	ha	number	
26	DAIRY COWS (A60)					
27	Autumn Calving	1,364.1	682.1	.0	0	0
28	All Year Calving	1,371.6	699.5	71.4	140	97933
29	Spring Calving	1,378.8	717.0	.0	0	0
30	REARING HEIFERS (I60)					
31	Aut Calving (26m)	284.4	179.2	.0	0	0
32	Spr Calving (30m)	269.9	186.2	13.8	20	3724
33	Aut Calving (30m)	282.5	197.8	14.0	20	3955
34	SUCKLER COWS (A90)					
35	Upl Wi Calving	427.4	260.7	.0	0	0
36	Upl Sp Calving	406.9	223.8	.0	0	0
37	Upl Su Calving	449.0	309.8	.0	0	0
38	Upl Au Calving	422.2	295.5	.0	0	0
39	WINTERING CALVES (I90)					
40	Spring Born Steer	731.0	87.7	.0	0	0
41	Spring Born Heifr	631.0	75.7	.0	0	0
42	Winter Born Steer	531.0	69.0	.0	0	0
43	Winter Born Heifr	546.4	71.0	.0	0	0
44	WINTER FINISHING (A115)					
45	Continental Steer	638.1	89.3	.0	0	0
46	Medium Steer	631.0	82.0	.0	0	0
47	Suckld Calf Steer	638.7	83.0	.0	0	0
48	Suckld Calf Heifr	631.0	69.4	.0	0	0
49	GRASS FINISHING (I115)					
50	Continental Steer	281.5	67.6	.0	0	0
51	Medium Steer	273.8	57.5	.0	0	0
52	Suckld Calf Steer	292.8	61.5	.0	0	0
53	Suckld Calf Heifr	279.0	55.8	.0	0	0

Fig. 3.12 Rapid whole farm budget spreadsheet (Cells R1:Y53).

	R	S	T	U	V	W	X	Y
54	DAIRY-BEEF FEEDING (A140)							
55	Cereal Bull Beef		n/a	74.0	.0	0	0	
56	Silage Bull Beef		1,039.8	166.4	8.8	55	9150	
57	18-20 Month Beef		553.6	160.6	.0	0	0	
58	22-24 Month Beef		507.3	213.1	.0	0	0	
59	Spring Yrlg Stores		569.5	74.0	.0	0	0	
60	Autumn Yrlg Stores		383.6	65.2	.0	0	0	
61	BREEDING EWES (A165)							
62	Upland Blackface		252.9	26.6	.0	0	0	
63	Upland F & St		264.0	26.7	.0	0	0	
64	Lowground F & St		309.1	31.2	2.0	20	624	
65	Lowground Early		339.2	25.1	.0	0	0	
66	FEEDING LAMBS (I165)							
67	Shortkeep Lambs		729.2	7.3	.0	0	0	
68	Longkeep Lambs		367.3	8.4	.0	0	0	
69	BREEDING SOWS (A220)							
70	3 Week Weaning		n/a	294	n/a	0	0	
71	4 Week Weaning		n/a	288	n/a	0	0	
72	FEEDING PIGS (I220)							
73	Pork		n/a	3.0	n/a	0	0	
74	Cutter		n/a	6.1	n/a	0	0	
75	Bacon		n/a	7.0	n/a	0	0	
76	Heavy		n/a	8.7	n/a	0	0	
77								
78	FORAGE CROPS (A200)							
79	Grazing (75N)				.0			
80	Grazing (125N)				.7			
81	Grazing (175N)				15.6			
82	Grazing (250N)				42.0			
83	Silage (220N)				11.2			
84	Silage (275N)				38.2			
85	Hay				1.2			
86	Swedes				.2			
87					-----			
88	TOTAL CROPS &GRASS (ha)				169.0			
89	Rough Grazing (ha)				5.4			
90					-----			
91	TOTAL FARM AREA (ha)				174.4			
92					-----			
93	Grass Equivalent of Rough Grazing				1.0		108	
94	ADJUSTED FARM AREA (ha)				170.0			
95					-----		---------	
96	TOTAL FARM GROSS MARGIN						143510	
97							---------	

Fig. 3.13 Rapid whole farm budget spreadsheet (Cells R54:Y97).

```
   |  AA  ||  AB  ||  AC  ||  AD  ||  AE  ||  AF  ||  AG  ||  AH  |

 1  EASYPLAN EASYPLAN EASYPLAN EASYPLAN EASYPLAN EASYPLAN EASYPLAN EASYPLAN
 2  (1)The GROSS OUTPUT & VARIABLE COSTS below relate to the system entered
 3     in the budget beginning at R8.
 4  (2)The FIXED COSTS are calculated on the basis of averages for Farm
 5     Type   8        (see page 339 Scottish Farm Management Handbook) but
 6     may be overwritten if alternative estimates are preferred.
 7  (3)Enter RENT & RATES at AD50, INTEREST RATE at AB52, HERITABLE PROPERTY
 8     VALUE at AG61, TENANT'S IMPROVEMENTS at AG63, & OWN CAPITAL at AG74.
 9  (4)If the labour cost is overwritten as paid labour only, the form of
10     the budget can be changed to show NET PROFIT by typing N while
11     pressing the ALT key.
12
13                            FARM BUDGET
14                            ===========
15  GROSS OUTPUT                                          £
16  ------------
17   CROPS                                            25235
18   MILK                                            142450
19   CATTLE                                           43475
20   SHEEP                                             1147
21   PIGS                                                 0
22                                                   -------
23                                                   212307
24  VARIABLE COSTS
25  --------------
26   SEED                                 4581
27   FERTILISER                          21298
28   CONTRACT & CASUAL                     350
29   SUNDRY CROP EXPS                     4995
30   FEED                                27079                    %
31   SUNDRY LSTK EXPS                    10494                  GROSS
32                                      -------     68797      OUTPUT
33                                                  -------     ------
34  FARM GROSS MARGIN                               143510        68
35  -----------------
36  FIXED COSTS
37  -----------
38   LABOUR   (incl. farmer & family)    58082                    27
39   MACHINERY
40    Repairs                   10988                                        5
41    Depreciation              17442                                        8
42    Fuel & Electricity         8547                                        4
43                             -------    36977                    17
44   PROPERTY REPAIRS                      5581                                3
45   MISCELLANEOUS                         9768                                5
46                                       -------    110408
47                                                  -------
48  SURPLUS BEFORE RENT & INTEREST                   33102        16
49  ------------------------------
50   RENT & RATES                            0                                0
51   INTEREST    ON   £    184292
52               AT     15.0%            27644                                13
53                                      -------     27644        13
54                                                  -------
55  NET SURPLUS   (Net Profit less charge for        5458         3
56  ===========           farmer & family labour)   =======
57  ==============================================================================
```

Fig. 3.14 Rapid whole farm budget spreadsheet (Cells AA1:AH57).

	AA || AB || AC || AD || AE || AF || AG || AH

```
58              ESTIMATED AVERAGE CAPITAL REQUIREMENTS
59              =========================================      £
60
61  HERITABLE PROPERTY                                       550000
62
63  TENANT'S IMPROVEMENTS & OTHER TENANT'S INGO (excluding        0
64     growing crops, crops in store and forage)
65  MACHINERY & EQUIPMENT                                     78489
66
67  BREEDING LIVESTOCK (Cows £   550      Sows £   135        78100
68     Lowground Ewes £ 55.0     Upland Ewes     £   50
69  WORKING CAPITAL (trading livestock, growing crops,        77703
70     crops in store, forage & other deadstock)
71                                                           -------        %
72  TOTAL AVERAGE CAPITAL REQUIRED                           784292     OWNED
73                                                                      -----
74     LESS: OWN CAPITAL (Net Worth)                         600000      76.5
75                                                           -------
76  ESTIMATED AVERAGE BORROWING REQUIREMENT                  184292
77  =========================================               =======
78
79  NOTES:  (1)To enter your name and a budget title go to AA90.
80          (2)The summary of the FARM SYSTEM PLAN which will appear in the
81             standard printout is shown at AA96.
82
83
```

Fig. 3.15 Rapid whole farm budget spreadsheet (Cells AA58:AH83).

```
|  AA  ||  AB  ||  AC  ||  AD  ||  AE  ||  AF  ||  AG  ||  AH  |
```

```
84    ************************************************************
85    *                        EASYPLAN                         *
86    *       a budgeting program devised by Roy Sutherland      *
87    *              SCOTTISH AGRICULTURAL COLLEGES              *
88    *             North College -- Economics Division          *
89    ************************************************************
90                     Date --    4/19/90
91      Budget prepared by --   Roy Sutherland
92
93      BUDGET TITLE : Example Dairy Farm
94      =========================================================
95
96                       FARM SYSTEM PLAN
97                       ================
98                Plus main performance assumptions
99                ---------------------------------
100   CROPPING              AREA              YIELD              PRICE
101   --------        hectares    acres   tonnes per ha.    £ per tonne
102   Winter Wheat        20.0      49        7                 100.0
103   Spring Barley       20.0      49        5.5                95.0
104   Winter Barley       10.0      25        6.5                95.0
105   Spring Oats           .0       0        0                    .0
106   Winter O S Rape     10.0      25        3.5               280.0
107   Protein Peas          .0       0        0                    .0
108   Potatoes Ware(MH)     .0       0        0                    .0
109   Potatoes Seed(HL)     .0       0        0                    .0
110   Other Crop            .0       0        0                    .0
111   Swedes                .2       0       75
112   Hay                  1.2       3        7.0
113   Silage              49.4     122       33
114   Grazing             58.3     144
115   Rough Grazing        5.4      13
116                      -----    ----
117   TOTAL              174.4     431
118                      -----    ----
119   LIVESTOCK            NUMBER              YIELD              PRICE
120   ---------                           litres per cow    p per litre
121   Dairy Cows                 140.0         5500              18.5
122   Heifers Reared per annum    40.0
123                                         AV SALE PRICE
124                                          £ per head
125   Suckler Cows                 .0                  .0    (CALVES)
126   Store Cattle (Spring sales)  .0                  .0
127   Store Cattle (Autumn sales)  .0                  .0
128   Winter Finishing Cattle      .0                  .0
129   Summer Finishing Cattle      .0                  .0
130   Intensive Bull Beef         55.0              569.0
131                                       LAMBING %     AV SALE PRICE
132                                                      £ per lamb
133   Ewes                        20.0        158.0          39
134   Feeding Lambs                .0                        0
135                                       PIGS REARED    AV SALE PRICE
136                                     PER SOW PER ANNUM   £ per pig
137   Sows                         .0          0              .0
138                                       FEED CONV RATIO
139   Feeding pigs                 .0          .0             .0
140
141   ==========================================================================
```

Fig. 3.16 Rapid whole farm budget spreadsheet (Cells AA84:AH141).

Crop variety selection

Purpose: To compare the economics of changing from a KNOWN cereal variety to a NEW one.

Author: Ian Howie

Spreadsheet Name: NEWGROW

4.1 Introduction

The spreadsheet (Fig. 4.1) compares the differences in yield, the main growing costs and grain price of a KNOWN variety with a NEW introduction. It can also be used to compare the growing of milling and feed varieties to assess the possible advantages.

The potential yield of the NEW crop is calculated by using the N.I.A.B. (National Institute of Agricultural Botany) yield index of both varieties to be compared and the expected yield of the established variety.

A number of variables can be introduced to take account of any differences in growing costs. The main areas covered are seed rate and costs, and any variations from the established variety in the costs of plant growth regulations (PGR's) and fungicides or other variable cost inputs.

4.2 Input data

All the input data is entered in columns B and C - column B for the KNOWN variety and column C for the NEW - and is as follows:

	Location
Variety names	B7:C7
NIAB yield indices	B8:C8
The expected yield of the existing variety	B9
Expected prices (£/t)	B12:C12
Seed rates (kg/ha)	B13:C13
Seed costs (£/t)	B14:C14

The differences in input costs per hectare, shown as a + or - against the NEW variety, take into account any differences between varieties due to disease, standing ability etc. Where there are increased costs they are entered as positive. Where there are savings, they are entered as negative.

	Location
Fungicide costs (£/ha)	C17
P.G.R. costs (£/ha)	C18
Other costs (£/ha)	C19

4.3 Output data

The spreadsheet does a series of calculations to show the Net benefit of changing varieties. This may or may not be a positive response.

(a) The spreadsheet firstly calculates the yield of the NEW variety C10. This is achieved by multiplying the expected yield of the KNOWN variety (B9) by the ratio of the N.I.A.B. yield index of the NEW variety (C8) to the N.I.A.B. yield index of the KNOWN variety (B8)

ie. yield of NEW variety = expected yield of KNOWN variety *
NIAB index of NEW variety / NIAB index of KNOWN variety

ie. C10 = B9 * C8 / B8

(b) These yield figures are then used to calculate the cash output of the KNOWN variety (B23) and the NEW variety (C23) by multiplying the yield (t/ha) (B9 or C10) by the price (£/t) (B12 or C12).

ie. cash output of KNOWN variety (£/ha) = Yield (t/ha)* price (£/t)

ie. B23 = B9 * B12
and similarly C23 = C10 * C12

(c) The costs (£/ha) of the NEW variety (C24) comprise of seed costs, fungicides, PGR's and other costs. Seed costs (£/ha) are calculated by multiplying the seed rate (kg/ha) (C13) by the seed cost (£/t) (C14) and by dividing by 1000. Fungicides, PGRs and other costs are already expressed in £/ha and so

ie. C24 = C13*C14/1000 + C17 + C18 + C19

The formula used to calculate costs (£/ha) of the KNOWN variety (B24) is similar

ie. B24 = B13*B14/1000 + B17 + B18 + B19

although if the user follows the data input instructions correctly entries at B17, B18 and B19 should be zero.

(d) The advantage or disadvantage in the output of the NEW variety is the difference between the output of each (B23 and C23)

ie. D23 = C23 - B23

(e) In a similar way the variations in growing costs are calculated by the difference in the costs of the two varieties (B24 and C24)

ie. D24 = C24 - B24.

(f) The benefit or otherwise of growing the NEW variety (D26) is obtained by adding the difference in the cash outputs (D23) to the difference in the growing costs (D24)

ie. D26 = D23 + D24.

This figure (D26) may be positive or negative. If it is positive, it shows the size of the advantage per hectare of changing to the NEW variety. If it is negative, it shows the loss per hectare of changing from the KNOWN variety.

All the formulas used in the spreadsheet are shown at Fig. 4.2

4.4 Other uses

The spreadsheet can also be used to compare growing milling with feed wheat or malting with feed barley. The final calculation (D26) will show the advantage or disadvantage of growing a specialist variety, assuming the appropriate quality premiums are achieved.

	A		B		C		D	

```
1    NEWGROW - a partial budget to compare two varieties - Ian Howie

2    =====================================================================
3    DATA INPUT SECTION
4                              KNOWN          NEW
5                              Variety        Variety
6                              --------------------------
7    Variety name             Slejpner       Worbridge
8    NIAB Yield Index         103            110
9    Expected yield (t/ha)    8.6
10   Calculated yield (t/ha)                 9.18
11
12   Expected price (£/t)     95             95
13   Seed rate (kg/ha)        180            160
14   Seed cost (£/t)          210            400
15
16   Other input cost variations ( + or - )
17   Fungicides (£/ha)                       15
18   PGR (£/ha)                              -7
19   Other costs (£/ha)                      0
20   -----------------------------------------------------------------
21   PARTIAL BUDGET                                       Benefit of
22                                                        new over old
23   Output (£/ha)            817            873          56
24   Costs (£/ha)             38             72           -34
25   =====================================================================
26   Net benefit of new variety (£/ha)                    21
27   =====================================================================
```

Fig. 4.1 Crop variety selection spreadsheet.

	A	B	C	D
1	NEWGROW - a partial budget to compare two varieties - Ian Howie			
2	==			
3	DATA INPUT SECTION			
4		KNOWN	NEW	
5		Variety	Variety	
6		-------	-------	
7	Variety name	Slejpner	Worbridge	
8	NIAB Yield Index	103	110	
9	Expected yield (t/ha)	8.6		
10	Calculated yield (t/ha)		B9*C8/B8	
11				
12	Expected price (£/t)	95	95	
13	Seed rate (kg/ha)	180	160	
14	Seed cost (£/t)	210	400	
15				
16	Other input cost variations (+ or -)			
17	Fungicides (£/ha)		15	
18	PGR (£/ha)		-7	
19	Other costs (£/ha)		0	
20				
21	PARTIAL BUDGET			
22				Benefit of new over old
23	Output (£/ha)	B9*B12	C10*C12	C23-B23
24	Costs (£/ha)	B13*B14/1000+B17+B18+B19	C13*C14/1000+C17+C18+C19	B24-C24
25		============================	============================	===========
26	Net benefit of new variety (£/ha)			D23+D24
27		============================	============================	===========

Fig. 4.2 Formulas for crop variety selection spreadsheet.

Seed growing and seed costs

Purpose: To compare a cereal crop for seed with crops grown for other uses. Also to compare the economics of growing from purchased seed or farm saved seed.

Author: Ian Howie

Spreadsheet Name: SEEDGROW

5.1 Introduction

The spreadsheet is in two parts (Fig. 5.1). The first part (A1:H45) compares the advantage of growing for seed over commercial production. It also shows the penalty incurred when a crop grown for seed is rejected or not sold for seed for some reason. The spreadsheet can also take into account any tonnage limitation in the seed contract and any extra costs involved such as certification charges.

The various options which can be considered are:

Option

1   Commercial crop grown from farm saved seed.
2   Commercial crop grown from purchased C2 seed.
3   Seed crop grown from Basic or C1 seed (adjusted for any tonnage limitation)
4   Crop grown for seed as in Option 3 but rejected.

To make a meaningful calculation, it is assumed in part one that the sales are all made at the same time.

In the second part (A47:H60), a further comparison is made between growing for seed and selling commercial ware grain at a later date to avoid selling at a depressed price immediately post harvest.

As the sales are delayed, the spreadsheet calculates the cost of the capital locked up in the grain until it is sold, and subtracts this amount from the sales figures to give a realistic comparison.

The spreadsheet can also be used to compare varieties, seed sources, yield, variations in quality and price premia and the timing of sales corrected for storage charges.

5.2 Input data

The input data is in two sections. In the first section (H5:H10) the following information is entered.

Location

H5	Commercial price of crop sold ex-harvest (£/t)
H6	Commercial price of crop sold later ex-store (£/t)
H7	Months stored
H8	Interest rate (%)
H9	Seed premium (£/t)
H10	Tonnage limitation per hectare of seed contract (t/ha)

In the second section (D23:F26) information on yields, seed rates, seed and other costs are entered for options 1, 2 and 3. The data for option 4 is assumed to be the same as that for option 3.

Location

D23:F23	Yield (t/ha)
D24:F24	Seed rate (kg/ha)
D25:F25	Seed cost (£/t)
D26:F26	Any other costs (£/ha)

5.3 Crops sold ex-harvest (A28:G45)

For each of the 4 options, a number of calculations are performed. The full set of formulas is given in Fig. 5.2 and a brief explanation is given below.

(a) Yield (t/ha) (D31:G31)

   For options 1, 2 and 3 these refer to the corresponding data entry cells in row 23 (eg. D31 = D23). For option 4 cell G31 refers to cell F23 (ie. seed crop yield).

(b) Price (£/t) (D32:G32)

   For options 1, 2 and 4 this is just the commercial price sold ex-harvest (H5) but for option 3, the seed premium (H9) has also to be added

   ie. $F32 = H5 + H9$

(c) Output (£/ha) (D34:G34)

   For options 1, 2 and 4 this is obtained by multiplying the yield by the price (eg. D34 = D31 * D32) but for option 3 an adjustment has to be made for the tonnage limitation per hectare of seed contract (H10). Any tonnage over that limitation is assumed to be sold at the commercial price

   ie. $F34 = H10 * F32 + (F31 - H10) * H5$

(d) Seed cost (£/ha) (D34:G35)

   For options 1, 2 and 3
   Seed cost (£/ha) = Seed rate (kg/ha) x seed cost (£/t)/1000

   eg. $D35 = D24 * D25/1000$

The seed cost for option 4 is the same as for option 3.

(e) Other costs (£/ha) (D36:G36)

For options 1, 2 and 3 these are the same as the input data values in row 26 (eg. D36 = D26). Option 4 is again the same as for option 3.

(f) Margin (£/ha) (D36:G38)

For all 4 options, Margin = Output - seed cost - other costs

eg. D38 = D34 - D35 - D36

(g) Benefit from growing seed crop (£/ha) (D41:E41)

The economics of options 1 and 2 are compared with those of growing the seed crop from Basic or C1 seed and the differences displayed in the cells D41 and E41.

eg. D41 = F38 - D38

A positive value indicates a benefit from growing the seed crop, a negative value the reverse.

(h) Penalty for rejected seed crop (£/ha) (G44)

This is the difference between the margins for options 3 and 4

ie. G44 = G38 - F38

5.4 Effect of delaying sales (A47:G60)

This part of the spreadsheet compares the earlier options with the further choice of delaying the sale of the commercial grain ex-combine and selling out of store at a later date, at an increased price (H6). As this delay in sales is also a delay in cash receipts, the spreadsheet calculates the cost of financing holding the grain in storage until a later date. The spreadsheet corrects the MARGIN according to the number of months that sales are delayed (H7) and the interest rate chosen (H8).

All comparisons in this section are made with seed sales ex-harvest (option 3).

(a) Output (£/ha) (D51:G51)

The new estimates of output are calculated by multiplying yields (row 23) by the commercial price sold ex-store (H6)

eg. D51 = D23 * H6

(b) Margin (£/ha) (D52:G52)

New margin = new output - seed cost - other costs

eg. D52 = D51 - D35 - D36

(c) Finance charges (£/ha) (D54:G54)

For each option, the cost of financing the delay in sales is calculated by applying the interest rate (H8/100) over the proportion of the year that the crop is held in store (H7/12) to the amount of money tied up in the stored crop. This amount is estimated as the average of the value of the crop ex-harvest and at sale (D34 + D51)/2.

Thus, eg. D54 = (D34 + D51)/2 * (H8/100) * (H7/12)

(d) Adjusted margin (£/ha) (D56:G56)

For each option, Adjusted margin = New margin - finance charges

eg. D56 = D52 - D54

(e) Benefit from growing seed crop (£/ha) (D56:G58)

The economics of all 3 options are compared with those of growing the seed crop from Basic or C1 seed and selling ex-harvest (F38).

eg. D58 = F38 - D56

Again, a positive value indicates a benefit from selling the seed crop ex-harvest, and vice-versa.

All the formulas used in the spreadsheet are shown at Fig. 5.2

```
    |   A    ||   B   ||   C  ||   D  ||   E   ||   F   ||   G   ||   H  |
1   SEEDGROW    To compare growing commercial grain crops with producing
2               seed crops, when sold ex-harvest or later ex-store. Ian Howie
3   ==============================================================================
4   INPUT DATA
5               Commercial price sold ex-harvest (£/t)                       100
6               Commercial price sold later ex-store (£/t)                   112
7               Months stored                                                  3
8               Interest rate (%)                                             14
9               Seed premium (£/t)                                            15
10              Tonnage limitation per hectare of seed contract             5.00
11              ------------------------------------------------------------------
12
13  OPTION                                                      COLUMN
14     1  :  Commercial crop grown from farm saved seed            D
15     2  :  Commercial crop grown from purchased (C2) seed        E
16     3  :  Seed crop grown from Basic or C1 seed                 F
17              (output adjusted for tonnage limitation)
18     4  :  Seed crop grown from Basic or C1 but rejected         G
19
20                                    Farm              Basic
21                                    saved      C2     or C1
22
23  Yield           t/ha              7.60      7.70    7.80
24  Seed rate       kg/ha              180       180     150
25  Seed cost       £/t                140       210     320
26  Other costs     £/ha                               12
27  ==============================================================================
28  CROPS SOLD EX HARVEST                                       Rejected
29                                                                seed
30
31  Yield           t/ha              7.60      7.70    7.80      7.80
32  Price           £/t                100       100     115       100
33  ------------------------------------------------------------------------------
34  Output          £/ha               760       770     855       780
35  Seed cost       £/ha                25        38      48        48
36  Other costs     £/ha                 0         0      12        12
37  ------------------------------------------------------------------------------
38  MARGIN          £/ha               735       732     795       720
39  ==============================================================================
40  Benefit from growing
41  seed crop       £/ha                60        63
42  ------------------------------------------------------------------------------
43  Penalty for rejected
44  seed crop       £/ha                                         -75
45  ==============================================================================
46
47  EFFECT OF DELAYING SALES.
48  Comparing seed sales ex-harvest with selling commercial crops ex-store
49  corrected for finance charges            Months in store       3
50
51  Output          £/ha               851       862             874
52  Margin          £/ha               826       825             814
53
54  Finance charges £/ha                28        29              29
55
56  ADJUSTED MARGIN £/ha               798       796             785
57  ==============================================================================
58  Benefit from growing               -3        -1              10
59  seed crop       £/ha
60  ==============================================================================
```

Fig. 5.1 Seed growing and seed costs spreadsheet.

	A	B	C	D	E	F	G	H
28	CROPS SOLD EX HARVEST							
29							Rejected	
30							seed	
31	Yield	t/ha		D23	E23	F23	F23	
32	Price	£/t		H5	H5+H9	H5	H5	
33								
34	Output	£/ha		D31*D32	E31*E32	H10*F32+(F31-H10)*H5	G31*G32	
35	Seed cost	£/ha		D24*D25/1000	E24*E25/1000	F24*F25/1000	F24*F25/1000	
36	Other costs	£/ha		D26	E26	F26	F26	
37								
38	MARGIN	£/ha		D34-D35-D36	E34-E35-E36	F34-F35-F36	G34-G35-G36	
39								
40	Benefit from growing							
41	seed crop	£/ha		F38-D38	F38-E38			
42								
43	Penalty for rejected							
44	seed crop	£/ha					G38-F38	
45								
46								
47	EFFECT OF DELAYING SALES.							
48	Comparing seed sales ex-harvest with selling commercial crops ex-store							
49	corrected for finance charges				Months in store			
50								
51	Output	£/ha		D23*H6	E23*H6	F23*H6	F23*H6	H7
52	Margin	£/ha		D51-D35-D36	E51-E35-E36		G51-G35-G36	
53								
54	Finance charges	£/ha		(D34+D51)/2*(H8/100)*(H7/12)	(E34+E51)/2*(H8/100)*(H7/12)	(F34+F51)/2*(H8/100)*(H7/12)	(G34+G51)/2*(H8/100)*(H7/12)	
55								
56	ADJUSTED MARGIN	£/ha		D52-D54	E52-E54		G52-G54	
57								
58	Benefit from growing							
59	seed crop	£/ha		F38-D56	F38-E56		F38-G56	
60								

Fig. 5.2 Formulas for seed growing and seed costs spreadsheet.

Crop partial budget

Purpose: To calculate the change in the annual farm profit that occurs when one crop is grown in preference to another and to assess the sensitivity of the result to changes in the values of some of the input data.

Authors: David Noble and Joe Morris

Spreadsheet Name: PBUDGET

6.1 Introduction

This spreadsheet (Figs. 6.2 and 6.3) computes the effect on farm profit of replacing one crop with another. Data requirements are specified in Section 6.3 and include only those costs which are affected by the proposed change. The analysis is therefore referred to as a partial budget. It shows the average annual changes that would occur in costs and revenues once the proposed change is fully operational.

One of the advantages of setting up a set of calculations on a spreadsheet is that by changing individual data values the effects of these changes on important output values are immediately computed. This is usually referred to as a sensitivity analysis. This spreadsheet has the added feature that it automatically performs a sensitivity analysis on important variables.

It should be of use to farmers and advisers.

6.2 Spreadsheet structure

There are three main parts to the spreadsheet (Fig. 6.1)

Input data section (A1:D19)
Partial budget calculations (A21:G40)
Sensitivity analyses (A41:G120)

The sensitivity analysis considers the effect on farm profit of changes in the values of important variables. The important variables for each crop are output price and yield, labour costs and total variable costs. There are three parts to the sensitivity analysis.

(i)   The change required in important variables to breakeven (A41:G60).

(ii)   The sensitivity of the budget (change in farm profit) to suggested changes in variables, taken one at a time (A61:G94).

(iii)   The sensitivity of the budget to changes in combinations of the variables (A95:G120).

The structure of the whole spreadsheet is shown in Fig. 6.1.

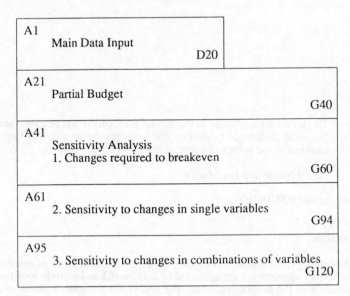

Fig. 6.1 Structure of the PBUDGET spreadsheet.

6.3 Data input

In addition, to the main data input, the ranges over which the sensitivity analyses are performed are specified as input data values (D67:D93 and B103:D19). These are explained in Sections 6.5.2 and 6.5.3.
The main data input is carried out in cells C2:D19 and is described in this section.

The data in column C are for the old (or existing) crop and those in column D are for the new (or proposed) crop. The same data are required for each crop. Specifically these are:

Location	Description
C2:D2	Crop name. In Supercalc, this has to be entered as a textual value, ie. enclosed first of all in quotes and then on the outside by brackets.
C3:D3	The area (ha) being changed. The spreadsheet is set up so that as soon as the value in C3 is entered, D3 is also set to that value.
C5:D5	Yield (t/ha)
C6:D6	Price (£/t)

C7:D7	Seed application rate (kg/ha)
C8:D8	Seed cost (£/t)
C9:D9	Fertiliser 1 application rate (t/ha)
C10:D10	Fertiliser 1 cost (£/t)
C11:D11	Fertiliser 2 application rate (t/ha)
C12:D12	Fertiliser 2 cost (£/t)
C13:D13	Costs of sprays (£/ha)
C14:D14	Machinery fixed costs (£) - these represent the changes that occur in average annual machinery fixed costs such as depreciation, interest on capital, shelter, tax and insurance.
C15:D15	Machinery variable costs (£/ha) - these represent the running costs of machinery and can again be calculated as in the BREAKEVN spreadsheet (Spreadsheet 11).
C16:D16	Cost of contractors (£/ha)
C17:D17	Any transport costs (£/ha)
C18:D18	Cost of part-time labour (£)
C19:D19	Any other costs (£/ha)

6.4 Partial budget calculations

There are four parts to the partial budget:

(a) Revenue lost through not growing the old crop
= Area (ha) of old crop * yield (t/ha) * price (£/t)

ie. C23 = C3 * C4 * C5

(b) Extra Revenue received through growing the new crop
= Area (ha) of new crop * yield (t/ha) * price (£/t)

ie. F23 = D3 * D4 * D5

(c) Extra costs incurred through growing the new crop (C23:C37). The formulas for these are virtually self-explanatory and can be seen in the printout at the end of this chapter. They consist in most cases of simply multiplying the cost (£/ha) by the area (ha). For seed, the cost (£/ha) has additionally to be calculated by multiplying the seed rate (kg/ha) by the seed cost (ie. C28 = D3 * D7 * D8/1000) and for fertilisers this has to be done for both fertilisers before adding them together.

eg. C29 = D3 * (D10*D11 + D12*D13)

For machinery both the fixed cost and variable cost components have to be added together with only the variable cost being multiplied by the area.

eg. C31 = D3*D15 + D14

The sum of all the extra costs is displayed at cell D37.

(d)   The costs saved through not growing the old crop (D28:D37). These are calculated in the same way as the extra costs incurred through growing the new crop.

The last line of the partial budget computes the change in farm profit by subtracting the reduced revenue and the extra costs from the extra revenue and the reduced costs,

ie. C39 = F23 + F37 - (C23 + C37)

The budget also displays the change in farm profit per hectare

ie. G39 = C39 / C3

6.5 Sensitivity analysis calculations

6.5.1 *Change required in important variables to breakeven (A41:G60)*

The partial budget is said to breakeven when the change in farm profit is zero. This section calculates by how much individual values have to change before this occurs. All the formulas involve dividing the present change in farm profit by the appropriate factor, and where necessary converting to a percentage. They are displayed in Fig. 6.4.

6.5.2 *Sensitivity to changes in single variables (A61:G94)*

For each of the important variables a best value, a most likely value, and a worst value are taken and the effect on the change in profit assessed.

Normally the most likely values will be the same as those in the main data input section but all values can be changed by the user. Specification of these values is performed in cells D67:D93.

The calculations for each of the variables are similar and will be described for the new crop price changes:

The "effect on profit" calculations (E67:E69) are performed by multiplying the change in price (from the original value) (£/t) by the yield (t/ha) and the area (ha),

eg. E67 = (D67 - D5) * D4 * D3

The single value in the "Range" column (F68) is the difference between the best and worst effects on the budget,

ie. F68 = E67 - E69

The "New change in profit" values (G67:G69) are just the original values plus the change (effect) that has occurred,

eg. G67 = C39 + E67

All these formulas are displayed in Fig. 6.5.

6.5.3 Sensitivity to changes in combinations of variables (A95:G120)

In this section the effect of combinations of changes in yield, price and costs of the new crop are considered. The nature of the calculation in each case is the same and is as follows:-

Increase in profit due to change =
    (New yield * New price - Old yield * Old price) * area - increase in costs

eg. E104 = (B103*C103 - D4*D5) * D3 - (D104-100)*C37/100

The full set of formulas is displayed in Fig. 6.5.

6.6 Example

The example data given in the spreadsheet (Fig. 6.2) are for a farmer considering discontinuing sugar beet production on 20 ha and substituting oil seed rape. One part-time worker is about to retire. A contractor is presently used for beet harvesting and would be used for cutting and windrowing the rape. The estimates of machinery fixed costs assume more rapid depreciation on the combine (due to the rape) and a depreciation saving on tractors and trailers presently used for carting the beet.

	A	B	C	D	E	F	G	H
1			OLD CROP	NEW CROP	===========================			
2	Crops		Beet	Rape	Partial Budget to			
3	Hectares		20	20	compare two crops			
4	Yield (t/ha)		40	2.8				
5	Price (£/t)		33	260	D.H.Noble & J.Morris			
6					Silsoe College			
7	Seed rate (kg/ha)		8	8	===========================			
8	Seed cost (£/t)		7000	3750				
9	Fertiliser 1 rate (t/ha)		.83	.63				
10	Fertiliser 1 cost (£/t)		125	125				
11	Fertiliser 2 rate (t/ha)		.83	.25	MAIN DATA INPUT			
12	Fertiliser 2 cost (£/t)		115	115	SCREEN			
13	Spray costs (£/ha)		140	100				
14	Machinery fixed costs (£)		1000	600				
15	: variable costs (£/ha)		110	60				
16	Contractor cost (£/ha)		150	35				
17	Transport cost (£/ha)		120	0				
18	Part-time labour cost(£)		3000	0				
19	Other costs (£/ha)		13	0				
20	===							
21	REVENUE LOST (£)				EXTRA REVENUE (£)			
22	----------------				------------------			
23		Beet	26400			Rape	14560	
24								
25	EXTRA COSTS (£)				COSTS SAVED (£)			
26	---------------				---------------			
27		Rape				Beet		
28	Seed		600				1120	
29	Fertilisers		2150				3984	
30	Sprays		2000				2800	
31	Machinery		1800				3200	
32	Contractor		700				3000	
33	Transport		0				2400	
34	Labour		0				3000	
35	Other		0				260	
36			-----------------				-----------------	
37			7250				19764	
38	---							
39	CHANGE IN FARM PROFIT		£674		CHANGE IN PROFIT/HA		£34	
40	===							
41								
42				SENSITIVITY ANALYSES				
43				====================				
44								
45			===					
46			Change required in important variables to breakeven					
47			--------------------------------------					
48					Change			
49			Variable		required			
50			--------------------------------------					
51								
52			Rape price (£/t)		-12.04			
53			Rape yield (t/ha)		-.13			
54			Rape costs (£/ha)		9.3%			
55			Beet price (£/t)		.84			
56			Beet yield (t/ha)		1.02			
57			Beet costs (£/ha)		-3.4%			
58			Extra labour cost		-22.5%			
59			===					
60								

Fig. 6.2 Crop partial budget spreadsheet (Cells A1:H60).

	A		B		C		D		E		F		G	|H|

```
 61  ================================================================================
 62                 Sensitivity to changes in single variables
 63  ================================================================================
 64                                              Effect on            New change
 65        Variable          Level        Value    profit    Range    in profit
 66  -------------------------------------------------------------------------------
 67                          Best          300      2240                 2914
 68         Rape             Most likely   260         0      4480        674
 69       price (£/t)        Worst         220     -2240                -1566
 70
 71                          Best          3.5      3640                 4314
 72         Rape             Most likely   2.8         0      5720        674
 73       yield (t/ha)       Worst         2.4     -2080                -1406
 74  -------------------------------------------------------------------------------
 75                          Best           36     -2400                -1726
 76         Beet             Most likely    33         0      4800        674
 77       price (£/t)        Worst          30      2400                 3074
 78
 79                          Best           50     -6600                -5926
 80         Beet             Most likely    40         0     13200        674
 81       yield (t/ha)       Worst          30      6600                 7274
 82  -------------------------------------------------------------------------------
 83                          Best         75.0%     1813                 2486.5
 84       Rape costs         Most likely 100.0%        0      3625        674
 85  (% of first estimate)   Worst       125.0%    -1813                -1138.5
 86
 87                          Best         75.0%    -4941                -4267
 88       Beet costs         Most likely 100.0%        0      9882        674
 89  (% of first estimate)   Worst       125.0%     4941                 5615
 90  -------------------------------------------------------------------------------
 91                          Best        150.0%     1500                 2174
 92   Labour saving          Most likely 100.0%        0      3000        674
 93  (% of first estimate)   Worst        50.0%    -1500                 -826
 94  ================================================================================
 95  =========================================================
 96    Sensitivity to changes in combinations of variables
 97  =========================================================
 98                                          Increase
 99               Rape       Rape     Rape   in profit
100               yield      price    costs  due to
101               (t/ha)     (£/t)    (%)    change (£)
102  --------------------------------------------------------
103                3.5        260     100.0%    3640
104                                   125.0%    1828
105
106                           220     100.0%     840
107                                   125.0%    -973
108  --------------------------------------------------------
109                2.8        260     100.0%       0
110                                   125.0%   -1813
111
112                           220     100.0%   -2240
113                                   125.0%   -4053
114  --------------------------------------------------------
115                2.4        260     100.0%   -2080
116                                   125.0%   -3893
117
118                           220     100.0%   -4000
119                                   125.0%   -5813
120  =========================================================
```

Fig. 6.3 Crop partial budget spreadsheet (Cells A61:H120).

```
         |  A   ||    B     ||   C   ||  D   ||  E   ||  F   |  G   ||H|
 1                                OLD CROP  NEW CROP  ==========================
 2    Crops                       ("Beet")  ("Rape")  | Partial Budget to      |
 3    Hectares                     20        C3       | compare two crops      |
 4    Yield (t/ha)                 40        2.8      |                        |
 5    Price (£/t)                  33        260      | D.H.Noble & J.Morris   |
 6                                                    | Silsoe College         |
 7    Seed rate (kg/ha)            8         8        ==========================
 8    Seed cost (£/t)              7000      3750
 9    Fertiliser 1 rate (t/ha)     .83       .63
10    Fertiliser 1 cost (£/t)      125       125
11    Fertiliser 2 rate (t/ha)     .83       .25          MAIN DATA INPUT
12    Fertiliser 2 cost (£/t)      115       115              SCREEN
13    Spray costs (£/ha)           140       100
14    Machinery fixed costs (£)    1000      600
15      : variable costs (£/ha)    110       60
16    Contractor cost (£/ha)       150       35
17    Transport cost (£/ha)        120       0
18    Part-time labour cost(£)     3000      0
19    Other costs (£/ha)           13        0
20    ======================================================================
21    REVENUE LOST (£)                         EXTRA REVENUE (£)
22    ----------------                         -----------------
23            C2             C3*C4*C5           D2         D3*D4*D5
24
25    EXTRA COSTS (£)                          COSTS SAVED (£)
26    ---------------                          ---------------
27            D2                                C2
28    Seed                D3*D7*D8/                     C3*C7*C8/1000
29    Fertilisers         D3*(D9*D10+D11*D12)           C3*(C9*C10+C11*C12)
30    Sprays              D3*D13                        C3*C13
31    Machinery           D3*D15+D1                     C3*C15+C14
32    Contractor          D3*D16                        C3*C16
33    Transport           D3*D17                        C3*C17
34    Labour              D18                           C18
35    Other               D3*D19                        C3*C19
36                        ------------------------------------------
37                        SUM(C28:C35)                  SUM(F28:F35)
38    -------------------------------------------------------------------
39    CHANGE IN FARM PROFIT    F23+F37-(C23+C37) CHANGE IN PROFIT/HA C39/C3
40    ======================================================================
41
42                        SENSITIVITY ANALYSES
43                        ====================
44
45           ==========================================================
46    Change required in important variables to breakeven
47           ------------------------------------------
48                                          Change
49                        Variable          required
50                        ------------------------------------------
51
52            D2          price (£/t)       -C39/(D3*D4)
53            D2          yield (t/ha)      -C39/(D3*D5)
54            D2          costs (£/ha)      100*C39/C37
55            C2          price (£/t)       C39/(C3*C4)
56            C2          yield (t/ha)      C39/(C3*C5)
57            C2          costs (£/ha)      -100*C39/F37
58                 Extra labour cost        -100*C39/(C18-D18)
59           ==========================================================
60
```

Fig. 6.4 Formulas for cells A1:G60 in Crop Partial Budget Spreadsheet.

Fig. 6.5 appears on pp. 60−61

	A ‖	B ‖	C ‖	D ‖	E ‖	F ‖	G ‖H‖
61							
62		Sensitivity to changes in single variables					
63							
64					Effect on		New change
65		Variable	Level	Value	profit	Range	in profit
66							
67			Best	300	(D67-D5)*D4*D3	E67-E69	C39+E67
68		D2	Most likely	260	(D68-D5)*D4*D3		C39+E68
69		price (£/t)	Worst	220	(D69-D5)*D4*D3		C39+E69
70							
71			Best	3.5	(D71-D4)*D5*D3	E71-E73	C39+E71
72		D2	Most likely	2.8	(D72-D4)*D5*D3		C39+E72
73		yield (t/ha)	Worst	2.4	(D73-D4)*D5*D3		C39+E73
74							
75			Best	36	(C5-D75)*C4*C3	E77-E75	C39+E75
76		C2	Most likely	33	(C5-D76)*C4*C3		C39+E76
77		price (£/t)	Worst	30	(C5-D77)*C4*C3		C39+E77
78							
79			Best	50	(C4-D79)*C5*C3	E81-E79	C39+E79
80		C2	Most likely	40	(C4-D80)*C5*C3		C39+E80
81		yield (t/ha)	Worst	30	(C4-D81)*C5*C3		C39+E81
82							
83			Best	75	(100-D83)*C37/100	E83-E85	C39+E83
84		D2 costs	Most likely	100	(100-D84)*C37/100		C39+E84
85		(% of first estimate)	Worst	125	(100-D85)*C37/100		C39+E85
86							
87			Best	75	(D87-100)*F37/100	E89-E87	C39+E87
88		C2 costs	Most likely	100	(D88-100)*F37/100		C39+E88
89		(% of first estimate)	Worst	125	(D89-100)*F37/100		C39+E89
90							
91		Labour saving	Best	150	(D91-100)*(C18-D18)/100	E91-E93	C39+E91
92		(% of first estimate)	Most likely	100	(D92-100)*(C18-D18)/100		C39+E92
93			Worst	50	(D93-100)*(C18-D18)/100		C39+E93
94							

```
95  ================================================================
96  Sensitivity to changes in combinations of variables
97  ================================================================
98
99                                               Increase
100  D2                                           in profit
101  yield     D2            D2                   due to
     (t/ha)    price         costs                change (£)
               (£/t)         (%)
102  ----------------------------------------------------------------
103  3.5       260           100     (B103*C103-D4*D5)*D3-(D103-100)*C37/100
104                          125     (B103*C103-D4*D5)*D3-(D104-100)*C37/100
105
106            220           D103    (B103*C106-D4*D5)*D3-(D106-100)*C37/100
107                          D104    (B103*C106-D4*D5)*D3-(D107-100)*C37/100
108
109  2.8       C103          D103    (B109*C109-D4*D5)*D3-(D109-100)*C37/100
110                          D104    (B109*C109-D4*D5)*D3-(D110-100)*C37/100
111
112            C106          D103    (B109*C112-D4*D5)*D3-(D112-100)*C37/100
113                          D104    (B109*C112-D4*D5)*D3-(D113-100)*C37/100
114  ----------------------------------------------------------------
115  2.4       C103          D103    (B115*C115-D4*D5)*D3-(D115-100)*C37/100
116                          D104    (B115*C115-D4*D5)*D3-(D116-100)*C37/100
117
118            C106          D103    (B115*C118-D4*D5)*D3-(D118-100)*C37/100
119                          D104    (B115*C118-D4*D5)*D3-(D119-100)*C37/100
120  ================================================================
```

Fig. 6.5 Formulas for cells A61:G120 in Crop Partial Budget Spreadsheet.

Perenniel crop replacement timing

Purpose: To determine the optimum age of replacement of a perennial crop at different discount rates.

Author: Nigel Williams

Spreadsheet Name: ORCHREPL

7.1 Introduction

An orchard or plantation is a typical longer term investment for which the cost of establishment is spread over several years. The cash flows increase at first, may continue at a stable level and then diminish as the productive capacity of the plants declines with age. The problems associated with this type of investment where there are uneven cash flows are (a) how to decide when to replace (grub) the crop and (b) how to compare the financial returns from it with returns from other perennial and annual crops.

The answer to the first question is to calculate the average annual return for a number of different assumed lives for the crop. The length of life giving the highest average annual return represents the optimum and the crop should be grubbed at the end of that period. The actual method of calculation used in the model is slightly more complex than using simple averages of the costs and returns because interest must be charged on the money invested in the project. This is incorporated into the model via the technique of discounting. The future cash flows are converted back to their present day values using discount factors. These present values can be summed to show the total benefit to be derived from keeping the perennial crop in production for any given number of years. Once this has been done the model amortises the total benefit over the life of the orchard to generate a constant equivalent annual net cash flow or equivalent annuity for each year of each different assumed life for the crop. The optimum length of life will be the one that generates the greatest equivalent annuity. This more complex approach gives greater accuracy in determining the optimum life for the project, although of course all the data used are bound to be estimates. The significant benefit of the more complex approach is that the equivalent annuity generated over the chosen life of the project can be directly compared with the returns from any other perennial crop, irrespective of its length of life and with the return from an annual crop or land-using livestock enterprise. The average annual cash flow cannot be used this way as it significantly overstates the return from the project since the cost of capital invested in the project is ignored.

The procedure for using the model is to calculate the expected net cash flow for each year of the project's life. These data are entered in cells C5 to C19. The interest rate is entered in cell G5. If the cash flows are expressed in today's money terms then the real interest rate (approximately the borrowing rate minus inflation rate) should be used.

The net cash flow for each year is then converted to its present value using the appropriate discount factor. The cumulative present value is calculated for appropriate intervals - in this case annually. These sums represent the net present value (NPV) or total benefit of the project if it was discontinued at any given point.

The NPV for each year is then converted to an equivalent annuity at the chosen discount rate using amortisation factors. The equivalent annuity represents the effective average annual cash flow in present value terms. The optimum life of the project is given by the year where the equivalent annuity is at a maximum.

If there are significant costs associated with removing the crop at the end of its life, then their discounted present value should be deducted from the NPV for each year under study before calculating the equivalent annuity.

7.2 Input data

The entire spreadsheet is displayed in Fig. 7.1. The data are entered on the first screen.

	Location
Net cash flow per year in £ per hectare	C5 : C19
Interest rate as a percentage	G5

7.3 Output data

Five sets of calculations are required to determine the optimum replacement age. The main output table (A21:H40) contains the following calculations.

(a) Net cash flow per year (B26:B40) repeated from the data entry section (C5:C14).

   eg. B26 = C5

(b) Total net cash flow to date (C26:C40) which is the cumulative cash flow to date.

   Total cash flow to date = net cash flow this year + total net cash flow last year.

   eg. C27 = C26 + B27

(c) Average annual cash flow (D26:D40) which is the average cash flow per year for a perennial crop of that age.

   $$\text{Average annual cash flow} = \frac{\text{total cash flow to date}}{\text{age (years)}}$$

   eg. D27 = C27 / A27

(d) Present value of the cash flow for the year (E26:E40) which is the discounted cash flow per year at the chosen interest rate (G5).

   PV of net cash flow = net cash flow * discount factor for year.

   eg. E27 = B27 * (1 + G5/100)^ -A27

(e)   Net present value (F26:F40) which is the cumulative net present value of the crop in each year of life.

Net present value = net present value in previous year +
present value of cash flow in this year.

eg. F27 = F26 + E27

(f)   Equivalent annuity (G26:G40) which is the net present value for each age of crop amortised to an equivalent annual value over that life.

Equivalent annuity = net present value * inverse annuity factor

eg. G27 = F27 * (G5/100) / (1- (1 + G5/100)^ -A27)

(g)   The replacement message (H26:H40) which indicates in which year replacement should take place by highlighting the year in which the equivalent annuity is at a maximum.

If the equivalent annuity in this year is greater than next year and it is greater than last year than print 'Replace' otherwise print a blank.

eg. H27 = IF(AND(G27>G28,G27>G26), ("Replace"), (""))

```
    |   A    ||    B    ||    C    ||    D    ||    E    ||    F    ||    G    ||    H    |

 1  Perennial Crop Replacement Model by Nigel Williams, Wye College.
 2  Used to determine when to grub a permanent crop.
 3
 4                        ************        Enter              ************
 5            Year 0  *   -8000  *            interest         *      10 *
 6  Enter       1  *   -1200  *            rate (%)           ************
 7  your        2  *   -1200  *
 8  net         3  *   -1600  *            Optimum replacement should
 9  cash        4  *    1000  *            occur at the end of the
10  flow        5  *    5000  *            crop year indicated below
11  for         6  *    6000  *            when equivalent annuity is
12  each        7  *    7000  *            at a maximum.
13  year        8  *    7000  *
14  in          9  *    6000  *            The equivalent annuity in
15  the        10  *    5000  *            that year is the maximum
16  box        11  *    3500  *            annual return from the crop.
17  to the     12  *    2000  *            Compare this with the return
18  right.     13  *    1000  *            from other annual or
19             14  *     500  *            perennial crops.
20  *****************************************************************
```

Age (years)	Net Cash Flow	Total Cash Flow to Date	Average Annual Cash Flow	P.V. of Net Cash Flow	N.P.V. @ 10%	Equiv. Annuity @ 10%	
	£	£	£	£	£	£	
0	-8000	-8000		-8000	-8000		
1	-1200	-9200	-9200	-1091	-9091	-10000	
2	-1200	-10400	-5200	-992	-10083	-5810	
3	-1600	-12000	-4000	-1202	-11285	-4538	
4	1000	-11000	-2750	683	-10602	-3345	
5	5000	-6000	-1200	3105	-7497	-1978	
6	6000	0	0	3387	-4110	-944	
7	7000	7000	1000	3592	-518	-106	
8	7000	14000	1750	3266	2747	515	
9	6000	20000	2222	2545	5292	919	
10	5000	25000	2500	1928	7220	1175	
11	3500	28500	2591	1227	8446	1300	
12	2000	30500	2542	637	9084	1333	Replace
13	1000	31500	2423	290	9373	1320	
14	500	32000	2286	132	9505	1290	

Fig. 7.1 Perennial crop replacement spreadsheet.

SPREADSHEET 8

Constant loan repayment

Purpose: To calculate constant loan repayments for a given combination of interest rate, loan amount and repayment period, on either a monthly or yearly basis.

Authors: Nicolas Lampkin and Nigel Chapman

Spreadsheet Name: LOANCALC

8.1 Introduction

The spreadsheet allows the calculation of constant loan repayments for a given combination of interest rate, loan amount and repayment period, on either a monthly or yearly basis.

It covers many situations which arise when long-term loans or mortgages are being considered, and allows for repayment period and/or size of loan to be adjusted at a given interest rate so that an affordable monthly or yearly repayment figure can be achieved.

The spreadsheet is not suited to dealing with short-term overdrafts or with several interest rates simultaneously, although it can be used to assess the effect on repayments of interest rate changes on a given combination of loan period and amount.

The speadsheet also gives a breakdown of interest payments, repayments of capital, and the outstanding balance at the end of each monthly or yearly period.

8.2 Input data

The whole spreadsheet is displayed in Figure 8.1. Only three items of data need to be entered:

C7 : interest rate as a percentage (either monthly or yearly)
C8 : the sum borrowed in pounds (or other currency unit)
C9 : the repayment period (either months or years)

8.3 Calculations

Figure 8.2 shows the cell entries in the top part of the spreadsheet. The main calculation is the constant repayment (C10). This is carried out using the formula:

$$\frac{L\,r}{1 - (1+r)^{-n}}$$

where L = the amount borrowed,
                 r = the interest rate expressed as a decimal,
                 n = the period of the loan.

ie. C10 = (C8*C7/100) / (1- (1+C7/100)^-C9)

In the payments analysis table, the following calculations have been used:

(a) For the period number (Column A), 1 has been entered into cell A16 and a formula to calculate each successive period into successive rows, ie. A16+1 into cell A17, A117+1 into cell A18 etc.

(b) The interest payment (Column B) is calculated as the balance outstanding at the end of the previous period multiplied by the interest rate. In period 1, this is based on the original data entered,

ie. B16 = C8 * C7 / 100

In all subsequent periods, the formula used relates to the balance outstanding at the end of the previous period,

eg. B17 = D16 * C7 / 100

(c) The capital repayment (Column C) is the constant repayment amount less interest, eg. C16 = C10-B16. However, in order to ensure that capital repayments are zero once the period of the loan has been exceeded (ie. the loan has been completely repaid), an IF statement is used. The IF statement can be interpreted as follows:

'If the period number (A16) is less than or equal to the period of the loan (C9), then the capital repayment is the constant repayment amount (C10) less the interest paid (B16), if not then the capital repayment is 0.'

ie. C16 = IF(A16<=C9, C10-B16, 0)

(d) The balance outstanding at the end of each period (Column D) is the balance outstanding at the end of the previous period less the capital repayment. In period 1, this is entered as D16 = C8-C16, referring to the original sum borrowed, but in all subsequent years the formulas are similar

eg. D17 = D16 - C17

(e) Once formulas have been entered into rows 16 and 17, those in row 17 can be copied to as many rows as time periods required. In the example illustrated with 40 time periods, the target range would be A18:A55.

```
         |   A   ||   B   ||   C   ||   D   ||      E      |
 1    SPREADSHEET TO CALCULATE CONSTANT LOAN REPAYMENTS
 2    **************************************************************
 3    Nicolas Lampkin and Nigel Chapman
 4    University College of Wales, Aberystwyth
 5    **************************************************************
 6    ENTER DATA IN C7, C8, C9:
 7    Interest rate          2.00% monthly (or annually)
 8    Sum borrowed        5000.00  pounds
 9    Loan period           36.00  months (or years)
10    Constant payment     196.16  pounds per month (or year)
11    **************************************************************
12    PAYMENTS ANALYSIS
13       Period   Interest  Capital  Balance
14       number     paid    repaid outstanding
15    --------------------------------------------------------------
16           1     100.00    96.16   4903.84
17           2      98.08    98.09   4805.75
18           3      96.11   100.05   4705.70
19           4      94.11   102.05   4603.65
20           5      92.07   104.09   4499.56
21           6      89.99   106.17   4393.38
22           7      87.87   108.30   4285.09
23           8      85.70   110.46   4174.63
24           9      83.49   112.67   4061.95
25          10      81.24   114.93   3947.03
26          11      78.94   117.22   3829.80
27          12      76.60   119.57   3710.24
28          13      74.20   121.96   3588.28
29          14      71.77   124.40   3463.88
30          15      69.28   126.89   3336.99
31          16      66.74   129.42   3207.57
32          17      64.15   132.01   3075.55
33          18      61.51   134.65   2940.90
34          19      58.82   137.35   2803.55
35          20      56.07   140.09   2663.46
36          21      53.27   142.90   2520.57
37          22      50.41   145.75   2374.81
38          23      47.50   148.67   2226.15
39          24      44.52   151.64   2074.50
40          25      41.49   154.67   1919.83
41          26      38.40   157.77   1762.06
42          27      35.24   160.92   1601.14
43          28      32.02   164.14   1437.00
44          29      28.74   167.42   1269.57
45          30      25.39   170.77   1098.80
46          31      21.98   174.19    924.61
47          32      18.49   177.67    746.94
48          33      14.94   181.23    565.71
49          34      11.31   184.85    380.86
50          35       7.62   188.55    192.32
51          36       3.85   192.32      .00
52          37        .00     .00      .00
53          38        .00     .00      .00
54          39        .00     .00      .00
55          40        .00     .00      .00
56    **************************************************************
```

Fig. 8.1 Spreadsheet to calculate constant loan repayments.

| A || B || C || D || E |

```
1    SPREADSHEET TO CALCULATE CONSTANT LOAN REPAYMENTS
2    **********************************************************************
3    Nicolas Lampkin and Nigel Chapman
4    University College of Wales, Aberystwyth
5    **********************************************************************
6    ENTER DATA IN C7, C8, C9:
7    Interest rate        2                    % monthly (or annually)
8    Sum borrowed         5000                 pounds
9    Loan period          36                   months (or years)
10   Constant payment     (C8*C7/100)/(1-(1+C7/100)^-C9)
11   **********************************************************************
12   PAYMENTS ANALYSIS
13       Period    Interest           Capital   Balance
14       number    paid               repaid outstanding
15   -------------------------------------------------------------------
16   1          C8*C7/100   IF(A16<=C9,C10-B16,0)    C8-C16
17   A16+1      D16*C7/100  IF(A17<=C9,C10-B17,0)    D16-C17
18   A17+1      D17*C7/100  IF(A18<=C9,C10-B18,0)    D17-C18
19   A18+1      D18*C7/100  IF(A19<=C9,C10-B19,0)    D18-C19
20   A19+1      D19*C7/100  IF(A20<=C9,C10-B20,0)    D19-C20
```

Fig. 8.2 Formulas used in cells A1:D20 of constant loan repayment spreadsheet.

SPREADSHEET 9

Investment appraisal with taxation and inflation

Purpose: To determine the gain from undertaking an investment in fixed capital, allowing for inflation and taxation.

Author: Nigel Williams

Spreadsheet Name: DCFTAX

9.1 Introduction

9.1.1 Discounted cash flows

The use of discounted cash flows (DCF) to appraise a capital investment is a well established technique in business management. Those unfamiliar with it are recommended to read a management text such as Barnard & Nix (1979). The essence of the technique is that money received in the future is worth less than money received now. The further into the future the money is received, the lower its present value. This is because money received today can be invested and earn interest so that it will accumulate over a given time period. The longer the time period, the greater the final sum. Equally, the higher the interest rate, the greater the final sum. Thus at higher interest rates, a given sum of money received in the future will have a lower present value today than if interest rates are lower.

The DCF technique consists of calculating the present value of all cash flows generated by a project (both positive and negative) using discount factors. If the sum of these present values (the net present value or NPV) is positive, then the decision maker will be better off. Strictly the NPV shows how much better off in today's money the decision maker will be. If the NPV is negative the decision maker will be worse off. The discount or interest rate used in the appraisal can be altered until the rate is found at which the NPV is zero. This is the breakeven discount rate and is effectively the percentage return on the investment. It is known as the internal rate of return (IRR). If the IRR is greater than the rate which money can earn in its next best investment, then the decision maker will be made better off by carrying out the investment.

Problems when using DCF techniques are caused by a number of factors. Two of the most important are taxation and inflation. These are fully dealt with in Williams (1986) but a brief summary of the methods of incorporating these factors is given below.

Inflation has the effect of reducing real interest rates since debt is repaid in depreciated currency. Thus it is necessary to differentiate between real (deflated) interest rates and nominal rates which are the rates normally quoted by lenders. There are two ways in which the DCF technique can handle inflation:

(a) The cash flows are discounted at the real (usually lower) rather than nominal interest rate. The real interest rate can be calculated by either deducting the inflation rate from the nominal interest rate (which gives an approximate value) or by using the following formula

$$R = \left[\frac{1 + r}{1 + i} - 1 \right] * 100$$

where   R = real interest rate as a percentage,
            r = nominal interest rate expressed as a decimal,
            i = inflation rate expressed as a decimal.

Thus with 18 per cent nominal interest and 10 per cent inflation, the real interest rate is 8 per cent, using the approximation, or, more accurately

$$\left[\frac{1.18}{1.10} - 1 \right] * 100 = 7.27\%$$

(b) The cash flows are inflated by the appropriate compounding factor (using the estimated inflation rate). These inflated cash flows are discounted at the nominal discount rate.

The two methods give identical answers in NPV terms, but in the former case the IRR is real and should be compared with the real interest rate. In the latter the IRR is nominal and should be compared with the nominal interest rate.

Taxation necessitates a number of adaptations. Interest payments attract tax relief thereby reducing the cost of money. The discount rate is therefore adjusted as follows:

$$PTDR = DR * (1 - T/100)$$

where   PTDR = post-tax discount rate expressed as a percentage,
            DR   = pre-tax discount rate expressed as a percentage,
            T   = tax rate expressed as a percentage

The cash flows are subject to tax which reduces their value as follows:

$$PTCF = CF * (1 - T/100)$$

where   PTCF = Post-tax cash flow,
            CF   = Pre-tax cash flow,
            T   = Tax rate expressed as a percentage

However, complications are created by the varying treatments of differing capital investments. Expenditure on non-depreciating assets (such as land) is not allowable against tax. Small capital items may be fully allowable in the year of purchase. Machinery may be allowable on the basis of writing down allowances calculated by the diminishing balance method. Other assets such as buildings may have writing down allowances calculated on the straight line basis. Each of these has implications for the post-tax cost of the capital investment.

The terminal value (if there is one) of the asset may cause problems. Capital gains tax is charged on the difference between the realisable value of an asset such as land and the purchase price indexed up for inflation. The difference between the terminal value of an item of machinery and its written down value will incur a tax penalty (or generate a tax relief) if it is positive (or negative).

All these possibilities have been incorporated into the model illustrated here.

9.1.2 Using the model

The model calculates the net present value and internal rate of return of a capital investment project. The length of life chosen for the project can be anything up to 15 years. Longer periods can be catered for by extending the tables.

The model allows for the effects of inflation by automatically inflating cash flows in each year by the estimated rate of inflation. The terminal value of the investment can be inflated at a different rate if required. This facility is most likely to be used if the investment is an asset such as land or buildings.

Both income and capital taxation can be handled in the model. Net cash flows are reduced by the estimated marginal rate of income taxation. Interest payments attract tax relief and thus the discount rate used in the appraisal is also reduced. Tax relief is also granted on depreciating capital items by means of writing down allowances (WDA). The model can accommodate either straight line or diminishing balance writing down allowances. It also allows the user to choose the annual percentage rates of WDA. The tax relief on these WDAs is calculated and then added to the net cash flow.

Taxation of the terminal value is less straightforward as it may be subject to capital gains tax (CGT) or to income tax depending on the type of investment.

(i)   If the investment is non-depreciating (ie. type 0 in the model), then CGT is charged on the difference between the terminal value (adjusted for inflation of capital items) and the original cost (adjusted for the rate of inflation allowable for CGT purposes).

(ii)   If the investment has diminishing balance WDAs (ie. type 1 in the model) then income tax is calculated on the difference between the terminal value (adjusted for inflation of capital items) and the written down value for tax purposes.

The model also shows the level of cash invested in the project in each year (the outstanding balance). This enables the decision maker to see if a project with a positive NPV is financially feasible, ie. whether it will generate sufficient surpluses in the early years to reduce the level of indebtedness.

9.2 Input data

The spreadsheet is displayed in Figs. 9.1 and 9.2. The data which should all be in today's values are entered in three sections.

(a)   Data relating to the investment opportunity

	Location
Discount rate (pre-tax, nominal) as a percentage	D6
Annual cash flow (if constant) in £	D7
(if not constant, enter zero and use section (b) below)	
Initial capital cost in £	D8
Expected life of project in years	D9
Expected terminal value of the project in £	D10
Marginal tax rate as a percentage	D11
Average capital gains tax rate as a percentage	D12
Expected inflation for capital items as a percentage	D13
Expected inflation for cash flows as a percentage	D14
Expected general inflation for CGT purposes as a percentage	D15
Annual writing down allowance as a percentage	D16
Choice of WDA profile: 0 = Nil	D17
1 = diminishing balance	
2 = straight line	

(b)   Data relating to irregular cash flows

	Location
Income per year for years 1 to 15 in £	F25:F39
Costs per year for years 1 to 15 in £	I25:I39

(c)   Estimate of internal rate of return

	Location
Estimate of internal rate of return as a percentage	F66

9.3 Intermediate calculations

A number of intermediate calculations are carried out before the main output tables are produced.

(a) Post-tax nominal interest rate (PTDR)

This is calculated in cell H20 using the formula

PTDR = Interest rate * (1 - tax rate/100)

ie. H20 = D6 * (1-D11/100)

(b) Post-tax real interest rates (RPTDR)

This is displayed for information in cell B20 but is not used in the model.

This is calculated using the formula

$$RPTDR = \left[\frac{1 + PTDR/100}{1 + inflation/100} - 1 \right] * 100$$

ie. B20 = (((1+H20/100)/(1+D14/100)) -1) * 100

(c) Total cash flow (K25:K39)

This is calculated by either taking the value entered in D7, or if that is equal to zero then the difference between cells F25 and I25. Should the project life in D9 be less than the year in C25 then zero is shown.

ie. K25 = IF(D9<C25, 0, IF(D7>0,D7,F25-I25))

9.4 The main output table

The main output table (A41:L80) contains the following calculations:

(a) Capital value (B45:B60)

This calculates the written down value of the initial investment (D8) in each year of the project's life (D9) according to the chosen writing down allowance function (D17). Thus the capital value will be calculated in one of the following three ways:

(i) If D17 = 0 the capital value remains unchanged,

(ii) If D17 = 1 the capital value is written down by the declining balance method,
Capital value in year n = original value * $(1\text{-writing down allowance}/100)^n$

(iii) If D17 = 2 and the capital has not already been written down to zero the capital value is written down by the straight line method,
Capital value in year n = original value * (1 - n * writing down allowance/100) unless this results in a negative value when it is set equal to zero.

eg. B46 = IF (A46>D9, 0, IF(D17=0, B45, IF(D17=1, B45*(1-D16/100)^A46,
IF(D17=2, MAX(B45*(1-(A46*D16/100)), 0), 0))))

(b) Cash flow (D45:D60)

This shows annual net cash flow (K25:K40) adjusted for inflation (D14) for each year of the project's life (D9). Otherwise it shows zero.

Cash flow in year n = total cash flow in year n * $(1 + \text{inflation rate}/100)^n$

eg. D46 = IF(A46>D9, 0, K25*(1+D14/100)^A46)

(c) Terminal value (F45:F60)

This shows the residual value of the project (D10) in the last year of its life (D9) adjusted for the expected rate of inflation (D13) for capital items. In all other years it shows zero.

Terminal value in year n = estimated capital value in year n * $(1 + \text{inflation rate}/100)^n$

eg. F46 = IF(A46=D9, D10*(1+D13/100)^A46, 0)

(d) Taxation allowance (H45:H60)

This calculates the tax relief gained on the writing down allowances on the capital investment for each year of the project's life (D9). Where there are no writing down allowance (D17 = 0), it shows zero.

Taxation allowance = (capital value last year - capital value this year) * tax rate/100

eg. H46 = IF(A46>D9, 0, (B45-B46)*D11/100)

Note that where there are no writing down allowances, this will show zero since the capital value remains the same each year.

(e) Taxation payments (I45:I60)

This calculates the tax payments on the net cash flow for each year of the project's life and the tax (either income (D11) or capital gains (D12)) on the terminal value of the project (D10) in its final year (D9).

The taxation in year n is calculated as follows:

(i)   If year > project life, then taxation = zero

(ii)   If year < project life, then taxation = - cash flow * income tax rate/100

(iii)   If year = project life and WDA = 1, then taxation =
        (- cash flow - terminal value + written down value) * income tax rate/100

(iv)   If year = project life and WDA <>1, then taxation =
        (-cash flow * income tax rate/100) - (terminal value - (written down value *
                    $(1 + \text{general inflation rate}/100)^n$)) * capital gains tax rate/100

eg. I46 = IF(A46>D9, 0, IF(A46<D9, -D46*D11/100, IF(AND(A46=D9,D17=1),
        (-D46-F46+B46)*D11/100, (-D46*D11/100) -
                        (F46-(B46*(1+D15/100)^A46))*D12/100)))

(f) Net cash flow (K46:K60)

This shows the sum of the various capital, cash and tax flows for each year of the project's life (D9).

Net cash flow = cash flow + terminal value + taxation allowances + taxation payments

eg. K46 = D46 + F46 + H46 + I46

except in year 0 when it is just the cost of the initial capital

ie. K45 = -B45

(g) Discounted cash flow (L45:L60)

This calculates the present value of the net cash flows for each year of the project's life (D9) at the post-tax nominal discount rate (H20).

$$\text{Discounted cash flow} = \frac{\text{net cash flow in year n}}{(1 + \text{discount rate}/100)^n}$$

eg. L46 = K46 / (1+H20/100)^A46

(h) Net present value (I62)

This shows the total of the discounted cash flows for each year of the project's life.

ie. I62 = SUM (L45:L60)

(i) Internal rate of return: post-tax (F71)

This shows the IRR as a percentage, using the post-tax discount rate.

ie. F71 = 100* IRR(F66/100, K45:K60)

(j) Internal rate of return: pre-tax (F72)

This calculates the pre-tax IRR that is equivalent to the post-tax IRR (F71).

$$\text{IRR pre tax} = \frac{\text{IRR post-tax}}{(1\text{-tax rate}/100)}$$

ie. F72 = F71 / (1-D11/100)

9.5 The secondary output table

The secondary output table (A81:L100) contains a calculation of the outstanding balance of the project as a check on feasibility. It contains the following calculations.

(a) Cash flow (B85:B100)

This shows the cash outflows and inflows before tax in each year of the project's life.

(i)   In year zero it shows the initial investment

ie. B85 = - B45

(ii)   In the remainder it shows the cash flow plus terminal value

eg. B86 = D46 + F46

(b) Tax flows (F85:F100)

This shows the sum of tax reliefs on writing down allowances and tax payments on cash flows.

eg. F86 = H46 + I46.

(c) Gross interest (H85:H100)

This calculates the interest on the outstanding balance in the previous year (L85) of the project at the pre-tax discount rate (D6) for each year of the project's life (D9). Otherwise it shows zero.

Gross interest in year n = interest rate/100 * outstanding balance in year n-1

eg. H86 = IF(A86>D9, 0, (D6/100)*L85)

(d) Tax relief (I85:I100)

This calculates the tax relief on the interest paid on the outstanding balance.

Tax relief = - gross interest * tax rate/100

eg. I86 = -H86 * (D11/100)

(e) Post-tax cash flow (K85:K100)

This shows the sum of the cash flow, tax flow (-), gross interest (-) and tax relief.

eg. K86 = SUM(B86:I86)

(f) Outstanding balance (L85:L100)

This calculates the outstanding balance in year n by adding the post tax cash flow in year n to the outstanding balance in year n-1 for each year of the project's life (D9). Otherwise it shows zero.

eg. L86 = IF(A86>D9, 0, L85+K86)

References

Barnard C.S. & Nix J.S. (1979). *Farm Planning and Control, (2nd Edition).* Cambridge University Press

Williams, N.T. (1986). *The Treatment of Taxation in Capital Investment Appraisal.* Agricultural Economics Research Unit, (Discussion Paper No. 103), Lincoln College, Canterbury, New Zealand.

```
  | A||   B   ||C||   D   |   F  ||G||   H   ||   I   ||J||   K   ||     L     |
1  DISCOUNTED CASH FLOW ALLOWING FOR TAXATION AND INFLATION
2  Nigel Williams, Wye College (University of London)
3
4  Assumptions made in the appraisal:
5              ************
6     Enter    *   13.60 * % Cost of Capital (Pre-tax, Nominal)
7     your     *    6000 * Annual Cash Flow (£)
8     data     *   50000 * Initial Capital Cost (£)
9     here     *      13 * Life of Project (yr)
10             *    5000 * Terminal Value (in today's money) (£)
11             *      25 * % Marginal Tax Rate
12             *       0 * % Capital Gains Tax
13             *       5 * % Expected Inflation for Capital Items
14             *       0 * % Expected Inflation for Cash Flows
15             *       0 * % Expected General Inflation for CGT Purposes
16             *      10 * % Writing Down Allowance
17             *       1 * W.D.A. (0=Nil, 1=Dim balance, 2=Straight line)
18             ***********
19 THIS IS EQUIVALENT TO THE FOLLOWING INTEREST RATES:
20       10.20 % (Post-tax, real)        10.20 % (Post-tax, nominal)
21 ENTER ANNUAL CASH FLOWS HERE                              Total
22                                                           Cash
23              Year        Income (£)         Costs (£)     Flow
24                       ***********        ***********
25               1     *         *       *         *      6000  PUT ZERO
26               2     *         *       *         *      6000  IN CELL
27               3     *         *       *         *      6000  D7 IF
28               4     *         *       *         *      6000  YOU WANT
29               5     *         *       *         *      6000  TO ENTER
30               6     *         *       *         *      6000  VARIABLE
31               7     *         *       *         *      6000  CASH
32               8     *         *       *         *      6000  FLOWS
33               9     *         *       *         *      6000  IN THIS
34              10     *         *       *         *      6000  SECTION
35              11     *         *       *         *      6000
36              12     *         *       *         *      6000
37              13     *         *       *         *      6000
38              14     *         *       *         *         0
39              15     *         *       *         *         0
40                       ***********        ***********
41 ********************************************************************************
42 Year  Capital   Cash    Terminal  Taxation  Taxation  Net Cash  Discounted
43       Value     Flow    Value     All'nce   Payments  Flow      Cash Flow
44
45  0    50000        0                    0         0    -50000    -50000
46  1    45000     6000        0        1250     -1500      5750      5218
47  2    40500     6000        0        1125     -1500      5625      4632
48  3    36450     6000        0        1013     -1500      5513      4119
49  4    32805     6000        0         911     -1500      5411      3669
50  5    29525     6000        0         820     -1500      5320      3274
51  6    26572     6000        0         738     -1500      5238      2925
52  7    23915     6000        0         664     -1500      5164      2617
53  8    21523     6000        0         598     -1500      5098      2344
54  9    19371     6000        0         538     -1500      5038      2102
55 10    17434     6000        0         484     -1500      4984      1887
56 11    15691     6000        0         436     -1500      4936      1696
57 12    14121     6000        0         392     -1500      4892      1525
58 13    12709     6000     9428         353      -680     15102      4272
59 14        0        0        0           0         0         0         0
60 15        0        0        0           0         0         0         0
```

Fig. 9.1 Spreadsheet for investment appraisal with taxation and inflation (Cells A1:L60).

```
        | A||   B   ||C|| D  |   F   ||G||   H   ||   I   ||J||   K   ||    L    |
61   *****************************************************************************
62   THE CASH FLOW HAS A NET PRESENT VALUE OF £       -9721 AT     10.2 % NOMINAL
63                                                                        DISCOUNT.
64   TO CALCULATE INTERNAL RATE OF RETURN, ENTER YOUR ESTIMATE OF IRR BELOW
65                              **************
66        Estimate of IRR % *        9   % *
67                              **************
68
69   THE CASH FLOW HAS INTERNAL RATES OF RETURN AS FOLLOWS:
70
71                 Post-tax      6.48  %
72                 Pre-tax       8.64  %
73
74   THESE SHOULD BE COMPARED WITH THE FOLLOWING INTEREST RATES:
75
76                 Post-tax     10.20  %
77                 Pre-tax      13.60  %
78
79
80   *****************************************************************************
81   CALCULATION OF OUTSTANDING BALANCE
82
83   Year   Cash                 Tax      Gross     Tax     Post-tax  Outstanding
84          Flow                 Flows    Interest  Relief  Cash Flow Balance
85      0   -50000                 0                        -50000    -50000
86      1    6000                -250     -6800     1700      650     -49350
87      2    6000                -375     -6712     1678      591     -48759
88      3    6000                -488     -6631     1658      539     -48220
89      4    6000                -589     -6558     1639      493     -47727
90      5    6000                -680     -6491     1623      452     -47275
91      6    6000                -762     -6429     1607      416     -46859
92      7    6000                -836     -6373     1593      385     -46474
93      8    6000                -902     -6320     1580      358     -46116
94      9    6000                -962     -6272     1568      334     -45782
95     10    6000               -1016     -6226     1557      314     -45468
96     11    6000               -1064     -6184     1546      298     -45170
97     12    6000               -1108     -6143     1536      285     -44885
98     13   15428                -327     -6104     1526    10523     -34361
99     14       0                   0         0        0        0          0
100    15       0                   0         0        0        0          0
```

Fig. 9.2 Spreadsheet for investment appraisal with taxation and inflation (Cells A61:L100).

SPREADSHEET 10

Irrigation system investment appraisal

Purpose: To investigate the economic feasibility of an investment in an unlined reservoir and irrigation equipment.

Authors: David Noble and Joe Morris

Spreadsheet Name: INVEST

10.1 Introduction

This spreadsheet is used to investigate the worth of an investment to irrigate an area of main crop potatoes. The investment involves an initial outlay to cover the cost of construction of a reservoir and the purchase of equipment such as irrigators, pipes and pumps. It also involves running costs to cover fuel, repairs and maintenance of equipment, labour and water abstraction.

These costs are compared with the benefits predicted to arise as a result of the investment. Benefits are assumed to be the value of extra yield of potatoes less any additional potato costs such as extra handling and storage costs.

The initial outlay occurs only once, whereas the running costs and the resultant benefits occur in each year of the project life. All future values are expressed in present money terms and the net present value (NPV) of the investment is calculated. The internal rate of return (IRR), the discount rate at which the NPV is zero, is also estimated. Readers unfamiliar with the terms NPV and IRR or their method of calculation are referred to Barnard & Nix (1979) or to Spreadsheet 9 in this book. The method used in this spreadsheet is to calculate annual cash flows without any allowance for inflation. The discount rate used in calculating NPV should therefore incorporate an allowance for inflation and the IRR thus calculated should be compared with the real (after inflation) discount rate.

It is recognised that there are important benefits attributable to the irrigation of potatoes other than that of extra yield. Irrigation can improve continuity and regularity of supply, reduce the risk of crop failure, significantly improve crop quality, and allow growers to exploit high prices in dry years when total potato output is low. Non-yield benefits could be incorporated into the example by adding benefit parameters. This is not done, however, in order to simplify presentation.

81

10.2 Example data

10.2.1 Capital costs

An irrigation system capable of applying 100 mm of water over an area of 24 ha of main crop potatoes is proposed. An unlined reservoir is to be constructed because direct abstraction from the water course is not possible. The cost of construction of the reservoir is estimated at £3000 (gross) per 4550 m^3 (1 million gallons) of storage capacity and in estimating the storage capacity required, allowance has to be made for evaporation and seepage losses. These are taken to be 50% of the annual water use.

The estimated costs of pipeline and hydrants are £800 per hectare (gross) and that of a hosereel irrigator capable of covering 24 ha applying 25 mm in a 5-day cycle is £15000 gross.

Pumps are required to pump from river to reservoir and from reservoir to field. The costs of these are estimated at £2300 gross and £7000 gross respectively.

At the end of 10 years, the values of the reservoir and pipes are estimated to be respectively 50% and 20% of their gross costs whereas the pumps and irrigator are assumed to have no remaining value.

Currently (1992) no grants are available for this sort of investment but it used to be that grants were available for investment in non-moveable items such as the reservoir. In some situations (eg. horticulture) grants are also available to offset the cost of investment in moveable items but not for field-scale arable production.

10.2.2 Running costs

The cost of pumping water from reservoir to field depends on fuel cost (14p/l), fuel use (9p/l) and pumping time (0.18 h/ha mm). The cost of pumping from river to reservoir is based on an estimate of £8 per 1000 m^3 water delivered to the reservoir.

The annual costs of repairs and maintenance are estimated for the reservoir, pipes, pumps and irrigators at 1%, 2%, 5% and 5% respectively of their gross costs.

The cost of winter abstraction of water is taken as £2.00 per 1000 m^3 and that of labour as £4.00/h at a labour requirement of 0.02 h/ha mm of water applied.

10.2.3 Benefits

It is assumed that water is the main determinant of potato yield. It is also assumed that the yield response of the crop to additional rainfall or irrigation is as in Table 10.1.

Rainfall + irrigation (mm) during May-August	Crop yield response (t/ha mm)
0 - 200	0.15
200 - 250	0.10
250 - 300	0.06
300 - 350	0.02

Table 10.1 Yield response of main crop potatoes to rainfall and irrigation

This represents a steadily decreasing response to additional water up to an assumed maximum obtainable yield of 50 t/ha at 350 mm of water applied.

The value of additional yield is estimated at £80/t with additional storage and handling costs (labour, bags, transport) estimated at £8/t. It is assumed that the extra output of potatoes does not result in increased expenditure on farm 'fixed' or 'overhead' costs such as machinery depreciation or regular labour.

On the basis of weather records for the locality over a 40-year time period, ten years have been selected at random to provide estimates of future rainfall over the life of the project. The effect of a different set or sequence of rainfall years on project NPV can be determined as required.

10.2.4 Water Application Rates

Water application is measured in mm. depth of water applied to a given surface area. The resultant unit of measurement is ha mm (eg. 100mm on 1 ha = 100 ha mm).

Also 1 mm depth applied on 1 hectare equals 10 m³ volume of water.

10.3 Structure of the spreadsheet

The spreadsheet has three main parts:

1. Main input data section (A5:D60), (Fig.10.1)
2. Calculation of capital and running costs (G5:I45), (Fig.10.1)
3. Annual calculation of costs and benefits including input of rainfall data (J1:W29) plus calculation of NPV and IRR (J31:M38), (Fig.10.2).

10.4 Input data requirements

10.4.1 Main data input area

Location	Data item
D7	Area to be irrigated (ha)
D8	Maximum annual application rate (mm)
D9	Additional reservoir storage required to allow for evaporation and seepage - as a percentage of annual water use.
	Gross costs
D13	Gross reservoir cost (£ per million gallons)
B13	1 million gallons expressed in m³
D14	Gross cost of pipes (£/ha)
D15	Gross input pump cost (£)
D16	Gross output pump cost (£)
D17	Gross cost of hosereel irrigator (£)
E13:E17	Terminal values - as percentages of gross cost of reservoir, pipes, input pump, output pump and irrigator respectively
	Grants available - as a percentage.
D21	On moveable assets (pipes, pumps, irrigator)
D22	On non-moveable assets (reservoir)
	Fuel costs - reservoir to field
D26	Pumping time (h/ha mm)

83

D27	Fuel use (l/h)
D28	Fuel cost (p/l)
D30	Fuel cost - from river to reservoir (£ per 1000 m^3) (it is also possible to change the basis of the cost, as the value of 1000 m^3 is stored in the cell B30)

Costs of repairs and maintenance - expressed as percentages of gross costs

D33	Reservoir
D34	Pipes
D35	Pumps
D36	Irrigator

D39	Cost of winter water abstraction (£ per 1000 m^3) (again the cost basis, 1000 m^3 can be changed in cell B39)
D41	Labour requirement (h/ha mm)
D42	Labour cost (£/h)
D46	Potato price (£/t)
D47	Additional storage and handling costs due to the increased tonnage of potatoes (£/t)
D49	Discount Rate - as a percentage. This should represent the real (after removing the effect of inflation) rate of interest.

10.4.2 Crop yield response data

This is set up in cells C56:D59 as a table similar to Table 10.1. It allows the crop yield response to water to be split into four intervals and a different yield response specified for each interval. Cells C56:C59 represent the upper limits of water applied in each interval and cells D56:D59 the respective crop yield responses (t/ha mm).

10.4.3 Rainfall data

This is entered in cells N11:W11 and represents the amounts of rain (mm) falling in the months of May to August over a 10 year period.

10.5 Output calculations

10.5.1 Capital costs (G5:I23)

Irrigation water required (ha mm) =
$\qquad$ Area to be irrigated (ha) * max. irrigation application (mm)

$\qquad$ ie. I8 = D7 * D8

Reservoir capacity (m^3) = 10 * Irrigation water required (ha mm)
$\qquad\qquad\qquad\qquad$ + allowance for evaporation and seepage (ha mm)

$\qquad$ ie. I9 = 10 * I8 * (1 + D9/100)

Gross reservoir cost = Cost (£/m^3) * Reservoir capacity (m^3)

$\qquad$ ie. I13 = D13/B13 * I9

Gross cost of pipes = Cost (£/ha) * Area (ha)

ie. I14 = D14 * D7

Gross cost of pumps = Cost of input pump (£) + cost of output pump (£)

ie. I16 = D15 + D16

Gross cost of irrigator, I17 = D17

Total gross cost, I19 = SUM(I13:I17)

Grants, where available, on costs of moveable and non-moveable assets,

ie. I20 = ((I14+I16+I17)*D20 + I13*D21) / 100

Net capital cost, I22 = I19 - I20

All the formulas used in this section are displayed in Fig. 10.3.

10.5.2 Annual running costs (£) (G25:I45)

Fuel cost : from reservoir to field = Pumping time (h/ha mm) * Fuel use (l/h)
* Fuel cost (£/l) * Irrigation water applied (ha mm)

ie. I28 = D26 * D27 * D28/100 * I8

Fuel cost : from river to reservoir = Fuel cost (£/m^3) * Reservoir capacity (m^3)

ie. I30 = D30/B30 * I9

Repairs and maintenance costs of reservoirs, pipes, pumps and irrigator are calculated separately in cells H33:H36 and their total displayed in cell I37. Each individual cost is obtained by multiplying the gross cost (I13:I17) by the corresponding repairs and maintenance percentage (D33:D36) eg. for the reservoir, H33 = I13 * D33/100.

Cost of water = Water cost (£/m^3) * Reservoir capacity (m^3)

ie. I39 = D39/B39 * I9

Labour cost = Labour required (h/ha mm) * Wage (£/h) * Irrigation water applied (ha mm).

ie. I42 = D41 * D42 * I8

Total running cost, I44 = SUM(I28:I42)

All the formulas used in this section are displayed in Fig. 10.3.

10.5.3 Crop yield response to irrigation water (N12:W12)

Because the yield response to water is non-linear (Table 10.1 and cells C56:D59) this calculation is quite complicated. The calculation of yield response to irrigation water in year 1 (N12) will be explained here. Calculations for other years are similar.

The calculation for each year is in two parts. The first part uses 4 hidden cells in rows 2:5, ie. for year 1 it uses cells N2:N5 (see Table 10.2). Each of the 4 hidden cells refers to the corresponding entry (C56:C59) in the crop yield response table.

The values in the example are D8 = 100, N11 = 190 and C56:C59 are 200, 250, 300 and 350 respectively. Thus the formula in each row first of all subtracts the rainfall (N11) from the upper limit of water applied in each yield response interval (C56) but limits this to a maximum of the irrigation water available (D8) ie. MIN(D8, C56-N11). However if the rainfall exceeds the upper limit, then this would result in a negative value so a lower limit of zero has to be set by using the MAX function.

Cell	Formula	Value in Example
N2	MAX(0, MIN(D8, C56-N11))	10
N3	MAX(0, MIN(D8, C57-N11))	60
N4	MAX(0, MIN(D8, C58-N11))	100
N5	MAX(0, MIN(D8, C59-N11))	100

Table 10.2 Formulas in hidden cells N2:N5

The second part of the calculation is in cell N12, where the answer is displayed. The formula used is

$$N12 = N2*D56 + (N3-N2)*D57 + (N4-N3)*D58 + (N5-N4)*D59$$

ie. it takes the yield response in each interval (D56:D59) and multiplies it by the amount of water applied in each interval (N2 or N3-N2 or N4-N3 or N5-N4) and adds them all up.

10.5.4 Annual benefits and costs (N14:W29)

The extra gross output each year = Response to irrigation water (t/ha)
                                       * Area irrigated (ha) * Value of crop (£/t)

ie. N14 = N12 * D7 * D46

The extra variable costs each year = Response to irrigation water (t/ha)
                                       * Area irrigated (ha) * Additional costs (£/t)

ie. N15 = N12 * D7 *D47

The net benefit each year is the difference between the extra gross output and the extra variable costs associated with potato production,

ie. N17 = N14 - N15

The capital costs are only incurred in year 0 of the project,

ie. M22 = I22

The annual recurrent costs would normally be equal to the annual running costs (I44). But these have been calculated assuming that all 100 mm of irrigation water have been applied. In some years (eg. year 2 in this example) due to high rainfall it is not necessary to apply the full 100 mm and so the annual running costs are adjusted proportionally,

ie. N23 = I44 * MIN(1, (C59-N11)/D8)

The terminal value of capital assets only arises in year 10, the assumed final year of the investment. It is obtained by multiplying together each gross cost by its percentage terminal value and summing (the terminal value is regarded as a negative cost),

ie. W25 = (E13*I13 + E14*I14 + E15*D15 + E16*D16 + E17*D17) /100

The total costs each year are the sum of any capital cost plus recurrent cost,

ie. N27 = N22 + N23

and in year 10, allowance is made for terminal values.

ie. W27 = W22 + W23 - W25

The Net Cash Flow each year is the difference between the extra gross margin and the total costs,

ie. N29 = N17 - N27

All the formulas used in the calculations for years 0 and 1 are shown in Fig. 10.4.

10.5.5 *Net present value and internal rate of return*

The net present value of the project is calculated in real terms using the NPV function adjusted for the capital cost in year 0,

ie. M35 = M29 + NPV(D49/100, N29:W29)

The internal rate of return is calculated using the IRR function (with an initial arbitrary guess of 0.15),

ie. M37 = IRR(0.15, M29:W29)

Reference

Barnard, C.S. and Nix, J.S. (1979). *Farm Planning and Control (2nd edition)*, Cambridge University Press.

	A || B || C || D || E || F || G || H || I

```
 1  ==================================================================================
 2  Irrigation system      -   compiled by David Noble and Joe Morris,
 3  investment appraisal        Silsoe College, Bedford, U.K.
 4  ==================================================================================
 5  INPUT DATA                                  CAPACITIES
 6
 7  Area (ha)                      24           Irrigation water
 8  Application rate (mm)         100                        (ha.mm.)       2400
 9  Additional storage (%)       50.0           Reservoir  (m^3)          36000
10  ----------------------------------------    ------------------------------
11  Gross costs                   Terminal      CAPITAL COST CALCULATION
12    Reservoir                   Value (%)                                  £
13    (£ per  4550 m^3)          3000   50      Gross reservoir cost      23736
14    Pipes (£/ha)                800   20      Gross pipe cost           19200
15    Input pump (£)             2300    0
16    Output pump (£)            7000    0      Gross pump cost            9300
17    Irrigator (£)             15000    0      Irrigator cost            15000
18  ----------------------------------------    ------------------------------
19  Grants                        (%)           Total gross cost          67236
20    Moveable assets              .0           Grants                     3560
21    Non-moveable assets        15.0           ------------------------------
22                                               Net capital cost          63676
23  ===========================================  ==============================
24
25  Fuel cost - to field                        ANNUAL RUNNING COSTS
26    Pumping time (h/ha.mm)       .18
27    Fuel use (l/h)                9
28    Fuel cost (p/l)              14           Fuel cost - out             544
29  Fuel cost - to reservoir
30    Cost/  1000 m^3 (£)           8           Fuel cost - in              288
31
32  Repairs & Maintenance                       Repairs & Maintenance cost
33    Reservoir (% of gross)      1.0             Reservoir      237
34    Pipes (% of gross)          2.0             Pipes          384
35    Pumps (% of gross)          5.0             Pumps          465
36    Irrigator (% of gross)      5.0             Irrigator      750
37                                                Total                    1836
38
39  Water (£/  1000 m^3)         2.00           Water cost                   72
40  Labour
41    required (h/ha.mm)          .02
42    wage (£/h)                 4.00           Labour cost                 192
43  ----------------------------------          ------------------------------
44                                               Total running cost         2933
45                                               ==============================
46  Potato price (£/t)          80.00
47  Additional costs (£/t)       8.00
48  ----------------------------------
49  Discount rate (%)           10.0
50  ----------------------------------
51                               Crop
52              Rainfall +       yield
53              irrigation       response
54                 (mm)          (t/ha.mm)
55              ----------------------
56                200            .15
57  CROP YIELD    250            .1
58  RESPONSE TABLE 300           .06
59                350            .02
60              ----------------------
```

Fig. 10.1 Irrigation system investment appraisal spreadsheet (Cells A1:I60).

	0	1	2	3	4	5	6	7	8	9	10
						Project years					
BENEFITS											
Total rainfall (mm)		190	260	225	170	175	135	30	205	170	260
Response to irrig. water (t/ha)		8.9	3.4	6	10.7	10.25	13.25	15	7.6	10.7	3.4
Extra gross output (£)		17088	6528	11520	20544	19680	25440	28800	14592	20544	6528
Extra variable costs (£)		1709	653	1152	2054	1968	2544	2880	1459	2054	653
Extra net benefits (£)		15379	5875	10368	18490	17712	22896	25920	13133	18490	5875
COSTS											
Capital costs (£)	63676										
Recurrent costs (£)		2933	2639	2933	2933	2933	2933	2933	2933	2933	2639
Terminal value of capital assets (£)											15708
Total costs (£)	63676	2933	2639	2933	2933	2933	2933	2933	2933	2933	-13069
Net cash flow (£)	-63676	12447	3236	7435	15557	14779	19963	22987	10200	15557	18944

Discount rate (%)	10
Investment period (yrs)	10
Net present value (£)	17427
Internal rate of return	15%

Fig. 10.2 Irrigation system investment appraisal spreadsheet (Cells J6:W39).

	A	B	C	D	E	F	G	H	I
1	==
2	Irrigation system	-		compiled by David Noble and Joe Morris,
3	investment appraisal			Silsoe College, Bedford, U.K.
4	==
5	INPUT DATA						CAPACITIES
6							
7	Area (ha)			24			Irrigation water
8	Application rate (mm)			100			(ha.mm.)	D7*D8
9	Additional storage (%)			50			Reservoir (m^3)	10*I8*(1+D9/100)
10	----------------------						
11	Gross costs						CAPITAL COST CALCULATION
12	Reservoir				Terminal Value (%)				£
13	(£ per 4550 m^3)			3000	50		Gross reservoir cost	D13/B13*I9
14	Pipes (£/ha)			800	20		Gross pipe cost	D14*D7
15	Input pump (£)			2300	0		
16	Output pump (£)			7000	00		Gross pump cost	D15+D16
17	Irrigator (£)			15000	0		Irrigator cost	D17
18	----------------------						
19	Grants				(%)		Total gross cost	SUM(I13:I17)
20	Moveable assets			0			Grants	((I14+I16+I17)*D20+I13*D21)/100
21	Non-moveable assets			15			Net capital cost	I19-I20
22							
23	==

```
24
25  Fuel cost - to field
26    Pumping time (h/ha.mm)  .18
27    Fuel use (l/h)            9
28    Fuel cost (p/l)          14          Fuel cost - out        D26*D27*D28/100*I8
29  Fuel cost - to reservoir
30    Cost/ 1000  m^3 (£)       8          Fuel cost - in         D30/B30*I9
31
32  Repairs & Maintenance                  Repairs & Maintenance cost
33    Reservoir (% of gross)    1             Reservoir I13*D33/100
34    Pipes     (% of gross)    2             Pipes     I14*D34/100
35    Pumps     (% of gross)    5             Pumps     I16*D35/100
36    Irrigator (% of gross)    5             Irrigator I17*D36/100
37                                            Total     SUM(H33:H36)
38
39    Water (£/ 1000  m^3)      2          Water cost             D39/B39*I9
40  Labour
41    required (h/ha.mm)      .02          Labour cost            D41*D42*I8
42    wage (£/h)                4
43  ---------------------------          ----------------------------------
44                                         Total running cost     SUM(I28:I42)
45                                        ==================================
```

ANNUAL RUNNING COSTS

Fig. 10.3 Formulas used in columns H and I of irrigation system investment appraisal spreadsheet.

```
     |  J    ||  K    ||  L    ||  M    ||                    N                          |
 1
 2                                          MAX(0,MIN(D8,C56-N11))
 3                                          MAX(0,MIN(D8,C57-N11))
 4                                          MAX(0,MIN(D8,C58-N11))
 5                                          MAX(0,MIN(D8,C59-N11))
 6
 7                                     0    1+M7
 8   BENEFITS
 9   -------------------------------------------------------------------------------
10
11   Total rainfall (mm)                    190
12   Response to irrig. water (t/ha)        N2*D56+(N3-N2)*D57+(N4-N3)*D58+(N5-N4)*D59
13   -------------------------------------------------------------------------------
14   Extra gross output (£)                 N12*D7*D46
15   Extra variable costs (£)               N12*D7*D47
16   -------------------------------------------------------------------------------
17   Extra net benefits (£)                 N14-N15
18   ===============================================================================
19
20   COSTS
21   -------------------------------------------------------------------------------
22   Capital costs (£)           I22
23   Recurrent costs (£)                    I44*MIN(1,(C59-N11)/D8)
24   Terminal value of
25     capital assets (£)
26   -------------------------------------------------------------------------------
27   Total costs (£)             M22+M23    N22+N23
28   ===============================================================================
29   Net cash flow (£)           M17-M27    N17-N27
30   ===============================================================================
31
32   Discount rate (%)  D49
33
34   Investment period (yrs)  |  10                                              |
35   ------------------------------------------------------------------------
36   Net present value (£)    |  M29+NPV(D49/100,N29:W29)                       |
37
38   Internal rate of return  |  IRR(.15,M29:W29)                               |
39   ------------------------------------------------------------------
40
```

Fig. 10.4 Formulas used in columns M and N of irrigation system investment appraisal spreadsheet.

Purchase combine v use contractor

Purpose: To compare the cost of owning and operating a combine harvester with the cost of hiring a contractor, for a range of harvested areas.

Authors: David Noble and Joe Morris

Spreadsheet name : BREAKEVN

11.1 Introduction

This spreadsheet compares the cost of owning and operating a combine harvester with that of hiring a contractor to carry out the cereal harvest. The comparison is carried out on the basis of average annual costs over the life of the machine with no consideration of year-to-year variations. There is no consideration of taxation effects.

For low hectarages the fixed costs per hectare of owning and operating a combine harvester are very high resulting in the fact that it is cheaper to hire a contractor. As the area harvested inceases the fixed costs per hectare decrease and there comes a point - referred to as the breakeven hectarage - when the total cost of owning and operating the harvester (fixed costs plus operating costs) exactly equals that of hiring a contractor. Costs are calculated for a range of hectarages and the breakeven hectarage computed.

A number of assumptions are made in the estimation of costs. These are explained in Section 3 and should be borne in mind when interpreting the results.

The spreadsheet should be of use to farmers making combine harvester 'buy or hire' decisions, and those who wish to determine average costs for different levels of machinery use. The spreadsheet can also be used to examine the sensitivity of combine costs to assumptions regarding purchase price, depreciation life, repairs and fuel costs. In addition the spreadsheet can show the effect on costs of different work rates as determined by speed, combine size, and field efficiency. It is also used as a student exercise in PC courses at Silsoe College. The construction of the spreadsheet is relatively straightforward reinforcing knowledge learnt in class about the COPY command and the IF function, as well as the students' understanding of the calculation of fixed and operating costs.

11.2 Input data

The input data is in three parts:

(a) Data for the cost of owning and operating combine (D6:D20)

Location

D6	Purchase price (£)
D7	Number of years (life) the combine is kept for
D8	Resale value - expressed as a percentage of purchase price
D9	Other fixed costs, eg shelter, insurance, taxes - expressed as a percentage of purchase price
D10	The economic life of the combine in hours.
D11	Costs of repairs and maintenance - expressed as a percentage of purchase price for each hour of life over its economic life
D12	Fuel use (l/h)
D13	Fuel price (p/l)
D14	Cost of oil and filters - as a percentage of fuel cost
D15	Driver's wage (£/h)
D16	Operating speed (km/h)
D17	Width of combine (m)
D18	Field efficiency, (%) ie. the percentage of time actually working in the field after deduction for idle travel/turning/waiting
D19	Interest rate - as a percentage
D20	Rate of inflation - as a percentage

(b) Data for the cost of hiring a contractor (G6:G7)

Location

G6	Standing charge irrespective of area harvested (often zero)
G7	Charge per hectare harvested (£/ha)

(c) Range of hectares for which the calculations are performed (C24:G24)

Currently the spreadsheet allows five values to be entered in this range. If more than five are required further values can be entered in H24, I24 etc. and the formulas in cells G28:G57 can be copied into columns H, I etc.

11.3 Calculations

Two intermediate calculations are performed before the main output table is produced.

(a) Capacity (ha/h) = $\dfrac{\text{speed (km/h) * width (m) * efficiency (\%)}}{1000}$

ie. G17 = D16 * D17 * D18/1000

(b) The real cost of capital (G20) is calculated using the formula,

$$r = \frac{1+i}{1+g} - 1$$

where r = real cost of capital (decimal),
　　　　i = nominal rate of interest (decimal),
　　　　g = rate of inflation (decimal),

ie. $G20 = (1 + D19/100)/(1 + D20/100) - 1$

The value stored in G20 is decimal but is displayed as a percentage.

The main output table (A22:G60) contains the following calculations.

(a) Fixed costs of owning the combine (C28:G32)

   (i) Depreciation of combine (C28:G28)

   Straight line depreciation is assumed over the life of the machine, ie.

   $$\text{Annual depreciation (£)} = \frac{\text{Purchase price (£) - Scrap value (£)}}{\text{Life of combine (yrs)}}$$

   ie. $C28 = D6 * (1 - D8/100) / D7$

   Entries at D28:G28 are set equal to C28 since this cost is assumed not to vary with use.

   (ii) Interest charges on borrowed capital (C29:G29)

   As an approximation, annual interest charges are estimated as the amount of interest paid on the average capital invested in the combine, ie.

   Annual interest (£) = (Purchase Price (£) + Scrap value (£)) / 2
   　　　　　　　　　* Real cost of capital

   ie. $C29 = D6 * (1 + D8/100)/2 * G20$

   Entries at D29:G29 are set equal to C29 since this cost does not vary with use.

   (iii) Other annual fixed costs (C30:G30)

   These are estimated as a percentage of the purchase price, ie.

   Other annual fixed costs (£) = Purchase price (£) * Other costs proportion

   ie. $C30 = D6 * D9/100$

   Entries at D30:G30 are set equal to C30 since this cost does not vary with use.

   (iv) The total fixed costs are obtained by summing the three fixed costs

   eg. $C32 = SUM(C28:C30)$

   Entries at D32:G32 are again set equal to C32.

95

(b) Combine operating costs (B36:G45)

Costs (£/ha) are calculated in column B (B36:B41). These are then multiplied by the hectarages in C24:G24 to obtain the corresponding costs (£) in columns C to G.

The individual costs per hectare are :

(i) Annual repairs and maintenance (B36)

As an approximation to the annual costs of repairs and maintenance a percentage of purchase price per hour of use is assumed. Thus

$$\text{Annual cost of repairs and maintenance (£/ha)} = \frac{\text{purchase price (£) * R \& M percentage}}{\text{economic life (h) * capacity (ha/h)}}$$

ie. B36 = D6 * D11 / (100 * D10 * G17)

$$(ii)\ \text{Annual fuel costs (£/ha)} = \frac{\text{fuel use (l/h) * fuel price (£/l)}}{\text{capacity (ha/h)}}$$

ie. B37 = D12 * D13 / (100 * G17)

(iii) Annual cost of oil and filters (£/ha) = annual fuel cost (£/ha) * oil and filters proportion

ie. B38 = B37 * D14/100

(iv) The driver's annual wage attributable to the harvesting operation is

Wage (£/ha) = wage (£/h) / capacity (ha/h)

ie. B39 = D15 / G17

(v) The total operating cost per hectare is obtained by summing the four operating costs,

ie. B41 = SUM(B36:B39)

The "Grand total" cost of owning and operating the combine is given in C43:G43 and is the sum of the fixed and operating costs.

eg. C43 = C32 + C41

The cost per hectare of owning and operating the combine is given in C45:G45 and is the Grand Total divided by the hectarage.

eg. C45 = C43 / C24

(c) Contractor's costs

There are only two components:

(i) The standing charge (C49:G49) is the same irrespective of area harvested and simply equals the input data value (G6).

(ii) The charge per hectare (B50) is again simply equal to the input data value (G7). This is then multiplied by the hectarages in C24:G24 to obtain the entries in C50:G50.

ie. Annual charge (£) = charge (£/ha) * hectares

eg. C50 = B50 * C24

The total contractor's charge (C52:G52) is the sum of the standing charge and variable charge,

eg. C52 = C49 + C50

The cost per hectare of hiring the contractor is given in C54:G54 and is the total contractor's charge divided by the hectarage.

eg. C54 = C52 / C24

(d) Comparison of costs

Determination of the minimum cost system (C57:G57) is achieved by comparing the costs per ha for each system.

eg. C57 = IF (C45 > C54, "Contract", "Purchase")

(e) Breakeven hectarage (B59)

The breakeven hectarage, X, occurs when the Grand Total cost of owning and operating the combine equals the total cost of hiring the contractor,

ie. where $FC_O + VC_O*X = FC_C + VC_C*X$

or where $X = (FC_O - FC_C) / (VC_C - VC_O)$

and FC_O = fixed cost of owning the combine,
VC_O = operating cost per hectare of the combine,
FC_C = contractor's standing charge,
VC_C = contractor's charge per ha.

This generates the spreadsheet equation

B59 = (C32 - C49) / (B50 - B41)

The spreadsheet is displayed in Figs. 11.1 and 11.2. Fig. 11.1 displays all the formulas used in the spreadsheet — with the exception of row 57. In row 57, because of the length of the formulas, only that for column C has been displayed. In this row, entries for columns D:G are obtained by copying across allowing both references to column C to change accordingly. Note that the column widths in Fig. 11.1 have had to be increased in order to display complete formulas. Fig. 11.2 shows the spreadsheet in the form in which it appears on the screen.

	A	B	C	D	E	F	G
1	BREAKEVN - Comparison of the costs of owning and operating a combine with						
2	the cost of hiring a contractor - D.H.Noble & J.Morris, Silsoe College						
3	==						
4	OWN COMBINE DATA					CONTRACTOR'S CHARGES (£)	
5							
6	Purchase price, (P) (£)			50000		Standing charge	500
7	Life on farm (yrs)			8		Charge per ha.	61.1
8	Resale value (% of purchase price, P)			10			
9	Other fixed costs (% of P)			1			
10	Economic life (h)			2000			
11	Repair cost over economic life (% of P)			60			
12	Fuel use (l/h)			33			
13	Fuel price (p/l)			17			
14	Oil & filter costs (% of fuel cost)			20			
15	Driver's wage (£/h)			3		INTERMEDIATE CALCULATIONS	
16	Operating speed (km/h)			4.8		Capacity (ha/h)	D16*D17*D18/1000
17	Width of combine (m)			5.5			
18	Field efficiency (%)			70			
19	Interest rate (%)			15		Real cost of	
20	Rate of inflation (%)			7		capital	(1+D19/100)/(1+D20/100)-1
21	==						
22				OUTPUT TABLE			
23	Hectares	100	150	200	250	300	
24							
25	Own combine:						
26	Fixed costs						
27	-------						
28	Depreciation	D6*(1-D8/100)/D7	C28	D28	E28	F28	
29	Interest	D6*(1+D8/100)/2*G20	C29	D29	E29	F29	
30	Other (shelter etc.)	D6*D9/100	C30	D30	E30	F30	
31							
32	Total	SUM(C28:C30)	C32	D32	E32	F32	
33	==						

		Per ha.					
34	Operating costs						
35	-----						
36	Repairs & maintenance	D6*D11/(100*D10*G17)	C24*B36	D24*B36	E24*B36	F24*B36	G24*B36
37	Fuel	D12*D13/(100*G17)	C24*B37	D24*B37	E24*B37	F24*B37	G24*B37
38	Oil & filters	B37*D14/100	C24*B38	D24*B38	E24*B38	F24*B38	G24*B38
39	Driver	D15/G17	C24*B39	D24*B39	E24*B39	F24*B39	G24*B39
40							
41	Total	SUM(B36:B39)	C24*B41	D24*B41	E24*B41	F24*B41	G24*B41
42	-----						
43	Grand total		C32+C41	D32+D41	E32+E41	F32+F41	G32+G41
44							
45	Cost per ha.		C43/C24	D43/D24	E43/E24	F43/F24	G43/G24
46	=====						
47							
48	Contractor:						
49	Standing charge		G6	G6	G6	G6	G6
50	Fixed charge per ha.	G7	C24*B50	D24*B50	E24*B50	F24*B50	G24*B50
51							
52	Grand total		C49+C50	D49+D50	E49+E50	F49+F50	G49+G50
53	-----						
54	Cost per ha.		C52/C24	D52/D24	E52/E24	F52/F24	G52/G24
55	=====						
56							
57	Minimum cost system		IF(C45>C54,"Contract","Purchase")				
58							
59	Breakeven hectarage	(C32-C49)/(B50-B41)					
60							

Fig. 11.1 Formulas for Purchase combine v Use contractor spreadsheet.

```
              |      A      ||   B   ||   C   ||   D   ||   E   ||   F   ||   G   |

 1   BREAKEVN - Comparison of the costs of owning and operating a combine with
 2        the cost of hiring a contractor - D.H.Noble & J.Morris, Silsoe College
 3   ===============================================================================
 4   OWN COMBINE DATA                            | CONTRACTOR'S CHARGES (£)
 5   ----------------                            | ------------------------
 6   Purchase price, (P) (£)              50000  | Standing charge        500
 7   Life on farm (yrs)                       8  | Charge per ha.       61.10
 8   Resale value (% of purchase price, P)  10.0 |_____
 9   Other fixed costs (% of P)            1.0   |
10   Economic life (h)                    2000   |
11   Repair cost over economic life (% of P) 60.0|
12   Fuel use (l/h)                         33   |
13   Fuel price (p/l)                       17   |
14   Oil & filter costs (% of fuel cost)  20.0   |_____
15   Driver's wage (£/h)                   3.00  | INTERMEDIATE CALCULATIONS
16   Operating speed (km/h)                4.8   |
17   Width of combine (m)                  5.5   | Capacity (ha/h)       1.85
18   Field efficiency (%)                 70.0   |
19   Interest rate (%)                    15.0   | Real cost of
20   Rate of inflation (%)                 7.0   |         capital       7.5%
21   ===============================================================================
22                                      OUTPUT TABLE
23
24                         Hectares     100     150     200     250     300
25   Own combine:                     ---------------------------------------
26   Fixed costs
27   -----------
28   Depreciation                     5625    5625    5625    5625    5625
29   Interest                         2056    2056    2056    2056    2056
30   Other (shelter etc.)              500     500     500     500     500
31                                    ---------------------------------------
32   Total                            8181    8181    8181    8181    8181
33                                    ---------------------------------------
34   Operating costs       Per ha.
35   ----------------
36   Repairs & maintenance    8.12     812    1218    1623    2029    2435
37   Fuel                     3.04     304     455     607     759     911
38   Oil & filters             .61      61      91     121     152     182
39   Driver                   1.62     162     244     325     406     487
40
41   Total                   13.38    1338    2007    2677    3346    4015
42                                    ---------------------------------------
43   Grand total                      9519   10189   10858   11527   12196
44                                    ---------------------------------------
45   Cost per ha.                    95.19   67.92   54.29   46.11   40.65
46   ===============================================================================
47
48   Contractor:
49   Standing charge                   500     500     500     500     500
50   Fixed charge per ha.    61.10    6110    9165   12220   15275   18330
51                                    ---------------------------------------
52   Grand total                      6610    9665   12720   15775   18830
53                                    ---------------------------------------
54   Cost per ha.                    66.10   64.43   63.60   63.10   62.77
55   ===============================================================================
56
57   Minimum cost system          Contract Contract Purchase Purchase Purchase
58
59   Breakeven hectarage    160.97
60   ===============================================================================
```

Fig. 11.2 Purchase combine v Use constractor spreadsheet.

Machinery replacement timing

Purpose: To determine the optimum age for the replacement of an item of machinery.

Author: Nigel Williams

Spreadsheet Name: MACHREPL

12.1 Introduction

The objective of the model is to identify the ideal length of time that a piece of machinery should be kept. This is influenced by two main factors: the fall in value of the machine (ie. depreciation) over time and the annual repair costs. Typically, the resale value of the machine falls rapidly during the first few years of life and then less rapidly after the fourth or fifth year. Repair costs are assumed to follow the reverse pattern, being low in the first few years and then rising as the machine ages. It is assumed that running costs, ie. fuel, insurance etc., are constant, irrespective of the age of the machine and therefore do not affect the decision.

The problem is to balance the high depreciation and low repair costs of early replacement against the low average depreciation but high average repair costs of keeping the machine longer. The problem is made more complex by the fact that interest needs to be charged on the average capital invested in the machine.

The model works by calculating the total cost of owning a machine for any number of years. The costs and returns generated in future years are converted back to their present day values using discount factors. This automatically allows for the interest charges. The discounted cost of owning a machine is the sum of the purchase price and the present value of the stream of running and repair costs less the present value of the machine's resale value. This computation provides the total cost of owning the machine for any given length of time. This calculation is repeated for each year of the machine's life.

The total cost of owning the machine must then be converted to an equivalent annual cost as this will vary with the length of time the machine is owned. The annual equivalent costs for each of these total costs is calculated using amortisation factors. The year which has the lowest annual equivalent cost is the point where replacement should take place, other things being equal, as this gives the lowest average annual cost of owning the machine.

An extension of the model incorporates the effects of different marginal tax rates and writing down allowances on the replacement decision. This enables the decision maker to examine the effects of changes in his tax situation on the replacement problem.

The spreadsheet contains depreciation formulas for a range of machine types. Most of these have been derived from data collected in the Ministry of Agriculture's Farm Business Survey (Cunningham, 1988). The remainder have been drawn from U.S. data (ASAE, 1987). The spreadsheet enables the user to select a depreciation schedule by entering two values which are incorporated into a depreciation formula. These two values are the initial depreciation, which shows the fall in value of the machine immediately it is purchased, and the subsequent depreciation, which reflects the fall in the value of the machine for each year of the machine's life (including the first). Thus a machine with initial depreciation of, say, 15 per cent and subsequent depreciation of, say, 10 per cent will be worth 24 per cent less at the end of its first year of life than its purchase price. Thereafter its resale value will fall by 10 per cent per year on a diminishing balance basis. This method mimics the observed fall in value of machinery more accurately than the conventional system of constant diminishing balance rates of depreciation but should the user prefer this latter method, a zero should be entered in the initial depreciation cell. The effects of these entries can be discovered by examining the data displayed in cells B65 to B80 which show how a machine of the value entered by the operator will depreciate according to the type of depreciation rates chosen.

There is a choice of four repair cost functions derived from UK survey data (type 1: Bates, Rayner & Custance, 1978, type 2: Culpin, 1975, type 3: Hunt & Bowers, 1970, type 4: Morris, 1988). The repair costs are a function of the machine's original cost and age. They are displayed in cells D43 to G57 as a percentage of original cost. Although replacement should ideally be related to hours of use, chronological age has been taken as a proxy for this given the difficulty of getting reliable data on the hours of use of machinery. However, three of the repair schedules included for illustrative purposes (ie. types 2,3 & 4) are based on hours of use (B43:B57) while the other (type 1) is based on chronological age (A43:A57). Cells C43 to C57 are left blank for the user to substitute his or her own estimates where necessary.

A third item of data required is the interest rate on borrowed (or own) capital. This allows for the cost of money 'tied up' in the machine during the time it is owned by the business. The model can also be adjusted to allow for taxation and inflation.

As the user will see, there is frequently relatively little difference between cost at the optimum age, and replacement slightly earlier or later. However, the model does identify the range of years within which the cost is near to a minimum. The actual decision on which year is ideal will often depend on other factors that cannot readily be incorporated in the model because of their qualitative nature.

Examples of factors that will tend to encourage early replacement include low interest rates, high secondhand values, high repair costs, rapid technological improvements in machinery, high levels of business confidence, high levels of tax reliefs on machinery investments, high penalties incurred through machinery breakdown etc.

12.2 Input data

The spreadsheet is displayed in Figs. 12.1 and 12.2. The data are entered in the three sections:

(a)   Data relating to the business environment

	Location
Initial capital cost in £	B9
Discount rate as a percentage	B10
Inflation rate as a percentage	B11
Tax writing down allowance as a percentage	B12
Marginal tax rate as a percentage	B13

These data are used to calculate the real discount rate (D17) and the post-tax discount rate (D18) using the formulas

D17 = ((1+B10/100)/(1+B11/100) -1) * 100
D18 = B10 * (100-B13) / 100

(b) Parameters for calculating the economic depreciation of the machine

	Location
Initial depreciation as a percentage	F38
Subsequent depreciation as a percentage	F39

Depreciation rates for a range of different machine types are displayed for information (B27:E35).

(c) A code number indicating the choice of repair cost function. Users may also enter their own data.

	Location
Code number in the range 0 to 4	F59
User's chosen repair costs per year as a percentage of original cost	C43:C57

12.3 Output data

The output data is in two tables showing without tax (A61:H80) and with tax (A81:J100) calculations. Both will incorporate inflation.

12.3.1 Before tax

(a) Age of the machine in years (A65:A80)

Age = preceding cell in column + 1 , eg. A66 = A65 + 1

(b) Value of the machine (B65:B80) showing the estimated value of the machine for each year of age (A65:A80).

Value of the machine = the original cost of the machine (B9) compounded by the rate of inflation (B11) and diminished by the depreciation function for that age (A65:A80).

Value of the machine = original cost $* C^N * A * B^N$, where
C = 1 + inflation factor/100
A = 1 - initial depreciation rate/100
B = 1 - subsequent depreciation rate/100
N = age in years

eg. B66 = B9 * ((1+B11/100)^A66) * (1-F38/100) * (1-F39/100)^A66

(c) Discounted secondhand value (C65:C80) showing the present value of the machine at the chosen discount rate (B10) for a given age (A65:A80)

$$\text{Discounted secondhand value} = \frac{\text{secondhand value}}{\text{inverse discount factor}}$$

eg. C66 = B66 / (1+(B10/100))^A66

(d) Repair cost showing the estimated cost of repairs for each year of the machine's life (D65:D80) based on the chosen repair cost function (F59) adjusted for inflation rate (B11) and age (A65:A80).

Repair cost = chosen repair cost function as a per cent of original cost (C43:G57) * original cost/100 * compound factor for inflation rate

eg. D66 = CHOOSE(F59,C43,D43,E43,F43,G43) * (B9/100) * (1+B11/100)^A66

(e) Discounted repair cost showing the present value of the repair cost (E65:E80) based on chosen discount rate (B10) and the machine age (A65:A80)

$$\text{Discounted repair cost} = \frac{\text{repair cost}}{\text{inverse discount factor}}$$

eg. E66 = D66 / (1+(B10/100))^A66

(f) Discounted holding cost (F65:F80) showing the present value of the total cost of owning the machine for each year of age (A65:A80).

Discounted holding cost = discounted holding cost for previous year + discounted second hand value in previous year - discounted second hand value this year + discounted repair cost this year.

eg. F66 = F65 + C65 - C66 + E66

(g) Equivalent annuity (G65:G80) showing the average cost in present value terms of keeping the machine to any particular age (A65:A80) at the chosen discount rate (B10).

$$\text{Equivalent Annuity} = \frac{\text{discounted holding cost}}{\text{annuity factor}}$$

eg. G66 = F66 * (B10/100) / (1-(1+B10/100)^-A66)

(h) The replacement message (H65:H80) which indicates in which year replacement should take place by highlighting the year in which the equivalent annuity is at a minimum.

If the equivalent annuity in this year is less than the preceding year and is less than the following year, then print "replace" otherwise print a blank.

eg. H66 = IF(AND(G66<G65,G66<G67), ("replace"), (" "))

12.3.2 After Tax

(a) Age of machine in years (A85:A100)

Age = preceding cell in column + 1 , eg. A86 = A85 + 1

(b) Value of the machine (B85:B100) showing the value of the machine for each year of age.

Value of the machine = value in "before tax" calculation, (B65:B80)

eg. B86 = B66

(c) Written down value (C85:C100) showing the written down value of the machine calculated using the annual writing down allowance (B12) for each year of age (A85:A100)

Written down value = original cost * writing down factor.

eg. C86 = B85 * ((100-B12)/100)^A86

(d) Tax on sale (D85:D100) showing the tax payable (or refundable) on the difference between the economic value of the machine (B85:B100) and the written down value (C85:C100) for each year of age (A85:A100) at the marginal tax rate (B13).

Tax on sale = (value of machine - written down value) * tax rate

eg. D86 = (B86-C86) * B13/100

(e) Post-tax writing down allowance (E85:E100) showing the tax relief on the writing down allowance at the marginal tax rate (B13) for that year.

Post-tax writing down allowance = (written down value in the previous year
                                                         - written down value in the current year) * tax rate.

eg. E86 = (C85-C86) * B13/100

(f) Post-tax repair cost (F85:F100) showing the cost of repairs in each year of age (A86:A100) after allowing for tax relief on the cost.

Post-tax repair cost = repair cost * tax adjustment factor.

eg. F86 = D66 * (100-B13)/100

(g) Cumulative repairs and writing down allowances (G85:G100) showing the present values of the accumulated post-tax writing down allowances and post-tax repair costs for each year of age.

Cumulative repairs and writing down allowances = value for previous year +
    (- post-tax writing down allowance in current year + post-tax repair cost in the
    present year) * post tax discount factor.

eg. G86 = G85 + (-E86+F86)*(1+D18/100)^-A86

(h) Discounted holding cost (H85:H100) showing the present value of the total post-tax cost of owning the machine for each year of age (A85:A100).

Discounted holding cost = original capital cost + cumulative repairs and writing down
    allowances + (- resale value + tax on sale) * post-tax discount factor.

eg. H86 = B85 + G86 + (-B86+D86)*(1+D18/100)^-A86

(i) Post-tax equivalent annuity (I85:I100) showing the average post-tax cost in present value terms of keeping the machine to any particular age (A86:A100).

Post-tax equivalent annuity = $\dfrac{\text{discounted holding cost}}{\text{post tax annuity factor}}$

eg. I86 = H86 * (D18/100) / (1-(1+D18/100)^-A86)

(j) Replacement message (J65:J100) which indicates in which year replacement should take place by highlighting the year in which the equivalent annuity is at a minimum as in 12.3.1 (h).

If the equivalent annuity in this year is less than the preceding year and is less than the following year then print "replace" otherwise print a blank.

eg. J86 = IF(AND(I86<I85,I86<I87), ("replace"), (" "))

References

American Society of Agricultural Engineers (1987) *Yearbook*. St. Joseph, Michigan, USA.

Bates, J.M., Rayner, A.J. & Custance, P.R. (1978) Inflation, tax allowance and the optimal timing of machinery replacement. *Oxford Agrarian Studies,* 87-104.

Culpin, C. (1975) *Profitable Farm Mechanisation* (3rd Edition). Crosby Lockwood Staples, London.

Cunningham, S. (1988) Adapting the diminishing balance method to cope with high rates of initial depreciation. Unpublished paper, University of Exeter.

Hunt, D.R. & Bowers, W. (1970) Application of Mathematical formulas to repair cost data. *Trans.Am.Soc.Ag. Eng.* **13**(6), 806-809.

Morris, J. (1988) Tractor repair costs *Farm Management* **6**(10) 433-441

```
   |  A  ||   B   ||   C   ||   D   ||   E   ||   F   ||   G   |

1   Calculating the optimum timing of machinery replacement
2   Nigel Williams (Wye College)
3
4   To calculate the optimum life of a piece of machinery enter the
5   data for your machine type and inspect the spreadsheet.  Replace
6   in the year in which the equivalent annuity is at a mininmum.
7
8            **************
9            *    5000 * initial capital cost (£)
10           *      12 * chosen discount rate (%)
11           *       0 * chosen inflation rate (%)
12           *      25 * chosen writing down allowance (% pa)
13           *      40 * chosen marginal tax rate (%)
14           **************
15
16  These data generate the following factors:
17   real discount rate (%)          12.00
18   post tax discount rate (%)       7.20
19
20
21  Research has shown that machines have the following average depreciation
22  rates.  The initial depreciation rate refers to the moment of purchase.
23  The subsequent depreciation rate refers to the following years, including
24  the first.
25                                    Initial   Subsequent
26                                       %          %
27          1  Tractor                   15         10
28          2  Combine Harvester         12         12
29          3  Forage Harvester          34         11
30          4  Baler                     15         13
31          5  Beet Harvester            12         16
32          6  Potato Harvester          47          6
33          7  Crawler                   32          8
34          8  Swather                   36         12
35          9  Other Machinery           40         12
36
37                                              **************
38  ENTER YOUR CHOICE HERE        Initial Depn (%)     *    15 *
39                                Subsequent Depn (%)  *    10 *
40                                              **************
41  Research has shown that machinery has the following repair cost functions.
42    Age     Hours    Type 0   Type 1   Type 2   Type 3   Type 4
43     1       800        0        1        7        2        2
44     2      1600        0        3       14        5        5
45     3      2400        0        4       21        9       10
46     4      3200        0        5       28       15       15
47     5      4000        0        7       35       21       21
48     6      4800        0        8       42       28       27
49     7      5600        0        9       48       36       34
50     8      6400        0       11       55       44       41
51     9      7200        0       12       62       53       49
52    10      8000        0       14       69       63       57
53    11      8800        0       15       76       73       66
54    12      9600        0       16       83       84       75
55    13     10400        0       18       90       96       84
56    14     11200        0       19       97      108       94
57    15     12000        0       20      104      120      104
58                                              **************
59  ENTER YOUR CHOICE OF REPAIR COST FUNCTION HERE    *     1 *
60  ********************************************************************************
```

Fig. 12.1 Machinery replacement timing spreadsheet (Cells A1:G60).

	A	B	C	D	E	F	G	H	I	J
	BEFORE TAX									
	Age of Machine	Value of Machine	Discounted 2nd-hand Value	Repair Cost	Discounted Repair Cost	Discounted Holding Cost	Equivalent Annuity			
	Years									
		£	£	£	£	£	£			
65	0	5000	5000	0	0	0	0			
66	1	3825	3415	68	60	1645	1843			
67	2	3443	2744	135	108	2424	1434			
68	3	3098	2205	203	144	3107	1293			
69	4	2788	1772	270	172	3712	1222			
70	5	2510	1424	338	192	4251	1179			
71	6	2259	1144	405	205	4736	1152			
72	7	2033	920	473	214	5175	1134			
73	8	1829	739	540	218	5573	1122			
74	9	1647	594	608	219	5937	1114			
75	10	1482	477	675	217	6271	1110			
76	11	1334	383	743	213	6579	1108			
77	12	1200	308	810	208	6862	1108	replace		
78	13	1080	248	878	201	7123	1109			
79	14	972	199	945	193	7365	1111			
80	15	875	160	1013	185	7589	1114			

	A	B	C	D	E	F	G	H	I	J
	AFTER TAX									
	Age of Machine	Value of Machine	Written Down Value	Tax on Sale	Post tax W. Down Allowance	Post tax Repair Cost	Cumul. Reps.& W.D.A.	Disc. Holding Cost	Post tax Equiv. Annuity	
	Years									
		£	£	£	£	£	£	£	£	
85	0	5000	5000	0	0	0	0	0		
86	1	3825	3750	30	500	41	-429	1031	1106	
87	2	3443	2813	252	375	81	-684	1539	854	
88	3	3098	2109	396	281	122	-814	1992	762	
89	4	2788	1582	483	211	162	-851	2403	713	
90	5	2510	1187	529	158	203	-820	2781	682	
91	6	2259	890	547	119	243	-738	3135	662	
92	7	2033	667	546	89	284	-618	3468	648	
93	8	1829	501	532	67	324	-471	3785	639	
94	9	1647	375	508	50	365	-303	4089	633	
95	10	1482	282	480	38	405	-119	4381	630	
96	11	1334	211	449	28	446	75	4663	628	
97	12	1200	158	417	21	486	277	4937	628	replace
98	13	1080	119	385	16	527	484	5202	629	
99	14	972	89	353	12	567	693	5459	632	
100	15	875	67	323	9	608	904	5710	635	

Fig. 12.2 Machinery replacement timing spreadsheet (Cells A61:J100).

Machinery depreciation schedule

Purpose: To calculate machinery depreciation on an historic and a current cost (ie. adjusted for inflation) basis.

Author: Nigel Williams

Spreadsheet Name: MACHDEPN

13.1 Introduction

This spreadsheet is used to calculate the depreciation (using the diminishing balance method) of a group of machines in any given year. The data required are the cost of each machine and its year of purchase. The operator also has to decide on the depreciation rate for each machine. The model gives the option of a different depreciation rate in the year of purchase from that used in subsequent years. This allows for the high initial loss in value that surveys indicate is the norm for agricultural machinery. There is, of course, no reason why the same depreciation rate should not be used for the first and subsequent years.

The model calculates the opening and closing valuation and depreciation for each machine and provides totals of these. The model also allows for the purchase and sale of machines during the year, and there is a 'fail-safe' device that indicates that a machine sold in a previous year should be deleted from the spreadsheet - although the model will show zeroes against it.

A further refinement of the model is that it will enable opening and closing valuations and depreciation to be calculated on a replacement cost basis, ie. adjusted for the effects of inflation. Briefly, inflation causes the book value of an asset to increase, at least in nominal terms, as the purchasing power of money falls. Failing to adjust for inflation will understate the cash values of these assets and similarly their depreciation. The former error leads to an understatement of net worth, or wealth of the business, and the latter to an overstatement of profit. The part of the template that adjusts all the values for inflation is in cells A61 to H80. The only additional information required is index numbers indicating the rate of inflation. These are entered for the relevant year in cells C21 to C39. These index numbers can be found in publications such as the Farm Management Pocketbook (Nix,1990) from whence the indices in the model were taken.

Ideally index numbers for each class of machinery (or failing that for farm machinery as a whole) should be used as machinery prices do not necessarily change exactly in line with inflation. Unfortunately these indices are not readily available. Where the user prefers to use different indices for different classes of machinery, it is recommended that a separate file is used for each class, with the relevant series of index numbers in each.

As well as showing the opening and closing valuation and the depreciation, the model calculates the holding gain for each machine. This is the increase in value of the machine from the previous year to the present. The holding gain is added to the opening valuation before depreciation is calculated and then subtracted to arrive at the closing valuation. The holding gain represents the increase in the value of the asset (before depreciation) due to the effects of inflation. It does not represent an increase in profit since it can only be liquidated by the sale of the machine. Any replacement machine would also have increased in cost due to the effects of inflation.

13.2 Input data

The spreadsheet is illustrated in Figs. 13.1 and 13.2. Data are entered in two sections.

13.2.1 Data relating to specific items of machinery.

	Location
Current crop year	B3
Machine name	B8 : B19
Year of purchase	C8 : C19
Original cost	D8 : D19
Depreciation rate in year of purchase as a percentage	E8 : E19
Depreciation rate in subsequent years as a percentage	F8 : F19
Sale value where sold in current year	G8 : G19
Sale year when sold in current year	H8 : H19

13.2.2 Price indices for the various years.

These data are contained in a LOOKUP table.

	Location
Year	B21 : B39
Price index	C21 : C39

An error message appears in cells F2:G4 if there are no indices for the crop year entered in B3.

13.3 Output data

The output data is in two tables showing historic cost (A41:H60) and current cost (A61:H80) valuations and depreciation.

13.3.1 Historic cost depreciation

(i) An error message (B46:B57) indicating whether or not the machine was sold in a year prior to the crop year (B3).

If the year of sale is greater than zero and less than the crop year then print DELETE, otherwise print OK.

eg. B46 = IF(AND(H8>0,H8<B3), ("DELETE"), ("OK"))

(ii) Opening valuation (D46:D57) showing the value of the machine at the start of the year.

If either the year of purchase (C8) is equal to the crop year (B3) or the machine was sold prior to the crop year then print zero, otherwise:

Opening valuation = original cost $* A * B^{N-1}$

where A = 1 - initial depreciation rate/100
       B = 1 - subsequent year's depreciation rate/100
       N = age in years

eg. D46 = IF(OR(C8=B3,B46=("DELETE")), 0, D8*((100-E8)/100) *
                                                    ((100-F8)/100)^(B3-1-C8))

(iii) Purchases (E46:E57) showing the cost of any purchases in the year.

If the year of purchase (C8) equals the crop year (B3) then print the purchase price (D8) otherwise print zero.

eg. E46 = IF(C8 = B3,D8,0)

(iv) Sales (F46:F57) showing the value of any machines sold in the year.

If the machine was sold prior to the crop year print zero, otherwise print the sale price (G8).

eg. F46 = IF(B46 = ("DELETE"),0,G8)

(v) Closing valuation (G46:G57) showing the value of the machine at the end of the year.

If either the sales (F46) are not equal to zero or the machine was sold prior to the crop year print zero, otherwise print the original cost (D8) times the depreciation factor.

Closing valuation = original cost $* A * B^{N}$

where A = 1 - initial depreciation rate/100
       B = 1 - subsequent depreciation rate/100
       N = age in years

eg. G46 = IF(OR(F46<>0,B46=("DELETE")), 0, D8*(100-E8)/100 *
                                                    ((100-F8)/100)^(B3-C8))

(vi) Depreciation (G46:G57) showing the depreciation in value of the machines during the year.

Depreciation = opening valuation + purchases - sales - closing valuation.

eg. H46 = D46 + E46 - F46 -G46

All of these values are totalled in cells D59:H59

eg. D59 = SUM (D46:D57) etc.

Each machine is assumed to fall in value by the first year depreciation (E8:E19) in the year of purchase and by the subsequent year's depreciation (F8:F19) thereafter.

13.3.2 *Replacement or current cost depreciation*

(a) An error message (B66:B77) as in (i) above

eg. B66 = B46 etc.

(b) Opening valuation (C66:C77) showing the value of the machine at the start of the year indexed to allow for the effects of inflation.

If year of purchase (C8) is zero then print zero otherwise:

$$\text{Opening valuation} = \frac{\text{historic opening valuation * last year's index}}{\text{index in the year of purchase}}$$

eg. C66 = IF (C8=0, 0, D46 * VLU(B3-1,B21:C39,1) / VLU(C8,B21:C39,1))

(c) Purchases (D66:D77) showing the cost of any purchases in the year as in (iii) above

eg. D66 = E46 etc.

(d) Holding gains (E66:E77) showing the increase in money value of the machine during the year as a result of inflation.

$$\text{Holding gain} = \frac{\text{opening valuation * this year's index}}{\text{last year's index}} - \text{opening valuation}$$

eg. E66 = C66 * VLU(B3,B21:C39,1) / VLU(B3-1,B21:C39,1) - C66

(e) Sale (F66:F77) showing the value of any machine sold in the year as in (iv) above

eg. F66 = F46

(f) Closing valuation (G66:G77) showing the value of machines at the end of the year indexed to allow for the effects of inflation.

$$\text{Closing valuation} = \frac{\text{Historic closing valuation * this year's index}}{\text{index in year of purchase}}$$

eg. G66 = IF(C8=0, 0, G46 * VLU(B3,B21:C39,1)/VLU(C8,B21:C39,1))

(g) Depreciation (H66:H77) showing the depreciation in value of the machine during the year after allowing for the increase in value caused by inflation.

Depreciation = Opening valuation + purchases + holding gains - sales - closing valuation

eg. H66 = C66 + D66 + E66 - F66 - G66

All these values are totalled in cells C79:H79

eg. C79 = SUM (C66:C77) etc.

Reference

Nix, J.S. (1990) *Farm Management Pocketbook (20th Edition)*. Wye College (University of London)

```
        |A||    B    ||    C    ||    D    ||    E    ||    F    ||    G    ||    H    |
1    Machinery Depreciation Calculation Program.  Nigel Williams, Wye College.
2        *************
3        *    1989 * Enter current crop year
4        *************
5           Machine      Year of  Original  Deprecn./year (%)      Sale      Sale
6      No Name           Purchase   Cost    First   Subseq'nt     Value      Year
7    *****************************************************************************
8       1 Tractor         1989     20000     15        10
9       2 Tractor         1988     20000     15        10
10      3 Tractor         1987     20000     15        10          15500      1989
11      4
12      5
13      6
14      7
15      8
16      9
17     10
18     11
19     12
20   *****************************************************************************
21      *      1976        215    *          Price Indices
22      *      1977        249    *
23      *      1978        270    *          Enter the price indices for
24      *      1979        306    *          the machine type of your choice,
25      *      1980        361    *          or general price indices.
26      *      1981        404    *
27      *      1982        439    *          You may also change the
28      *      1983        459    *          range of years.
29      *      1984        482    *
30      *      1985        511    *
31      *      1986        528    *
32      *      1987        551    *
33      *      1988        575    *
34      *      1989        605    *
35      *      1990               *
36      *      1991               *
37      *      1992               *
38      *      1993               *
39      *      1994               *
40   *****************************************************************************
41   Historic Cost Depreciation
42
43      No                      Opening  Purchases   Sales   Closing   Deprec'n
44                              Valuation                    Valuation
45
46      1         OK                  0     20000        0     17000       3000
47      2         OK              17000         0        0     15300       1700
48      3         OK              15300         0    15500         0       -200
49      4         OK                  0         0        0         0          0
50      5         OK                  0         0        0         0          0
51      6         OK                  0         0        0         0          0
52      7         OK                  0         0        0         0          0
53      8         OK                  0         0        0         0          0
54      9         OK                  0         0        0         0          0
55     10         OK                  0         0        0         0          0
56     11         OK                  0         0        0         0          0
57     12         OK                  0         0        0         0          0
58                                -------   -------  -------   -------    -------
59   Totals                       32300     20000    15500     32300       4500
60                                =======   =======  =======   =======    =======
```

Fig. 13.1 Machinery depreciation schedule spreadsheet (Cells A1:H60).

|A||	B ||	C ||	D ||	E ||	F ||	G ||	H	
61	Replacement Cost Depreciation Calculation							
62								
63	No		Opening	Purchases	Holding	Sales	Closing	Deprec'n
64			Valuation		Gains		Valuation	
65								
66	1	OK	0	20000	0	0	17000	3000
67	2	OK	17000	0	887	0	16098	1789
68	3	OK	15966	0	833	15500	0	1299
69	4	OK	0	0	0	0	0	0
70	5	OK	0	0	0	0	0	0
71	6	OK	0	0	0	0	0	0
72	7	OK	0	0	0	0	0	0
73	8	OK	0	0	0	0	0	0
74	9	OK	0	0	0	0	0	0
75	10	OK	0	0	0	0	0	0
76	11	OK	0	0	0	0	0	0
77	12	OK	0	0	0	0	0	0
78			-------	-------	-------	-------	-------	-------
79	Totals		32966	20000	1720	15500	33098	6088
80			=======	=======	=======	=======	=======	=======

Fig. 13.2 Machinery depreciation schedule spreadsheet (Cells A61:H80).

SPREADSHEET 14

Financing machinery acquisition

Purpose: To compare the costs of acquiring farm machinery by different financing methods.

Author: Joe Morris

Spreadsheet Name : FINANCE

14.1 Introduction

This spreadsheet (Figs. 14.2 and 14.3) compares the costs of acquiring farm machinery by different financing methods, namely; purchase with cash from own funds, purchase by bank loan, hire purchase, leasing and contract hire.

Longer-life, more expensive farm machinery, together with falling farm profits make it more difficult nowadays to pay for new equipment from annual profits or short-term current account overdrafts.

In response, financing institutions have designed schemes for machinery purchase which spread the cost of the asset over its revenue earning life, or allow the machinery user to make best advantage of available capital allowances.

The following comments are made about the financing methods. The methods are demonstrated in the spreadsheet with example data listed in Section 14.3 below.

Purchase with cash from own funds involves one immediate downpayment equivalent to the full capital cost of the asset. The owner purchaser derives benefit from setting subsequent capital allowances against income tax. Cash purchases can enable buyers to negotiate favourable discounts.

Where annual profits are high, cash purchases in any one year may allow full exploitation of tax allowances, especially first year allowances.

Cash purchases may also be part of a replacement schedule whereby selected machines are replaced each year out of revenue. The disadvantages of cash purchases are that it requires a large 'up front' commitment of funds, it reduces subsequent flexibility of financing, and if profits are lower than expected, it may not allow full advantage to be taken of tax allowances.

Many farmers purchase for cash, but use their *overdraft facility* as a source of short term borrowing. This is a flexible, informal, and often cheap source of credit with interest paid only on the current account deficit. The disadvantages are that it is liable to recall, it ties up the overdraft facility, and it is difficult to assess real interest charges. Like cash purchase, the use of the overdraft may encourage investments to be regarded as a residual activity, only possible if there is enough cash or short term credit.

Where assets are acquired with purposely borrowed funds a general principle of financing is to match the term of borrowing to the life of the asset such that capital repayments and interest charges are paid out of earnings. Longer life machinery should encourage longer term borrowing.

Hire purchase (HP) involves a specified down payment (equity stake) followed by equal annual payments which comprise the balance of the Capital Value plus interest on the initial sum borrowed. The purchaser, as eventual owner, accrues tax allowances on the HP charges. HP is generally considered high cost, but can be attractive during periods of high or variable interest rates, especially if favourable prices or interest rates can be negotiated when trade is slack. HP companies prefer moveable assets as security.

Leasing involves the purchase of rights to exclusive use of an asset over an agreed period, without ownership. The lessee makes periodic (monthly, quarterly, annual etc.) payments in advance which are tax deductible. However in the UK, it is only possible to set against tax lease charges that reflect the useful life of the asset. Accelerated lease payments, where large initial payments are made, cannot all be claimed as tax deductible expenses. Capital allowances accrue to the lessors which may be reflected in the lease charges to the lessee. The lessor may derive capital allowances at (higher) corporation tax rates compared to the lessees who may pay lower tax rates, or if times are hard, none at all.

Most commonly, charges are levied to recover Principal, Interest and expenses over a PRIMARY period of one to five years. Payment 'up front' effectively represents an equity stake. A SECONDARY period can last up to 15 years at a nominal charge or as a % of original cost. The lessee has an option to buy (through a 3rd party) or sell at the end of the primary period and gets 85 - 100% of the sale price. The remaining value of the asset is an important factor in influencing the net cost to the farmer/lessee. Sometimes resale value is accepted as downpayment for a new lease. Lease agreements usually commit the user to insure, repair and maintain the asset and avoid negligent use.

Contract hire, as the name implies, involves the hire of a machine for an agreed period. In return for periodic payments, the farmer has exclusive use and all major repairs are met by the owner/contractor. At the end of the contract period, eg. 3 years, the machine returns to the contractor and is replaced with another new one. The contractor sets charges to recover the expected depreciation and repair costs of the machine. The hirer can set 100% of contract charges against tax.

Charges are relatively high because the risks are borne by the contractor. Usually there are restrictions on use. Contract hire is not particularly attractive to careful users, but more suited to heavy users, those who need to keep up-to-date equipment, or those who want to retain flexibility over fleet size (eg. organizations providing machinery services).

In the example, charges to recover repair cost elements of the contract hire have been omitted in order to allow comparison with other financing methods.

14.2 Spreadsheet structure

The structure of the spreadsheet is displayed in Fig. 14.1.

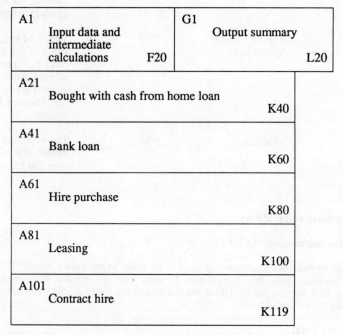

Fig. 14.1 Structure of the FINANCE spreadsheet.

14.3 Input data (D5:D11)

Example input data is contained within Fig. 14.2.

Location	Variable	Value in Example	Explanation
D5	Purchase Price	£20,000	The initial (net of discount) price of the asset (£20,000 for a tractor)
D6	Repayment Period	4 years	The term of the loan or financing agreement
D7	Interest Rate	12%	The commercial rate of interest to be paid
D8	Marginal Rate of Tax	25%	The % rate at which tax is levied on taxable income

117

D9	First Year Allowance	25%	The % of the initial asset value that can be charged as a writing down allowance against taxable income, but claimed $1\frac{1}{2}$ years in arrears
D10	Annual Capital Allowance	25%	The % of the remaining value of the asset which can be charged as a writing down allowance against tax in each year of life, claimed $1\frac{1}{2}$ years in arrears
D11	Inflation	6%	The expected average annual rate of inflation over the life of the asset

14.4 Intermediate calculations

14.4.1 Hidden calculations (F7:F10)

Throughout the spreadsheet reference will need to be made to the values in cells D7:D10 expressed as fractions rather than percentages. In order to avoid repeated division of these values by 100, they are divided by 100 at the outset and the result stored (with a hidden format) in cells F7:F10. Thus

$$F7 = D7 / 100 ,$$
$$F8 = D8 / 100 \text{ etc.}$$

The values in F7:F10 are then used in the remainder of the spreadsheet.

14.4.2 The real discount rate (D12)

The real discount rate is the real cost of borrowing money after adjusting for inflation, as determined by:

$$\frac{1 + \text{interest rate (F7)}}{1 + \text{inflation rate (F11)}} - 1$$

This is first of all calculated (hidden) in F12 as a fraction

$$\text{ie. } F12 = (1 + F7) / (1 + F11) - 1$$

and then displayed as a percentage in D12

$$\text{ie. } D12 = 100 * F12$$

14.5 Output data

14.5.1 Bought with cash from own capital (A21:K40)

Purchasing with cash from own funds, involves a down payment in year 0 (now) of £20,000. Although the full capital cost of the asset is committed immediately, the purchaser can set a writing down allowance of the asset against taxable income over the asset's life. Assuming the purchaser is making profits against which tax can be claimed (and this may not necessarily be the case in practice!), the tax allowances generate negative costs (ie. savings) over the machine's life. In Britain, annual capital allowances are currently 25% of remaining value. This implies a life of about 8 years which is that used in the example.

(a) Cash out (C27)
   The capital cost of the machine (D5)

(b) First year (F/y) allowance (E29)

   The first year allowance is a tax saving calculated as:
   initial purchase price * first year allowance * marginal tax rate

   Usually this is received about 18 months in arrears, during the second year.

   ie. E29 = D5 * F9 * F8

(c) Annual capital (A/c) allowances (F30:K30)

   Capital allowances are calculated using the diminishing balance method, that is as a constant % of the remaining value at the beginning of each year. This writing down allowance is claimed against tax at the relevant tax rate.

   The remaining value at the beginning of each year is determined by the expression:

   $P * (1 - d)^n$

   where:

   P is the purchase price
   d is the annual capital allowance as a decimal
   n is the year concerned

   Annual allowance = remaining value * annual writing down allowance * marginal tax rate.

   This annual allowance is received in arrears. For example, the allowance arising in Year 2 is paid during Year 3,

   ie. F30 = D5 * (1 - F10) ^ D25 * F10 * D8   and thereafter

       G30 = (1 - F10) * F30
       H30 = (1 - F10) * G30 etc.

(d) Net annual cost (C32:K32)

   This shows the sum of the cash flows for each year over a nominal eight year financing period. For instance for Year 3:

   Net annual cost = cash out - first year allowance - annual allowance ie. F32 = F27 - F29 - F30

In Years 2 through to 8 net annual costs are negative showing the beneficial effects of tax savings.

(e) Net Cost (C34)

This shows the sum of all the net annual costs over the eight year period.

ie. C34 = SUM(C32:K32)

(f) Net Present Cost (C36)

This shows the present value sum of net annual costs discounted at the relevant discount rate. This takes account of the time value of money : £1 occurring later in time has a lower present value than £1 occurring earlier, because the latter could be invested to generate interest in the intervening period. Annual cash flows are multiplied by a factor $1/(1 + r)^n$ (where r is the discount rate as a decimal and n is the year in which the cash flow occurs) to give 'present value' annual cash flows. These are summed to give the net present cost at the relevant discount rate. A change in the discount rate changes the net present cost.

The calculation uses the net present value function of the spreadsheet:

ie. C36 = C32 + NPV(F12,D32:K32)

The discounted net present cost is greater than the undiscounted net cost because discounting reduces the present value of benefits associated with future tax savings.

14.5.2 *Bank Loan (A41:K60)*

Acquisition of the asset is by means of a bank loan taken out over a given repayment period. Annual loan repayments are constant. In addition to capital allowances for depreciation, the borrower can set interest charges against taxable income.

(a) Repayments (A46:K48)

The annual cost of repayments is given in row 48. These assume a constant annual repayment with interest charged on the amount outstanding at year beginning according to the formula:

$$P * \frac{r}{1 - (1 + r)^{-n}}$$

where:

P is the amount borrowed
r is the commercial interest rate
n is the loan period

Thus in year 1, D48 = D5 * F7 / (1 - (1 + F7)^-D6)

In further years, the spreadsheet uses the IF function to determine whether or not a loan repayment should be made in that year. For example, if the cash flow year (say Year 3) is less than the loan period (say, 4 years) a repayment is made, otherwise repayment is zero.

This facility allows the spreadsheet to accommodate different loan periods automatically. In the example, for year 3:

F4 = IF(F43>D6, 0, D48)

Because F43 (3) is not greater than D6(4), then a repayment is made according to the formula. If F43 had been greater than D6 then no repayment would be made.

A repayment in any one year comprises a charge for interest and a contribution towards paying off the amount originally borrowed. These are separately identified because the interest charges are allowable against tax. Row 47 identifies the interest charges. Row 46 identifies the amount of principal paid off each year.

Row 47 uses an IF function to determine whether a loan repayment has been made in a particular year. If it has, then interest is charged on the amount outstanding, ie. the original loan less the repayments of the principal to date.

Thus D47 = IF(D48>0, D5 * F7, 0),
    E47 = IF(E48>0, D47 - D46 * F7, 0)
    F47 = IF(F48>0, E47 - E46 * F7, 0) etc.

For each year the repayments of the principal (Row 46) are then determined by calculating the difference between the annual loan repayment and the annual interest charge.

eg. F46 = F48 - F47

The principal repayment increases relative to interest charges during the later years of the loan period.

(b) First Year and Annual Allowances (E50 and F51:K51)

The borrower acquires ownership of the asset and is therefore able to set writing down allowances against income taxation as described in Section 14.5.1.

ie. E50 = E29 and
    F51 = F30,   G51 = G30 etc.

(c) Relief on Interest (E52:K52)

The interest component of loan repayments identified in Row 47 can be set against tax and relief obtained in the following year. Thus:

relief on interest in one year = interest payment in previous year * marginal tax rate

eg. F52 = E47 * F8

(d) Net Annual Cost (D54:K54)

This is derived by subtracting the sum of the first year allowance, annual allowances and the relief on interest from the annual cost

eg. F54 = F48 - F50 - F51 - F52

(e) Net cost and net present cost (C56,C58)

These are calculated as described in Section 14.5.1

ie. Net cost, C56 = SUM(D54:K54)
Net present cost, C58 = NPV(F12,D54:K54)

14.5.3 Hire Purchase (A61:K80)

Acquisition of the asset is by means of a down payment followed by equal annual repayments over a hire purchase (HP) period.

(a) Down Payment (C65)

A down payment is usually specified in the HP agreement as a percentage of the asset value. In the example, the deposit depends on the HP period:

Deposit = asset value / loan period
ie. C65 = D5 / D6

(b) Repayments (D68:K70)

Repayment for hire purchase includes two elements; the repayment of the amount borrowed (that is the asset value less the down payment : the purchase element) and the charge for interest (the 'hire charge' element) on the amount borrowed.

The annual repayment of the amount borrowed is set at the amount borrowed (asset value less deposit) divided by the loan period (years).

ie. D68 = (D5 - C65) / D6

and the IF function is used thereafter in row 63 to test to see if the loan repayment period has expired

eg. E68 = IF (E63>D6, 0, D68)

A similar approach is used to determine annual interest charges which are based on the original amount borrowed (and not the amount outstanding as was the case with the loan repayment method):

ie. D69 = (D5 - C65) * F7 and
eg. E69 = IF (E63>D6, 0, D69)

The sums of annual principal and interest payments are shown in Row 70.

(c) First Year and Annual Allowances (E72 and F73:K73)

The HP holder is deemed to be acquiring eventual ownership and can therefore draw capital allowances as described in Section 14.5.1.

ie. E72 = E29 and F73 = F30 etc.

(d) Relief on Interest (E74:K74)

The interest payments made under the HP agreement are tax allowable in arrears as described in Section 14.5.2.

eg. E74 = D69 * F8

(e) Net Annual Costs, Net Cost and Net Present Cost (C76:K76, C78, C80)

These are derived as described in Section 14.5.2. Thus

Net annual cost in year 1, D76 = D65 + D70 - D72 - D73 - D74
Net cost,   C78 = SUM (C76:K76)
Net present cost,   C80 = C76 + NPV(F12,D76:K76)

14.5.4 Leasing (A81:K100)

Acquisition of the asset is by means of a series of annual lease payments made over an agreed period. Ownership does not transfer to the lessee. The lessee does not qualify for capital allowances, but the annual lease payments can be set against tax.

(a) Repayments (D88:K90)

Annual repayments are made up of two components; a repayment of the principal and a charge for interest on the value of the asset. The annual repayment of the principal is the asset value divided by the length of the lease in years.

ie. D88 = D5 / D6

Again the IF function is used thereafter in row 88 to test to see if the lease period has expired

eg. E88 = IF (E85>D6, 0, D88)

Annual interest charges are calculated using a similar method, with interest charged on the original asset value.

ie. D89 = D5 * F7 and
eg. E89 = IF (E85>D6, 0, D89)

The total leasing rental is the sum of principal and interest payments.

eg. D90 = D88 + D89

(b) Relief on Rental (E92:K92)

The lease payments are tax deductable, one year in arrears. Thus in Year 2:

Tax Relief = Rental in Year 1 * tax rate

ie. E92 = D90 * F8

(c) Net annual cost (D94:K94), net cost sum (C96) and net present cost (C98) are calculated as described in Section 14.5.2. Thus

Net annual cost in year 1, D94 = D90 - D92
Net cost,   C96 = SUM(D94:K94)
Net present cost,   C98 = NPV (F12,D94:K94)

In some cases lease payments are made 'up front' or in advance, sometimes monthly, sometimes quarterly. This affects the timing of cash flows and could affect the net present cost. For instance if a 6 month advance payment is required this could be shown in Year 0 in a similar way to that of the HP deposit. This would increase the net present sum in the example from £22,829 to £23,683. The adjustment could be accommodated in the spreadsheet calculations if required, but it is not done so here.

14.5.5 Contract Hire (A101:K119)

This method involves a constant annual payment in return for the services of a machine which is replaced regularly, say every three or four years, and fully maintained by the contractor. The example assumes that the machine acquired under the various financing plans provides eight years of service. Hence, contract hire payments over an eight year period are assumed, although the machine itself is likely to be replaced with a new one after three or four years.

(a) Repayments (D107:K109)

Repayments comprise two elements; a charge for the asset and a charge for interest. In practice, contract hire charges include a charge for repairs and maintenance but these are left out in the example to allow comparison between other financing methods.

The estimate for the asset charges uses an average annual rate of depreciation based on the capital allowance rate (D10) and the assumption that the tractor is replaced with a new one at the interval specified for repayment period (D6).

Thus, the annual charge for 'depreciation' is given by:

$$D107 = (D5 - D5 * (1 - F10) \wedge D6) / D6$$

and the rest of the entries in row 107 are set equal to D107

eg. E107 = D107

The annual interest payments are based on the original asset value. Thus

D108 = D5 * F7 and E108 = D108 etc.

It may be considered more appropriate to set the replacement interval independent of the loan repayment period (D6). Many hire schemes may replace tractors every three years or so. The replacement period could be specified as a separate cell in the input data matrix, for example (D13) = 3 years. The formula for 'depreciation' given above would then contain the variable D13 instead of D6.

The total hire payment (row 109) is the sum of the principal and interest payments

eg. D109 = D107 + D108

(b) Relief on Payments (E111:K111)

The hire payments are eligible for tax allowance one year in arrears. Thus,

eg. E111 = D109 * F8

(c) Net Annual Cost, Net Cost Sum, and Net Present Cost (D113:K113, C115, C117)

These are calculated as described in Section 14.5.2. Thus

D113 = D109 - D111
C115 = SUM(D113:K113)
C117 = NPV(F12, D113:K113)

The same comments are relevant to contract hire payments made in advance, as for 'up front' payments on leases. For example, a six month up front payment would increase the net present sum from £29,712 to £30,372 in the example shown.

14.6 Output summary

A table is presented in cells G3:L11 which summarises the net costs and net present costs of the financing alternatives. This table draws its results from relevant parts of the spreadsheet. For example, the net cost (I7) and net present cost (K7) of the cash purchase method are taken from C28 and C30 respectively.

To assist a comparison of the options, net cost and net present cost are expressed as an index of the cash purchase option (the latter being set at 100). The index in column J is calculated by dividing the corresponding entry in column I by I7 and multiplying by 100

eg. J8 = I8 / I7 * 100

and similarly the index in column L is calculated by dividing the corresponding entry in column K by K7 and multiplying by 100

eg. L8 = K8 / K7 * 100

By way of example, the table below summarises the estimates for the basic assumptions referred to in Section 14.3 above.

In terms of net cost (undiscounted), the cash purchase appears significantly cheaper than other options. Loans, hire purchase and leasing are about 30% to 40% more expensive, and contract hire over twice the cost of outright purchase. The latter option, however, always guarantees a relatively new machine maintained at full design specification.

If the costs of the financing options are discounted to give the net present cost, the difference between the options is significantly reduced. Loan, hire purchase and leasing are between 10% and 20% more expensive, and contract hire 1.75 times greater than outright purchase for the example given.

The use of discounting favours the 'borrowing' options which defer payments until later. This is a point that financing organizations like to emphasize.

The spreadsheet can also be used to test the sensitivity of financing options to changes in important variables such as loan period, interest rates, or tax rates. Generally, higher interest rates and lower tax rates make financing machinery acquisition more expensive, but the effect, particularly of higher real interest rates, is moderated by the use of the discounting method.

METHOD	NET COST	INDEX	NET PRESENT COST	INDEX
Cash	15667	100	16492	100
Loan	20421	130	18146	110
Hire Purchase	21067	134	19386	118
Lease	22200	142	19728	120
Contract Hire	36362	232	28841	175

Index shows cost relative to cash purchase (100), assumed loan or repayment period - 4 years.

The preceeding example assumed that the asset was kept and provided services for eight years on the farm, except for contract hire where the user was assured the services of a relatively new machine. In this respect, the financing methods assume the same residual value for the asset, that is its remaining value at the end of eight years. This will be about 10% of initial value assuming a 25% diminishing balance rate of depreciation, $(1-0.25)^8$. In practice it may be that different financing arrangements are associated with different replacement timing and residual value. For instance, at the end of a lease the asset may be sold and the realised value retained by the lessee or used to renegotiate a new lease. This complication could be incorporated into the spreadsheet by making, for example, the loan or lease period equal to the life of the asset on the farm, calculating a remaining value, and terminating relevant tax allowances. Remaining value estimates, based on a diminishing balance method, would need to be the same for all financing methods. In theory, remaining value is independent of financing method, although in practice the care of and intensity of asset use by the farmer may not be. In order to keep the presentation of the spreadsheet simple, however, these complications have been avoided by assuming a fixed eight year life and ignoring residual value.

Formulas for columns C to G of the spreadsheet are set out in Figs. 14.4 and 14.5.

	A		B		C		D		E		F	

```
1    FINANCING MACHINERY ACQUISITION
2
3    DATA SET
4
5    Purchase price (£)            20000.00
6    Repayment period (years)          4.00
7    Interest rate                    12.0 %
8    Marginal rate of tax             25.0 %
9    First year allowance             25.0 %
10   Annual capital allowance         25.0 %
11   Inflation rate                    6.0 %
12   Real discount rate                5.7 %
13
14
15
16
17
18
19
20   ------------------------------------------------------------
21
22   BOUGHT WITH CASH FROM OWN CAPITAL
23
24
25   Years                      0          1          2          3
26
27   Cash out              20000
28
29   F/y allowance                                 1250
30   A/c allowance                                            938
31
32   Net annual cost       20000          0      -1250       -938
33
34   Net cost sum          15667
35
36   Net present cost      16492
37
38
39
40   ------------------------------------------------------------
41   BANK LOAN
42
43   Years                      0          1          2          3
44
45   Repayments:
46   Principal                          4185       4687       5249
47   Interest                           2400       1898       1335
48   Annual cost                        6585       6585       6585
49
50   F/y allowance                                 1250
51   A/c allowance                                            938
52   Relief on interest                             600        474
53
54   Net annual cost                    6585       4735       5173
55
56   Net cost sum          20421
57
58   Net present cost      18146
59
60   ------------------------------------------------------------
```

Fig. 14.2 Financing machinery acquisition spreadsheet (Cells A1:L60).

	G	H	I	J	K	L
1						
2						
3	SUMMARY					
4					NET	
5			NET	INDEX	PRESENT	INDEX
6	METHOD		COST		COST	
7	Cash		15667	100	16492	100
8	Loan		20421	130	18146	110
9	Hire purchase		21067	134	19386	118
10	Lease		22200	142	19728	120
11	Contract hire		36362	232	28841	175
12						
13	Index shows cost relative to cash purchase (100)					
14	assumed loan or repayment period			4.00years		
15						
16						
17						
18						
19						
20	---					
21						
22						
23						
24						
25		4	5	6	7	8
26						
27						
28						
29						
30		703	527	396	297	222
31						
32		-703	-527	-396	-297	-222
33						
34						
35						
36						
37						
38						
39						
40	---					
41						
42						
43		4	5	6	7	8
44						
45						
46		5879	0	0	0	0
47		706	0	0	0	0
48		6585	0	0	0	0
49						
50						
51		703	527	396	297	222
52		334	176	0	0	0
53						
54		5548	-704	-396	-297	-222
55						
56						
57						
58						
59						
60	---					

	A	B	C	D	E	F
61	HIRE PURCHASE					
62						
63	Years		0	1	2	3
64						
65	Down payments		5000			
66						
67	Repayments:					
68	Principal			3750	3750	3750
69	Interest			1800	1800	1800
70	Annual cost			5550	5550	5550
71						
72	F/y allowance				1250	
73	A/c allowance					938
74	Relief on interest				450	450
75						
76	Net annual cost		5000	5550	3850	4163
77						
78	Net cost sum		21067			
79						
80	Net present cost		19386			
81	--					
82						
83	LEASING					
84						
85	Years		0	1	2	3
86						
87	Repayments:					
88	Principal			5000	5000	5000
89	Interest			2400	2400	2400
90	Leasing rental			7400	7400	7400
91						
92	Relief on rental				1850	1850
93						
94	Net annual cost			7400	5550	5550
95						
96	Net cost sum		22200			
97						
98	Net present cost		19728			
99						
100	--					
101						
102	CONTRACT HIRE					
103						
104	Years		0	1	2	3
105						
106	Repayments:					
107	Principal			3418	3418	3418
108	Interest			2400	2400	2400
109	Hire payments			5818	5818	5818
110						
111	Relief on hire				1454	1454
112						
113	Net annual cost			5818	4363	4363
114						
115	Net cost sum		36362			
116						
117	Net present cost		28841			
118						
119	===					

Fig. 14.3 Financing machinery acquisition spreadsheet (Cells A61:L119).

| | G || H || I || J || K || L |

Row	G	H	I	J	K	L
61						
62						
63	4	5	6	7	8	
64						
65						
66						
67						
68	3750	0	0	0	0	
69	1800	0	0	0	0	
70	5550	0	0	0	0	
71						
72						
73	703	527	396	297	222	
74	450	450	0	0	0	
75						
76	4397	-977	-396	-297	-222	
77						
78						
79						
80						
81	---					
82						
83						
84						
85	4	5	6	7	8	
86						
87						
88	5000	0	0	0	0	
89	2400	0	0	0	0	
90	7400	0	0	0	0	
91						
92	1850	1850	0	0	0	
93						
94	5550	-1850	0	0	0	
95						
96						
97						
98						
99						
100	---					
101						
102						
103						
104	4	5	6	7	8	
105						
106						
107	3418	3418	3418	3418	3418	
108	2400	2400	2400	2400	2400	
109	5818	5818	5818	5818	5818	
110						
111	1454	1454	1454	1454	1454	
112						
113	4363	4363	4363	4363	4363	
114						
115						
116						
117						
118						
119	===					

```
         |   A   ||   B   ||        C        ||         D          |
 1   FINANCING MACHINERY ACQUISITION
 2
 3   DATA SET
 4
 5   Purchase price (£)            20000
 6   Repayment period (years)      4
 7   Interest rate                 12
 8   Marginal rate of tax          25
 9   First year allowance          25
10   Annual capital allowance      25
11   Inflation rate                6
12   Real discount rate            100*F12
13
14
15
16
17
18
19
20   -----------------------------------------------------------------
21
22   BOUGHT WITH CASH FROM OWN CAPITAL
23
24
25   Years            0                    C25+1
26
27   Cash out         D5
28
29   F/y allowance
30   A/c allowance
31
32   Net annual cost  C27-C29-C30          D27-D29-D30
33
34   Net cost sum     SUM(C32:K32)
35
36   Net present cost C32+NPV(F12,D32:K32)
37
38
39
40   -----------------------------------------------------------------
41   BANK LOAN
42
43   Years            0                    C43+1
44
45   Repayments:
46   Principal                             D48-D47
47   Interest                              IF(D48>0,D5*F7,0)
48   Annual cost                           D5*F7/(1-(1+F7)^-D6)
49
50   F/y allowance
51   A/c allowance
52   Relief on interest
53
54   Net annual cost                       D48-D50-D51-D52
55
56   Net cost sum     SUM(D54:K54)
57
58   Net present cost NPV(F12,D54:K54)
59
60   -----------------------------------------------------------------
```

Fig. 14.4 Formulas for financing machinery acquisition spreadsheet (Cells A1:G60).

	E			F			G	

SUMMARY

%	D7/100	METHOD
%	D8/100	Cash
%	D9/100	Loan
%	D10/100	Hire purchase
%	D11/100	Lease
	(1+F7)/(1+F11)-1	Contract hire

Index shows cost relati
assumed loan or repayme

D25+1	E25+1	F25+1
D5*F9*F8		
	D5*(1-F10)^D25*F10*F8	(1-F10)*F30
E27-E29-E30	F27-F29-F30	G27-G29-G30

D43+1	E43+1	F43+1
E48-E47	F48-F47	G48-G47
IF(E48>0,D47-D46*F7,0)	IF(F48>0,E47-E46*F7,0)	IF(G48>0,F47-F46*F7,0)
IF(E43>D6,0,D48)	IF(F43>D6,0,D48)	IF(G43>D6,0,D48)
E29		
	F30	G30
D47*F8	E47*F8	F47*F8
E48-E50-E51-E52	F48-F50-F51-F52	G48-G50-G51-G52

```
        |   A    ||   B    ||          C          ||            D            |
61    HIRE PURCHASE
62
63    Years                   0                        C63+1
64
65    Down payments           D5/D6
66
67    Repayments:
68    Principal                                        (D5-C65)/D6
69    Interest                                         (D5-C65)*F7
70    Annual cost                                      D68+D69
71
72    F/y allowance
73    A/c allowance
74    Relief on interest
75
76    Net annual cost         C65+C70-C72-C73-C74 D65+D70-D72-D73-D74
77
78    Net cost sum            SUM(C76:K76)
79
80    Net present cost        C76+NPV(F12,D76:K76)
81    --------------------------------------------------------------
82
83    LEASING
84
85    Years                   0                        C85+1
86
87    Repayments:
88    Principal                                        D5/D6
89    Interest                                         D5*F7
90    Leasing rental                                   D88+D89
91
92    Relief on rental
93
94    Net annual cost                                  D90-D92
95
96    Net cost sum            SUM(D94:K94)
97
98    Net present cost        NPV(F12,D94:K94)
99
100   --------------------------------------------------------------
101
102   CONTRACT HIRE
103
104   Years                   0                        C104+1
105
106   Repayments:
107   Principal                                        (D5-D5*(1-F10)^D6)/D6
108   Interest                                         D5*F7
109   Hire payments                                    D107+D108
110
111   Relief on hire
112
113   Net annual cost                                  D109-D111
114
115   Net cost sum            SUM(D113:K113)
116
117   Net present cost        NPV(F12,D113:K113)
118
119   ==============================================================
```

Fig. 14.5 Formulas for financing machinery acquisition spreadsheet (Cells A61:G119).

	E			F			G	

```
D63+1                   E63+1                   F63+1


IF(E63>D6,0,D68)        IF(F63>D6,0,D68)        IF(G63>D6,0,D68)
IF(E63>D6,0,D69)        IF(F63>D6,0,D69)        IF(G63>D6,0,D69)
E68+E69                 F68+F69                 G68+G69

E29
                        F30                     G30
D69*F8                  E69*F8                  F69*F8

E65+E70-E72-E73-E74     F65+F70-F72-F73-F74     G65+G70-G72-G73-G74
```

```
D85+1                   E85+1                   F85+1


IF(E85>D6,0,D88)        IF(F85>D6,0,D88)        IF(G85>D6,0,D88)
IF(E85>D6,0,D89)        IF(F85>D6,0,D89)        IF(G85>D6,0,D89)
E88+E89                 F88+F89                 G88+G89

D90*F8                  E90*F8                  F90*F8

E90-E92                 F90-F92                 G90-G92
```

```
D104+1                  E104+1                  F104+1

D107                    E107                    F107
D108                    E108                    F108
E107+E108               F107+F108               G107+G108

D109*F8                 E109*F8                 F109*F8

E109-E111               F109-F111               G109-G111
```

==

Pig fattening budget

Purpose: To calculate gross margins and net profits for a pig fattening enterprise, from a range of physical and financial data. The spreadsheet also allows critical levels to be determined for the key production parameters.

Author: Charles Course

Spreadsheet Name: PIGCOSTS

15.1 Introduction

This spreadsheet calculates the gross margin per pig that can be achieved from fattening weaners through to a range of different weights. The value of all parameters and variables can be changed by the user.

The output produced is a gross margin budget both per pig and for the whole unit. Fixed costs can then also be deducted to give the net margin or net profit for the whole unit. Performance parameters such as food cost per kilo live weight gain etc. can be calculated.

The spreadsheet is divided into four main sections:

Input data (Rows 7:25)
Intermediate calculations (Rows 33:38)
Gross margin calculations (Rows 45:65)
Fixed costs and net margin (Rows 67:77)

The whole spreadsheet is shown in Figs. 15.1 and 15.2.

15.2 Input data

The following items of data are entered into the first screen:

Data	Location
Size of unit (no. of pigs)	D7
Weaner price (£/head)	D8
Weaner weight (kg)	D9
Liveweight at slaughter (kg)	D10
Killing out %	D11

Output price (p/kg deadweight)	D12
Food conversion ratio (FCR) during fattening period	D13
Food cost (£/tonne)	D14
Number of weeks from purchase to sale	D15
Mortality (%)	D16
Transport and marketing costs (£/pig)	D17
Miscellaneous cost (£/pig)	D18
Veterinary and medicine costs (£/pig)	D19
Overtime labour cost (£/hour)	D20
Overtime labour required (hours/week)	D21
Cost of electricity consumed in unit in full year (£)	D22
Cost of water consumed in unit in full year (£)	D23
Rate of interest (%)	D24
Rate of inflation (%)	D25

15.3 Intermediate calculations

The following intermediate calculations are made

(a) Food consumption per pig (kg)
       = Total liveweight gain (kg) * food conversion ratio

   ie. $D33 = (D10 - D9) * D13$

(b) Food cost per pig (£) = Food consumption per pig (kg) * Food price (£/kg)

   ie. $D34 = D33 * (D14/1000)$

(c) Food cost (p) per kilo liveweight gain = Food cost per pig / liveweight gain

   ie. $D35 = D34 / (D10-D9) * 100$

(d) Number of pigs fattened per year
       = Number of batches fattened per year * size of batch

   The number of batches fattened per year is based on the length of time taken to fatten
   each batch of pigs plus 1 week for cleaning the unit

   ie. $D36 = (52 / (D15 + 1)) * D7$

(e) Average deadweight per pig (D37) is calculated from the liveweight at slaughter and the
   killing out %

   ie. $D37 = D10 * (D11/100)$

(f) Real rate of interest (D38) is calculated from the nominal rate of interest (D24) and the
   rate of inflation (D25) using the formula

$$\text{Real rate of interest} = \frac{1 + \text{nominal rate}}{1 + \text{inflation rate}} - 1$$

   ie. $D38 = ((1 + D24/100) / (1 + D25/100) - 1) * 100$

15.4 Output data

(a) The output data is presented in the form of a gross margin budget on a per head basis. The revenue (E49) is calculated for the deadweight (D37) and the deadweight price (D12).

ie. E49 = D37 * (D12/100)

From this is deducted the purchase price of the weaner (D8) and an allowance for mortality. The mortality allowance (E51) is calculated on the average value of pigs in the herd (E49 + E50) / 2 less an allowance for food saved D34*(D16/100)

ie. E51 = (D16/100 * (E49+E50)/2) - D34*(D16/100)

Variable costs are listed in cells E56 to E59 and are taken from the input data and intermediate calculations. Deducting variable costs directly from output gives gross margin per pig (F62).

The average weekly gross margin of the unit (F65) is given by dividing total annual gross margin (gross margin per pig * number of pigs) by 52.

ie. F65 = (F62 * D36) / 52

(b) The net margin, or profit, of the unit can also be determined by deducting the appropriate weekly fixed costs from the total gross margin. In the example, electricity, water, additional labour and interest on capital are deducted to give a profit before rent, permanent labour, machinery costs etc. Any other fixed costs can be included to suit the user. Interest on capital is calculated as the real rate (D38) on the average capital invested (E49 + E50) / 2. This is then converted to a per week basis by multiplying by the number of pigs (D36) and dividing by the 52 weeks in the year.

ie. E72 = (D38/100) * ((E48+E49)/2) * D36/52

The complete set of formulas is shown in Fig. 15.3.

```
        | A ||              B              || C || D || E || F |

1   Pigcosts   -  C. P. Course
2   * * * * * * * * * * * * * * * * * * * * * * * * * * * * * * * *
3   *                                                          *
4   *   User Entered Data                                      *
5   *   ------------------                                     *
6   *                                                          *
7   *   No. pigs in unit                        160           *
8   *   Weaner Price (£/head)                     32          *
9   *   Weaner weight (kg)                       31.2         *
10  *   Liveweight at slaughter (kg)              74          *
11  *   Killing out %                             72          *
12  *   Output Price (p/kg d'wt)                 117          *
13  *   Food Conversion Ratio (FCR)              2.6          *
14  *   Food cost (£/tonne)                      182          *
15  *   No. of weeks to fatten                    10          *
16  *   Mortality (%)                              1           *
17  *   Transport & Marketing costs (£/pig)      1.3          *
18  *   Miscellaneous costs (£/pig)               .5          *
19  *   Vet & Med. costs (£/pig )                1.1          *
20  *   Overtime Labour costs (£/hour)             5           *
21  *   Overtime Labour used (hrs/wk)              3           *
22  *   Electricity cost (£/year)                300          *
23  *   Water costs (£/year)                     120          *
24  *   Rate of interest (%)                      15          *
25  *   Rate of Inflation (%)                      7           *
26  *                                                          *
27  * * * * * * * * * * * * * * * * * * * * * * * * * * * * * * * *
28
29
30      Intermediate Calculations
31      -------------------------
32
33      Food consumption per pig (kg)           111.28
34      Food cost per pig (£)                    20.25
35      Food cost per kg l'wt gain (p)           47.32
36      No. pigs fattened per year              756.36
37      Average Deadweight (kg)                  53.28
38      Real Interest rate (%)                    7.48
39
```

Fig. 15.1 Pig fattening budget spreadsheet (Cells A1:F39).

```
        | A ||                 B                 ||  C  ||  D  ||  E  ||  F  |

40      ------------------------------------------------------------------------
41
42        Output Data
43        -----------
44
45        Gross Margin per pig
46        --------------------                                        £/head
47
48        Sale Value                        53.28 kg d'wt
49                                    @      117 p/kg          62.34
50          less    Cost of weaner                            32.00
51                  Mortality                                   .27
52
53        Output                                                       30.07
54
55        Variable Costs
56        Food                                               20.25
57        Transport & marketing                               1.30
58        Miscellaneous                                        .50
59        Vet. & Med.                                         1.10
60        Total Variable Costs                                         23.15
61
62        Gross Margin (£/pig)                                          6.92
63        ------------------------------------------------------------------------
64
65        Unit Gross Margin (£/week)                                  100.59
66
67        Fixed Costs (£/week)
68
69        Electricity                                         5.77
70        Water                                               2.31
71        Additional Labour                                  15.00
72        Interest on Capital                                51.30
73        Total Fixed Costs (£/week)                                   74.37
74
75        Net Margin (£/week)                                          26.22
76
77        Net Margin (£/year)                                        1363.20
78      ------------------------------------------------------------------------
```

Fig. 15.2 Pig fattening budget spreadsheet (Cells A40:F78).

	B	|| C ||	D ||	E ||	F	
30	Intermediate Calculations							
31	------------------------							
32								
33	Food consumption per pig (kg)			(D10-D9)*D13				
34	Food cost per pig (£)			D33*(D14/1000)				
35	Food cost per kg l'wt gain (p)			D34/(D10-D9)*100				
36	No. pigs fattened per year			(52/(D15+1))*D7				
37	Average Deadweight (kg)			D10*(D11/100)				
38	Real Interest rate (%)			((1+D24/100)/(1+D25/100)-1)*100				
39								
40	---							
41								
42	Output Data							
43	-----------							
44								
45	Gross Margin per pig							
46	--------------------				£/head			
47								
48	Sale Value		D37	kg d'wt				
49			@ D12	p/kg	D37*(D12/100)				
50	less Cost of weaner			D8				
51	Mortality			(D16/100*(E49+E50)/2)-D34*(D16/100)				
52								
53	Output				E49-E50-E51			
54								
55	Variable Costs							
56	Food			D34				
57	Transport & marketing			D17				
58	Miscellaneous			D18				
59	Vet. & Med.			D19				
60	Total Variable Costs				SUM(E56:E59)			
61								
62	Gross Margin (£/pig)				F53-F60			
63	---							
64								
65	Unit Gross Margin (£/week)				(F62*D36)/52			
66								
67	Fixed Costs (£/week)							
68								
69	Electricity			D22/52				
70	Water			D23/52				
71	Additional Labour			D20*D21				
72	Interest on Capital			(D38/100)*(E49+E50)/2*D36/52				
73	Total Fixed Costs (£/week)				SUM(E69:E72)			
74								
75	Net Margin (£/week)				F65-F73			
76								
77	Net Margin (£/year)				F75*52			
78	---							

Fig. 15.3 Formulas for pig fattening budget spreadsheet.

Labour profile

Purpose: To estimate monthly labour requirements and availability on the basis of farm data or published standard data.

Authors: Nicolas Lampkin and Nigel Chapman

Spreadsheet Name: LABOUR

16.1 Introduction

The spreadsheet allows the estimation of monthly labour requirements and availability on the basis of farm data or published standard data. The standard data is contained in two tables which form part of the spreadsheet and can be referenced by the formulas.

The spreadsheet is appropriate in most situations where the construction of a labour profile is appropriate. Users should, however, be aware of the limitations of labour profiles as a labour planning tool. In particular:

* labour profiles rely on average data which take no account of the fixed time element required to perform a certain task;

* the data do not always take into account different labour requirements under different soil conditions, levels of mechanisation, building and field layout etc.;

* labour profiles on a monthly basis do not pay adequate attention to gang work and to the need to complete some tasks in a very short period (less than one month and other tasks which it may be possible to complete over a period of more than one month;

* the seasonal distribution of labour requirements will vary in different locations and does not necessarily accord with the monthly distributions assumed here.

16.2 Spreadsheet structure

The spreadsheet is in four parts :

(i)   calculation of the monthly labour requirements for the specified farm input data (A1:Q54)
(ii) estimation from standard data of the monthly labour availability (A61:Q98)
(iii) calculation of the monthly labour surplus/deficit (A106:Q114)
(iv) standard data for the monthly crop labour requirements (AA1:AR78)

143

16.3 Standard data

The standard data used in this example has been obtained from Nix (1989), with some minor modifications and additions. Reference should be made to the original text for details of the assumptions made in arriving at the labour requirement and availability estimates.

Labour requirements are given in cells AA1:AR76 (Figs. 16.1 and 16.2) and labour availabilities in cells A61:P73 (Fig. 16.4).

As a check that data has been entered correctly, it is advisable to use a formula in column AQ to calculate the annual labour requirements per hectare or unit of each enterprise.

eg. AQ8 = SUM(AE8:AP8)

The standard data table can be easily adapted to include data from other sources, or different types of data such as Standard Man Days. It is important, however, that the code numbers (Column AA) are in ascending order if new rows are added.

The 999 code in cell AA77 is used where a blank should appear in the output table (ie. no enterprise has been selected). For this to work, a space should be entered as a textual value, ie. as (" "), in cells AB77 and AC77. Cells AA77:AC77 can easily be moved lower if the table needs to be extended.

Also, in Supercalc 4, for the LOOKUP function to work properly when referencing the lookup table specified as AA8:AP500, ie. extending below the data, a value greater than 999, eg. 1000, should be entered in cell AA78.

16.4 Input data

The spreadsheet consists of two sections illustrated in Figs 16.3 and 16.4. Data is entered in two columns only, A and D. Column A contains the codes which allow the standard data table to be referenced. The correct code can be identified most easily by referring to a hard copy of the standard data table. The code 999 is used where no further enterprises are to be selected in a particular group.

Column D contains the hectarages and numbers of stock of each enterprise or activity to be included in the farm plan, as well as the full-time worker equivalents represented by each of the individuals working on the farm. Where the code 999 is used in column A, the hectarage should be set to 0 for neatness, but this is not essential as the monthly labour requirements will still work out as 0.

The enterprises have been grouped into five groups (a maximum of six is possible), to allow a graph to be produced showing the labour profile and the contribution of each group of enterprises to it.

16.5 Calculations

The calculations for each group are identical. Those for the first group (arable crops) are explained below. Although the formulas seem complex, they are relatively straightfoward to assemble - extensive use can be made of the Copy command. The complete spreadsheet takes a little bit of time to recalculate, so it is advisable to work with the spreadsheet in manual recalculation mode.

16.5.1 Labour requirements

(a) Enterprise names (columns B and C)

These are obtained by using the VLOOKUP function to reference the standard data table, the main body of which is contained in cells AA8:AP500. (Note that not all the rows or columns specified for the data table have been used, allowing space for further expansion).

In Supercalc4, any text referred to by the VLOOKUP function has to be stored as a textual value and the maximum number of characters that can be stored in one cell in this manner is limited to 9. For this reason two columns (AB and AC) are required to store the enterprise names, and two columns (B and C) are required to display those that are referenced. Thus

B9 = VLOOKUP(A9,AA8:AP500,1) and
C9 = VLOOKUP(A9,AA8:AP500,2)

The vertical lookup function VLOOKUP used in B9 works by referring to the code in A9, finding the same code in the standard data table column AA, and reproducing the data contained 1 cell to the right. Thus the formula in B9 has the effect of reproducing the text in column AB, and similarly the formula in C9 reproduces the text in column AC.

(b) Monthly labour requirements (columns E to P)

Again the VLOOKUP function is used to obtain the standard data for the appropriate month from AA8:AP500. This is then multiplied by the hectarage or number of stock to obtain the monthly labour requirement in hours.

Thus for January,   E9 = VLOOKUP(A9,AA8:AP500,4) * D9 ,
for February,   F9 = VLOOKUP(A9,AA8:AP500,5) * D9 etc.

These formulas can then be copied into rows 10 to 13 making sure that the specification of the LOOKUP table AA8:AP500 is not changed.

The total monthly labour requirement is given in row 15 by

eg. E15 = SUM(E9:E13)

(c) Annual labour requirements (column Q)

These are given for each enterprise in rows 9 to 13,

eg. Q9 = SUM(E9:P9)

and for all arable crops in cell Q15,

ie. Q15 = SUM(Q9:Q13)

(d) Total farm labour requirements (Row 53)

The total farm labour requirement is obtained by summing the labour requirements of each of the five groups. These totals are given monthly in columns E to P,

eg. E53 = E15 + E24 + E33 + E42 + E51

145

and annually in column Q,

ie. $Q53 = Q15 + Q24 + Q33 + Q42 + Q51$

16.5.2 *Monthly labour availability*

As mentioned in Section 16.3 the standard data for the calculations of labour availability are stored in cells A61:P73. Entries in rows 72 and 73 are calculated by multiplying the adjusted ordinary hours (row 69) by either the field percentage workable (row 70) or the stock percentage workable (row 71),

eg. $E72 = E69 * E70 / 100$
or $E73 = E69 * E71 / 100$

This section uses the standard data to estimate the available hours (excluding overtime) for each individual working on the farm. The labour is split into two sections - field work and livestock - reflecting the different skills and available working hours of the two groups.

In each section the amount of labour available in each month is estimated by extracting the relevant standard data for a full-time equivalent worker using the VLOOKUP function and multiplying this by the data value entered in column D (the proportion of full-time equivalent worker),

eg. $E78 = VLOOKUP(A78,A72:P73,4) * D78$

Monthly totals of available labour are given in rows 86 (field work) and 97 (stock work),

eg. $E86 = SUM(E78:E84)$

Annual totals for each type of worker are given in column Q,

eg. $Q78 = SUM(E78:P78)$

16.5.3 *Labour surplus/deficit*

The final table of the spreadsheet (Cells A106:Q114) brings together labour required and available labour to indicate potential surplus or deficit situations.

The fieldwork surplus/deficit (row 110) is calculated by subtracting from the labour available for fieldwork the labour required for arable, horticultural and forage crops.

eg. $E110 = E86 - E15 - E24 - E33$

Similarly, the labour surplus/deficit for stockwork (row 113) is calculated using

eg. $E111 = E97 - E42 - E51$

The surplus/deficit for the whole farm (row 113) is calculated by adding the surpluses or deficits for fieldwork and stockwork together,

eg. $E113 = E110 + E111$

Finally, formulas to calculate the annual surpluses/deficits are entered in cells Q110, Q111 and Q113,

eg. $Q110 = SUM(E110:P110)$

16.6 Labour Profile Graph

The labour profile graph (Fig. 16.5) can be produced as a Stacked-Bar Chart, using the grouped enterprise labour requirements as variables. However, since the manner in which graphs are produced varies from spreadsheet package to package, no details are given here.

Reference

Nix J.S. (1989) *Farm Management Pocketbook* (20th Edition). Wye College, University of London.

	AA		AB		AC		AD		AE		AF		AG		AH		AI	

MONTHLY LABOUR PROFILE SPREADSHEET

Nicolas Lampkin and Nigel Chapman (04/1990)　　　University C

****

STANDARD DATA FOR MONTHLY LABOUR REQUIREMENTS　　Data from Ni

	Data	Hectares/						
	CodeEnterprise	numbers	Jan	Feb	Mar	Apr	May	

8	100 W Wheat Av	1	0	0	.5	1.1	.3
9	101 W Wheat Pr	1	0	0	.3	.8	.2
10	105 S Wheat Av	1	0	0	3.7	.6	1.1
11	106 S Wheat Pr	1	0	0	2.5	.5	.7
12	110 W Barley Av	1	0	0	.5	1.1	.3
13	111 W Barley Pr	1	0	0	.3	.8	.2
14	115 S Barley Av	1	0	0	3.7	.6	1.1
15	116 S Barley Pr	1	0	0	2.5	.5	.7
16	120 W Oats Av	1	0	0	.5	1.1	.3
17	121 W Oats Pr	1	0	0	.3	.8	.2
18	125 S Oats Av	1	0	0	3.7	.6	1.1
19	126 S Oats Pr	1	0	0	2.5	.5	.7
20	130 Straw bale Av	1	0	0	0	0	0
21	131 Straw bale Pr	1	0	0	0	0	0
22	140 Sugar Beet Av	1	.5	0	5.7	3.5	3.1
23	141 Sugar Beet Pr	1	.4	0	4.9	3	.4
24	150 Dried Peas Av	1	0	.2	3.4	.6	2.5
25	151 Dried Peas Pr	1	0	.1	2.4	.4	1.8
26	160 W Fld beans Av	1	0	0	0	0	0
27	161 W Fld beans Pr	1	0	0	0	0	0
28	165 S Fld beans Av	1	0	1	2	0	0
29	166 S Fld beans Pr	1	0	.7	1.4	0	0
30	170 Oilseed Rape Av	1	0	0	.5	.5	0
31	171 Oilseed Rape Pr	1	0	0	.3	.3	0
32	200 MC Potatoes Av	1	0	0	5.7	12.2	2.2
33	201 MC Potatoes Pr	1	0	0	2.5	3.7	.8
34	205 Early Pots Av	1	0	1.6	18.6	2.3	1.2
35	206 Early Pots Pr	1	0	1	6	.8	0
36	208 2nd E Pots Av	1	0	0	10.7	8.2	2.9
37	209 2nd E Pots Pr	1	0	0	4.1	2	.8
38	300 1-yr Ley u/s Av	1	0	0	.9	.9	.6
39	301 1-yr Ley u/s Pr	1	0	0	.5	.5	.3
40	305 3-yr Ley u/s Av	1	0	0	.7	.7	.6
41	306 3-yr Ley u/s Pr	1	0	0	.5	.5	.3
42	310 1yrLey DDAut Av	1	0	0	.6	.6	.6
43	311 1yrLey DDAut Pr	1	0	0	.3	.3	.3
44	315 3yrLey DDAut Av	1	0	0	.6	.6	.6
45	316 3yrLey DDAut Pr	1	0	0	.3	.3	.3
46	320 1yrLey DDSpr Av	1	0	0	3	1.8	.3
47	321 1yrLey DDSpr Pr	1	0	0	2.1	1.2	.3
48	325 3yrLey DDSpr Av	1	0	0	1.4	.9	.6
49	326 3yrLey DDSpr Pr	1	0	0	1	.7	.3
50	330 Perm Pasture Av	1	0	0	.6	.6	.6

Fig. 16.1 Standard data section of labour profile spreadsheet (Cells AA1:AR50).

```
     | AJ || AK || AL || AM || AN || AO || AP || AQ ||      AR      |
1
2    ollege of Wales, Aberystwyth
3    ************************************************************
4    x's Farm Management Handbook, 1989, adjusted in some cases
5
6       Jun    Jul   Aug   Sep   Oct   Nov   Dec Total          Notes
7    -------------------------------------------------------------
8        .3      0   2.6   2.4   3.6    .6     0  11.4
9        .2      0   1.7   1.7   2.5    .4     0   7.8
10        0      0    .9   1.9    .7   1.1    .7  10.7
11        0      0    .7   1.3    .4    .9    .4   7.4
12       .3      1   2.5   1.5   4.2     0     0  11.4
13       .2     .5   1.8   1.1   2.9     0     0   7.8
14        0      0   2.8     0    .7   1.1    .7  10.7
15        0      0     2     0    .4    .9    .4   7.4
16       .3      0   3.5   1.5   4.2     0     0  11.4
17       .2      0   2.3   1.1   2.9     0     0   7.8
18        0      0     2    .8    .7   1.1    .7  10.7
19        0      0   1.5    .5    .4    .9    .4   7.4
20        0      0   3.1   2.7     0     0     0   5.8
21        0      0   2.1   1.8     0     0     0   3.9
22      3.1    1.6     0   3.1  12.7  14.5   1.7  49.5
23       .4     .3     0     2   7.9   9.2   1.2  29.7
24       .2    2.2   2.5     1   1.8   1.1    .2  15.7
25       .2    1.4   1.6    .5   1.2    .7    .2  10.5
26       .6      0   3.4   2.5   4.2     0     0  10.7
27       .4      0   2.6   1.7   2.8     0     0   7.5
28       .6      0     0   3.4     0     0   2.5   9.5
29       .4      0     0   2.6     0     0   1.7   6.8
30        0    2.9   4.6   3.3    .3    .3     0  12.4
31        0    2.1   3.1   2.1    .2    .2     0   8.3
32      3.3    2.7    .6   7.4  28.3   8.2    .6  71.2 Excluding
33        0    1.3    .4   7.3  28.2   5.5    .4  50.1 labour for
34       35      0     0     0     0   1.9    .6  61.2 picking and
35       30      0     0     0     0   1.3    .4  39.5 riddling
36       .9     10    20     0     0   1.9    .6  55.2 (usually
37        0     10    20     0     0   1.3    .4  38.6 casual)
38       .6     .6    .3    .6     0     0     0   4.5
39       .3     .3    .2    .3     0     0     0   2.4
40       .6     .6    .3    .3     0     0     0   3.8
41       .3     .3    .2    .2     0     0     0   2.3
42       .6     .6     5   3.2     0     0     0  11.2
43       .3     .3   3.4   2.2     0     0     0   7.1
44       .6     .6   1.9   1.4     0     0     0   6.3
45       .3     .3   1.4     1     0     0     0   3.9
46       .6     .6    .3     0    .9   1.4    .7   9.6
47       .3     .3    .2     0    .5     1    .5   6.4
48       .6     .6    .2     0    .6     1    .6   6.5
49       .3     .3    .2    .2    .3    .3    .2   3.8
50       .6     .6    .3    .2     0     0     0   3.5
```

	AA ||	AB || AC ||	AD ||	AE ||	AF ||	AG ||	AH ||	AI |
51	331	Perm Pasture Pr	1	0	0	.3	.3	.3
52	340	Hay Av	1	0	0	0	0	0
53	341	Hay Pr	1	0	0	0	0	0
54	345	Silage Av	1	0	0	0	0	6.8
55	346	Silage Pr	1	0	0	0	0	5.1
56	350	Kale growing Av	1	0	0	.5	2.6	1.9
57	351	Kale growing Pr	1	0	0	.3	1.8	1.5
58	400	Dairy 60cow hrd	1	3.3	3.3	3.3	3	2.7
59	401	Dairy 80cow hrd	1	2.9	2.9	2.9	2.7	2.4
60	402	Dairy 100cow hrd	1	2.5	2.5	2.5	2.4	2.2
61	410	AB Calf 0-12m Av	1	1	1	1	.3	.3
62	411	AB Calf 0-12m Pr	1	.7	.7	.7	.2	.2
63	415	SB Calf 0-12m Av	1	1.3	1.3	1.3	2.6	2.6
64	416	SB Calf 0-12m Pr	1	.6	.6	.6	1.9	1.9
65	420	Repl Unit Av	1	3.7	3.7	3.7	1.4	1.4
66	421	Repl Unit Pr	1	2.1	2.1	2.1	.9	.9
67	450	Sheep Av	1	.3	.3	1	.4	.3
68	451	Sheep Pr	1	.25	.25	.75	.3	.25
69	500	Brdng Sow Av	1	2.7	2.7	2.7	2.7	2.7
70	501	Brdng Sow Pr	1	1.8	1.8	1.8	1.8	1.8
71	505	Br/Fat Pork Av	1	5.8	5.8	5.8	5.8	5.8
72	506	Br/Fat Pork Pr	1	3.7	3.7	3.7	3.7	3.7
73	550	Lay Hens 5000/work	1	.05	.05	.05	.05	.05
74	551	Lay Hens 8000/work	1	.0325	.0325	.0325	.0325	.0325
75	560	TabBirds20000/work	1	.0075	.0075	.0075	.0075	.0075
76	561	TabBirds50000/work	1	.005	.005	.005	.005	.005
77	999							
78	1000							

Fig. 16.2 Standard data section of labour profile spreadsheet (Cells AA51:AR78).

	AJ		AK		AL		AM		AN		AO		AP		AQ			AR	
51	.3		.3		.2		.2		0		0		0		1.9				
52	8.8		4.4		0		0		0		0		0		13.2				
53	6.6		3.3		0		0		0		0		0		9.9				
54	3.4		0		0		0		0		0		0		10.2				
55	2.5		0		0		0		0		0		0		7.6				
56	.6		0		0		0		0		0		2.5		8.1				
57	.4		0		0		0		0		0		1.7		5.7				
58	2.7		2.7		2.7		2.7		3		3.3		3.3		36				
59	2.4		2.4		2.4		2.4		2.8		2.9		2.9		32				
60	2.1		2.1		2.1		2.2		2.4		2.5		2.5		28				
61	.3		.3		.3		.3		2.6		2.6		2.6		12.6				
62	.2		.2		.2		.2		1.9		1.9		1.9		9				
63	2.6		1		1		1		1.3		1.3		1.3		18.6				
64	1.9		.7		.7		.7		.6		.6		.6		11.4				
65	1.4		1.4		1.4		1.4		3.7		3.7		3.7		30.6				
66	.9		.9		.9		.9		2.1		2.1		2.1		18				
67	.4		.2		.2		.25		.25		.2		.2		4				
68	.3		.15		.15		.15		.15		.15		.15		3				
69	2.7		2.7		2.7		2.7		2.7		2.7		2.7		32.4				
70	1.8		1.8		1.8		1.8		1.8		1.8		1.8		21.6				
71	5.8		5.8		5.8		5.8		5.8		5.8		5.8		69.6				
72	3.7		3.7		3.7		3.7		3.7		3.7		3.7		44.4				
73	.05		.05		.05		.05		.05		.05		.05		.6				
74	.0325		.0325		.0325		.0325		.0325		.0325		.0325		.39				
75	.0075		.0075		.0075		.0075		.0075		.0075		.0075		.09				
76	.005		.005		.005		.005		.005		.005		.005		.06				
77																			
78																			

```
        | A ||    B    ||   C    ||    D    || E || F ||  G  || H |
1   MONTHLY LABOUR PROFILE SPREADSHEET
2   Nicolas Lampkin and Nigel Chapman (04/1990)          Univer
3   ***************************************************************
4   MONTHLY LABOUR REQUIREMENTS (HOURS)
5   Data                         Hectares/
6   Code Enterprise              numbers   Jan   Feb   Mar   Apr
7   ---------------------------------------------------------------
8   Arable Crops (Codes 100-199)
9      101 W Wheat Pr                10      0     0     3     8
10     105 S Wheat Av                15      0     0    56     9
11     110 W Barley Av               30      0     0    15    33
12     130 Straw bale Av             55      0     0     0     0
13     140 Sugar Beet Av             15      8     0    86    53
14                                  ---   ---   ---   ---   ---
15        Total                     125     8     0   159   103
16  ---------------------------------------------------------------
17  Horticultural Crops (Codes 200-299)
18     200 MC Potatoes Av            10      0     0    57   122
19     208 2nd E Pots Av             10      0     0   107    82
20     999                            0      0     0     0     0
21     999                            0      0     0     0     0
22     999                            0      0     0     0     0
23                                  ---   ---   ---   ---   ---
24        Total                      20      0     0   164   204
25  ---------------------------------------------------------------
26  Forage Crops (Codes 300-399)
27     315 3yrLey DDAut Av           60      0     0    36    36
28     999                            0      0     0     0     0
29     999                            0      0     0     0     0
30     999                            0      0     0     0     0
31     999                            0      0     0     0     0
32                                  ---   ---   ---   ---   ---
33        Total                      60      0     0    36    36
34  ---------------------------------------------------------------
35  Grazing Livestock (Codes 400-499)
36     402 Dairy 100cow hrd         100    250   250   250   240
37     450 Sheep Av                 200     60    60   200    80
38     999                            0      0     0     0     0
39     999                            0      0     0     0     0
40     999                            0      0     0     0     0
41                                  ---   ---   ---   ---   ---
42        Total                     300    310   310   450   320
43  ---------------------------------------------------------------
44  Intensive Livestock (Codes 500-599
45     505 Br/Fat Pork Av            20    116   116   116   116
46     550 Lay Hens 5000/work      3000    150   150   150   150
47     999                            0      0     0     0     0
48     999                            0      0     0     0     0
49     999                            0      0     0     0     0
50                                  ---   ---   ---   ---   ---
51        Total                    3020    266   266   266   266
52  ---------------------------------------------------------------
53        FARM TOTAL                       584   576  1075   929
54  ***************************************************************
```

Fig. 16.3 Monthly labour requirements section of labour profile spreadsheet.

```
        |  I  ||  J  ||  K  ||  L  ||  M  ||  N  ||  O  ||  P  ||  Q  |
1
2       sity College of Wales, Aberystwyth
3       ***********************************************************
4
5
6        May   Jun   Jul   Aug   Sep   Oct   Nov   Dec   Total
7       ---------------------------------------------------------
8
9          2     2     0    17    17    25     4     0      78
10        17     0     0    14    29    11    17    11     161
11         9     9    30    75    45   126     0     0     342
12         0     0     0   171   149     0     0     0     319
13        47    47    24     0    47   191   218    26     743
14       ---   ---   ---   ---   ---   ---   ---   ---     ---
15        74    58    54   276   286   352   238    36    1642
16       ---------------------------------------------------------
17
18        22    33    27     6    74   283    82     6     712
19        29     9   100   200     0     0    19     6     552
20         0     0     0     0     0     0     0     0       0
21         0     0     0     0     0     0     0     0       0
22         0     0     0     0     0     0     0     0       0
23       ---   ---   ---   ---   ---   ---   ---   ---     ---
24        51    42   127   206    74   283   101    12    1264
25       ---------------------------------------------------------
26
27        36    36    36   114    84     0     0     0     378
28         0     0     0     0     0     0     0     0       0
29         0     0     0     0     0     0     0     0       0
30         0     0     0     0     0     0     0     0       0
31         0     0     0     0     0     0     0     0       0
32       ---   ---   ---   ---   ---   ---   ---   ---     ---
33        36    36    36   114    84     0     0     0     378
34       ---------------------------------------------------------
35
36       220   210   210   210   220   240   250   250    2800
37        60    80    40    40    50    50    40    40     800
38         0     0     0     0     0     0     0     0       0
39         0     0     0     0     0     0     0     0       0
40         0     0     0     0     0     0     0     0       0
41       ---   ---   ---   ---   ---   ---   ---   ---     ---
42       280   290   250   250   270   290   290   290    3600
43       ---------------------------------------------------------
44
45       116   116   116   116   116   116   116   116    1392
46       150   150   150   150   150   150   150   150    1800
47         0     0     0     0     0     0     0     0       0
48         0     0     0     0     0     0     0     0       0
49         0     0     0     0     0     0     0     0       0
50       ---   ---   ---   ---   ---   ---   ---   ---     ---
51       266   266   266   266   266   266   266   266    3192
52       ---------------------------------------------------------
53       707   692   733  1112   980  1191   895   604   10076
54       ***********************************************************
```

```
         | A ||    B    ||   C    ||    D    || E || F || G || H |
61   **************************************************************
62   MONTHLY LABOUR AVAILABILITY (Hours)
63                            Proportion
64   Data                     of full-time
65   Code   Description       worker    Jan   Feb   Mar   Apr
66   -------------------------------------------------------------
67   Standard data (from Nix's Farm Management Handbook, 1989,
68          Tot Ord Hours        1     177   160   172   161
69          Adj Ord Hours        1     148   134   149   139
70          % workable - field         50    50    60    65
71          % workable - stock         80    80    80    90
72       10 Field Worker - avl hrs     74    67    89    90
73       11 Stockperson - avl hrs     118   107   119   125
74   -------------------------------------------------------------
75   Available Labour (individuals/hours excluding overtime)
76   -------------------------------------------------------------
77   Field work
78       10 Farmer             .5      37    34    45    45
79       10 Spouse              0       0     0     0     0
80       10 Other Family       .1       7     7     9     9
81       10 Full-time worker    1      74    67    89    90
82       10 Part-time worker   .75     56    50    67    68
83       10 Casual Labour       0       0     0     0     0
84       10 Contractors         0       0     0     0     0
85                                    ----  ----  ----  ----
86   Avail. Field Labour       2      174   157   210   212
87   -------------------------------------------------------------
88   Stock
89       11 Farmer             .5      59    54    60    63
90       11 Spouse             .5      59    54    60    63
91       11 Other Family        0       0     0     0     0
92       11 Full-time worker    2      237   214   238   250
93       11 Part-time worker   .5      59    54    60    63
94       11 Casual Labour       0       0     0     0     0
95       11 Contractors         0       0     0     0     0
96                                    ----  ----  ----  ----
97   Avail. Stock Labour       4      414   375   417   438
98   **************************************************************
99
100
101
102
103
104
105
106  **************************************************************
107  LABOUR SURPLUS / DEFICIT (excl. overtime)
108         Description                Jan   Feb   Mar   Apr
109  -------------------------------------------------------------
110         Fieldwork                  166   157  -149  -130
111         Stock                     -162  -201  -299  -148
112                                    ----  ----  ----  ----
113         Whole Farm                   5   -43  -448  -278
114  **************************************************************
```

Fig. 16.4 Monthly labour availability and surplus/deficit section of labour profile spreadsheet.

```
         |  I  ||  J  ||  K  ||  L  ||  M  ||  N  ||  O  ||  P  ||  Q  |

61      *********************************************************
62
63
64
65      May    Jun    Jul    Aug    Sep    Oct    Nov    Dec    Total
66      -----------------------------------------------------------
67      adjusted in some cases)
68         171    170    177    169    172    177    172    161    2039
69         151    150    157    150    152    153    144    135    1762
70          70     75     75     75     70     65     50     50     755
71          90     90     90     90     90     80     80     80    1020
72         106    113    118    113    106     99     72     68    1115
73         136    135    141    135    137    122    115    108    1500
74      -----------------------------------------------------------
75
76      -----------------------------------------------------------
77
78          53     56     59     56     53     50     36     34     557
79           0      0      0      0      0      0      0      0       0
80          11     11     12     11     11     10      7      7     111
81         106    113    118    113    106     99     72     68    1115
82          79     84     88     84     80     75     54     51     836
83           0      0      0      0      0      0      0      0       0
84           0      0      0      0      0      0      0      0       0
85        ----   ----   ----   ----   ----   ----   ----   ----    ----
86         248    264    277    264    250    234    169    159    2619
87      -----------------------------------------------------------
88
89          68     68     71     68     68     61     58     54     750
90          68     68     71     68     68     61     58     54     750
91           0      0      0      0      0      0      0      0       0
92         272    270    283    270    274    245    230    216    2999
93          68     68     71     68     68     61     58     54     750
94           0      0      0      0      0      0      0      0       0
95           0      0      0      0      0      0      0      0       0
96        ----   ----   ----   ----   ----   ----   ----   ----    ----
97         476    473    495    473    479    428    403    378    5248
98      *********************************************************
99
100
101
102
103
104
105
106     *********************************************************
107
108     May    Jun    Jul    Aug    Sep    Oct    Nov    Dec    Total
109     -----------------------------------------------------------
110         87    129     60   -332   -193   -401   -170    111    -665
111        -70    -84    -21    -44    -57   -128   -153   -178   -1544
112       ----   ----   ----   ----   ----   ----   ----   ----    ----
113         17     45     38   -375   -251   -529   -323    -67   -2209
114     *********************************************************
```

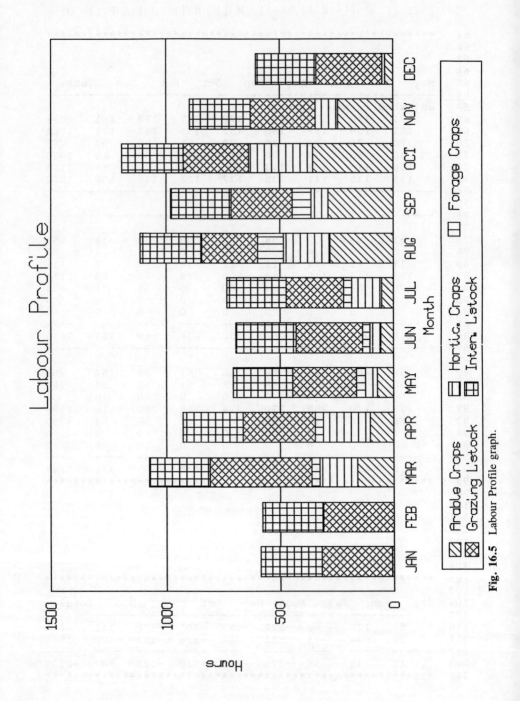

Fig. 16.5 Labour Profile graph.

Fertiliser tank contents

Purpose: To ascertain the quantity of liquid contained in a cylindrical container lying on its side, by measuring the height of the liquid.

Authors: Graham Bunn, Jonathan Bunn

Spreadsheet Name: TANK

17.1 Introduction

Liquid fertiliser deliveries are made into an old cylindrical tank for which graduated content scales are no longer available. If the tank had been erected so that its flat base were on the ground, measurement of its contents would have been a simple task, but lying on its side, as it does, a method of calculating its contents proved to be more difficult.

By entering the dimensions of the tank and measuring the height of the liquid, its contents are now calculated mathematically.

The spreadsheet would be of use to anyone with any cylindrical container in this orientation and could include anything from water ballasted land rollers to irrigation pipes.

Checks are now kept with measurements taken following a delivery of liquid fertiliser for comparison with invoices and applications can now be monitored more accurately.

17.2 Input data

The spreadsheet (Fig. 17.1) is extremely easy to use. Only three items of input are required:-

(a) Cell D10: The radius of the container (cm)

(b) Cell D11: The length of the container (cm)

(c) Cell D13: The depth of the liquid (cm)

17.3 Output data

Cells located at B16 and B17 show the output:

(a) B16 uses the formula:

$$\text{Vol} = L \left[r^2 \cos^{-1}((r-d)/r) - (r-d) \sqrt{\{r^2 - (r-d)^2\}} \right]$$

where   L = length of tank
                     r = radius
                     d = depth of liquid

This translates into the spreadsheet formula:

B16 = (D10^2*ACOS((D10-D13)/D10) - SQRT(D10^2-(D10-D13)^2) * (D10-D13))
                                                          * D11/1000

The formula
(i)   finds the area of the triangle ABC (Fig.17.3) in the segment of the circle that is part filled with liquid.
(ii)   calculates the total area of the segment now that the angle in the centre at B is known.
(iii) subtracts one from the other to give the area of liquid in the part segment.
(iv) multiplies by the length of the tank and converts to litres to give volume.

(b) B17 multiplies B16 by 0.22 to convert litres to gallons.

Both the formulas used in the spreadsheet are shown in Fig. 17.2.

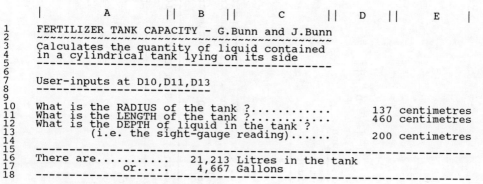

```
|       A        ||   B  ||     C       ||   D  ||    E     |
 1   FERTILIZER TANK CAPACITY - G.Bunn and J.Bunn
 2   ~~~~~~~~~~~~~~~~~~~~~~~~~~~~~~~~~~~~~~~~~~~~~~~~~~~
 3   Calculates the quantity of liquid contained
 4   in a cylindrical tank lying on its side
 5   ----------------------------------------------
 6
 7   User-inputs at D10,D11,D13
 8   --------------------------
 9
10   What is the RADIUS of the tank ?............         137 centimetres
11   What is the LENGTH of the tank ?............         460 centimetres
12   What is the DEPTH of liquid in the tank ?
13           (i.e. the sight-gauge reading)......        200 centimetres
14
15   ----------------------------------------------------------------------
16   There are...........    21,213 Litres in the tank
17           or.....     4,667 Gallons
18   ----------------------------------------------------------------------
```

Fig. 17.1 Fertiliser tank contents spreadsheet.

159

```
        |   A    ||    B    ||    C    ||   D   ||   E   ||
    |------------------------------------------------------------
 1  | FERTILIZER TANK CAPACITY - G.Bunn and J.Bunn
    |------------------------------------------------------------
 2  |
 3  | Calculates the quantity of liquid contained
 4  | in a cylindrical tank lying on its side
    |------------------------------------------------------------
 5  |
 6  |
 7  | User-inputs at D10,D11,D13
 8  |
    |------------------------------------------------------------
 9  |
10  | What is the RADIUS of the tank ?..........  137    centimetres
11  | What is the LENGTH of the tank ?..........  460    centimetres
12  | What is the DEPTH of liquid in the tank ?
13  |    (i.e. the sight-gauge reading)......     200    centimetres
    |------------------------------------------------------------
14  |
15  |
16  | There are........  (D10^2*ACOS((D10-D13)/D10)-SQRT(D10^2-(D10-D13)^2)*(D10-D13))*D11/1000
17  |        or......  B16*.22  Gallons
18  |
    |------------------------------------------------------------
```

Fig. 17.2 Formulas for fertiliser tank contents spreadsheet.

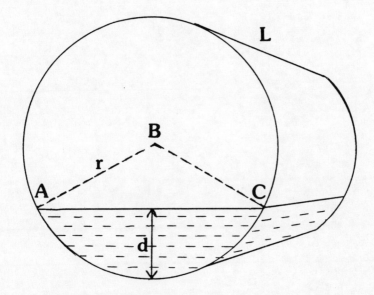

Fig. 17.3 Diagrammatic representation of the formula in cell B16.

Beet invoice analysis

Purpose: To analyse the British Sugar plc Weekly Beet Invoice, advising growers of loads delivered to their account.

Author: Graham Bunn

Spreadsheet Name: BEET

18.1 Introduction

Sugar Beet growers will be familiar with the format of part of this spreadsheet (Fig. 18.1) as it is based on the Weekly Beet Invoice. The computer, once the information is recorded, will extract maximum and minimum values and averages, and collate totals to provide the user with figures to transport to a Gross Margin Account or Field Record Book.

Of necessity, the spreadsheet requires loads delivered from each field to be recorded separately which in some cases may prove difficult particularly if they are drawn from a large clamp. There is no reason, however, why a block of fields may not be grouped together and treated as one area, as long as the grower is aware that the more fields included in the block the less detailed will be the results for future husbandry decisions.

This particular spreadsheet was instrumental on one occasion in discovering a brick! A very high tare figure had been overlooked until the totals made it plain that something was amiss. Subsequent enquiry at the factory confirmed that indeed a brick had been found in the sample taken at the weighbridge. A financial adjustment was then made to the load to the benefit of the grower.

The summary section (A7:Q25) has been placed above the individual load records so that more than the displayed 14 loads, as shown in the example, can be catered for more easily.

18.2 Spreadsheet structure

The spreadsheet can be divided into four main areas :

A3:P5   INPUT   Field Details and the running total of deliveries to date.

A7:Q25   OUTPUT   Summary Section showing the totals including, in rows 24 and 25, the totals to be carried forward.

A27:P28   INPUT   Four items of financial data, as advised by British Sugar.

A31:R50 INPUT	Details of each beet delivery. The layout of this section corresponds to that of the Weekly Beet Invoice received from British Sugar. It is placed last on the spreadsheet since it is of variable length, ie. the number of rows will depend on the number of deliveries.	

18.3 Input requirements

Location	Input Item	Recorded in Example
C3	Field Reference No.	101
F3	Field/Block Name	Alder Carr
O4	Previous Clean Deliveries (t)	3459.20
E5	Size of field or block (Ha)	5.41
O5	Previous Adjusted Deliveries (t)	4206.04
J27	Price per Tonne (this may require adjustment at the end of the season if "C" Quota Beet have been delivered)	27.00
O27	N.F.U. Levy taken from invoice in pence per tonne	6.56
J28	Transport Allowance (£/t) (this varies depending on distance from factory)	1.82
O28	Research and Experimental Levy taken from invoice in pence per tonne	9.00

Details of each load are recorded in columns A:R, one load per row starting at row 37. For row 37 entries are :

Location	Input Item	Recorded in Example
A37	Date of delivery	0301 (3rd Jan)
B37	Gross Weight of load (t)	18.66
C37	Top tare deduction (%)	8
D37	Total tare deduction (%)	17
E37	CALCULATED - not input	
F37	Amino Acid Score	69
G37	Sugar Content (%)	18.0
L37	Early or Late Delivery Bonuses (£)	(blank)
O37	Haulage Deduction (£) (Some growers elect to have their haulier paid direct from this statement)	(blank)

Subsequent loads are recorded at A38 etc.

18.4 Calculations

Some calculations concerning individual deliveries of beet are performed in the beet deliveries section (A33:R50) but the main body of calculations are performed in the Summary Section (A7:Q25).

18.4.1 Individual delivery analysis (A33:R50)

There are several calculations in each row of this section. Examples are given for row 37.

(a) Deducts the percentage of tare from the total weight to arrive at the clean weight (t)

ie. E37 = B37 * (1-D37/100)

(b) If the sugar content of any load of beet varies from 16%, the clean weight is multiplied by a factor to obtain what is referred to as the adjusted weight. The factor is calculated in column H from the formula:

factor = 0.91 - 0.1*(15-G37)   if G37 < 15
        = 0.91 + 0.09*(G37-15)   if G37 >= 15

where G37 is the sugar content (%) of the load. Column H is of width 0, so is effectively hidden.

ie. H37 = IF(G37<15, .91- .1*(15-G37), .91+ .09*(G37-15))

(c) The adjusted weight (t) is calculated by multiplying the clean weight (rounded to 2 decimal places) by the factor calculated in column H.

ie. I37 = ROUND(E37,2) * H37

(d) The value (£) of the load is calculated by multiplying the adjusted weight (t) by the price per tonne.

ie. J37 = I37 * J27

(e) The allowance (£) paid by British Sugar for transport is calculated but this time based on the clean tonnage, not adjusted.

ie. K37 = E37 * J28

(f) The NFU Levy (£) is calculated by multiplying adjusted tonnage by the value in O27 and converting to pounds.

ie. M37 =I37 * O27/100

(g) The Research and Experimental Levy (£) is calculated by multiplying adjusted tonnage by the value in O28 and converting to pounds.

ie. N37 =I37 * O28/100

(h) All growers credits (£) are added

ie. P37 = J37+K37+L37

(i) All growers debits (£) are added

ie. Q37 = M37+N37+O37

(j) The net value of the load (£) is calculated

ie. R37 = P37 - Q37

These formulas are copied down to succeeding rows, keeping any reference to cells J27, J28, O27 and O28 unchanged.

18.4.2 Summary Section (A7:Q25)

In Column I a number of calculations are performed :

(a)   The gross weight per hectare is calculated from the total weight delivered divided by field/block area.

ie. I10 = SUM(B37:B201) / E5

(b)   The clean weight per hectare is calculated from the total weight delivered divided by field/block area.

ie. I12 = SUM(E37:E201) / E5

(c)   The clean weight is subtracted from the gross weight to show the tare per hectare.

ie. I14 = I10 - I12

(d)   The adjusted weight per hectare is calculated from the total adjusted weight divided by field/block area.

ie. I16 = SUM(I37:I201) / E5

(e)   The total grower's income per hectare is calculated from the sum of total credits (column P) divided by the field/block area.

ie. I18 = SUM(P37:P201) / E5

(f)   The total of all deductions per hectare is calculated from the sum of total debits (column Q) divided by field/block area.

ie. I20 = SUM(Q37:Q201) / E5

(g)   Net income per hectare is calculated from total income less total deductions.

ie. I22 = I18 - I20

Each of the above values is then converted to a "per acre" value (J10:J22) by dividing the corresponding value in column I by 2.471.

A further set of summary calculations are performed in column Q :

Item	Location	Formula
Number of loads delivered	Q7	COUNT(B37:B201)
Highest Top Tare	Q8	MAX(C37:C201)
Lowest Top Tare	Q9	MIN(C37:C201)
Average Top Tare	Q10	AV(C37:C201)
Highest Total Tare	Q11	MAX(D37:D201)
Lowest Total Tare	Q12	MIN(D37:D201)
Average Total Tare	Q13	AV(D37:D201)
Highest Sugar Content	Q14	MAX(G37:G201)
Lowest Sugar Content	Q15	MIN(G37:G201)
Average Sugar Content	Q16	AV(G37:G201)

Item	Location	Formula
The total gross weight delivered for the field/block is the sum of the individual deliveries.	Q17	SUM(B37:B201)
The total clean weight delivered for the field/block is the sum of the clean weights of the individual deliveries.	Q18	SUM(E37:E201)
The total adjusted weight delivered for the field/block is the sum of the adjusted weights of the individual deliveries.	Q19	SUM(I37:I201)
The highest value of Amino Nitrogen	Q20	MAX(F37:F201)
The average value per clean tonne is the total net value divided by the total clean tonnage.	Q21	SUM(R37:R201)/Q18
The total net income is the sum of the net values of the individual deliveries.	Q22	SUM(R37:R201)

Finally two calculations are performed in column O :

(a) The clean weight delivered on this spreadsheet is added to the deliveries carried forward from previous spreadsheets.

   ie. O24 = O4 + Q18

(b) The adjusted weight delivered on this spreadsheet is added to the deliveries carried forward from previous spreadsheets

   ie. O25 = O5 + Q19

All the formulas used in the spreadsheet are shown in Figs. 18.2 and 18.3.

```
 |A||  B  || C ||  D   ||  E  ||  F  || G ||  H  ||  I  || J || K || L || M || N || O || P || Q || R

1   SUGAR BEET RETURN ANALYSIS - G.Bunn
2
3   FIELD/S...... 101      NAME...Alder Carr          PREVIOUS CLEAN DELIVERIES TO DATE... 3459.20 Tonnes
4                                                     PREVIOUS ADJUSTED DELIVERIES TO DATE 4206.04 Tonnes
5   TOTAL HECTARES..........      5.41
6
7   SUMMARY                          PER       PER        No. of Loads Delivered.......       14
8                                   HECTARE   _ACRE       Tops Tare :-    Highest...          9%
9   (Details of                                                          Lowest...           6%
10  individual loads  Gross Weight Delivered (t) ..  46.50   18.82                      Average..    7%
11  can be found at   Clean Weight Delivered (t) ..  39.48   15.98       Total Tare :-  Highest...   20%
12  A31 and below)                                                                      Lowest...   11%
13                    Tare Delivered (t) ..........   7.02    2.84                      Average.    15%
14                                                                       Sugar Content :- Highest... 18.1%
15                    Total Adjusted Weight (t) ...  45.64   18.47                        Lowest...  17.1%
16                                                                                        Average.  17.7%
17                    Total Income (£) ............ 1304.16  527.78      Gross Weight Delivered (t) ...  251.58
18                                                                       Clean Weight Delivered (t) ...  213.58
19                    Total Deductions (£) ........   7.10    2.87       Total Adjusted Weight (t) ....  246.92
20                                                                       Amino Nitrogen Maximum.......      140
21                    Net Income (£) ..............  1297.05  524.91     Av. Income per Clean Tonne (£) .  32.85
22                                                                       Total Net Income of Crop (£) .  7017.06
23
24                                                    NEW CLEAN DELIVERIES TO DATE...... 3672.78 Tonnes
25                                                    NEW ADJUSTED DELIVERIES TO DATE.... 4452.96 Tonnes
26
```

	Price per Tonne @ 16%.	27.00		N.F.U. Levy	6.56 p. / Tonne
	Transport Allowance £/t	1.82		R & E Levy	9.00 p. / Tonne

								[GROWERS CREDITS]		[GROWERS DEBITS]						
Date	Total Weight (t)	Tops Tare (%)	Total Tare (%)	Clean Weight (t)	Amino Nitro	Sugar (%)	Adjusted Weight (t)	Beet Value (£)	Trans Allow (£)	EDB! LDB! (£)!	NFU Levy (£)	R E Levy (£)	Haulage (£)	Total CREDITS (£)	Total DEBITS (£)	NET VALUE (£)
0301	18.66	8	17	15.49	69	18.0	18.2782	493.51	28.19		1.20	1.65		521.70	2.84	518.86
"	14.54	8	13	12.65		18.1	15.0409	406.10	23.02		.99	1.35		429.13	2.34	426.79
0401	19.66	6	15	16.71		18.1	19.8682	536.44	30.41		1.30	1.79		566.86	3.09	563.76
"	19.30	6	12	16.98		17.3	18.9667	512.10	30.91		1.24	1.71		543.01	2.95	540.06
::	19.40	7	15	16.49	136	17.7	19.0130	513.35	30.01		1.25	1.71		543.36	2.96	540.40
"	19.30	6	17	16.02		17.5	18.1827	490.93	29.15		1.19	1.64		520.09	2.83	517.26
::	19.10	6	13	16.62		17.9	19.4620	525.47	30.24		1.28	1.75		555.72	3.03	552.69
::	15.04	9	18	12.33		17.8	14.3275	386.84	22.45		.94	1.29		409.29	2.23	407.06
::	19.10	7	12	16.81	50	18.1	19.9871	539.65	30.59		1.31	1.80		570.24	3.11	567.13
::	19.36	8	16	16.26	133	18.0	19.1868	518.04	29.60		1.26	1.73		547.64	2.99	544.66
::	19.08	6	19	15.45		17.6	16.9796	458.45	28.13		1.11	1.53		486.58	2.64	483.93
::	18.84	7	20	15.07		17.6	17.2401	465.48	27.43		1.13	1.55		492.91	2.68	490.23
::	18.76	7	12	16.51		17.5	18.7389	505.95	30.05		1.23	1.69		535.99	2.92	533.08
::	11.44	6	11	10.18	140	17.6	11.6459	314.44	18.53		.76	1.05		332.97	1.81	331.16

Fig. 18.1 Beet invoice analysis spreadsheet.

	A	B	C	D	E	F	G	H	I
1	SUGAR BEET RETURN ANALYSIS - G.Bunn								
2									
3	FIELD/S...... 101			NAME..........Alder Carr					
4									
5	TOTAL HECTARES.........5.41								
6									PER
7	SUMMARY								HECTARE
8									
9	(Details of								
10	individual loads			Gross Weight Delivered (t) ...					SUM(B37:B201)/E5
11	can be found at			Clean Weight Delivered (t) ...					SUM(E37:E201)/E5
12	A31 and below)								
13				Tare Delivered (t)					I10-I12
14									
15				Total Adjusted Weight (t)					SUM(I37:I201)/E5
16									
17				Total Income (£)					SUM(P37:P201)/E5
18									
19				Total Deductions (£)					SUM(Q37:Q201)/E5
20									
21				Net Income (£)					I18-I20
22									
23									
24									
25									
26									

		Price per Tonne @ 16% ..£						
		Transport Allowance £/t						

Row	Date	Total Weight (t)	Tops Tare (%)	Total Tare (%)	Clean Weight (t)	Amino Nitro	Sugar (%)		Adjusted Weight (t)
33–35	Date	Total Weight (t)	Tops Tare (%)	Total Tare (%)	Clean Weight (t)	Amino Nitro	Sugar (%)		Adjusted Weight (t)
37	0301	18.66	8	17	B37*(1-D37/100)	69	18	IF(G37<15,.91-.1*(15-G37),.91+.09*(G37-15))	ROUND(E37,2)*H37
38	"	14.54	8	13	B38*(1-D38/100)		18.1	IF(G38<15,.91-.1*(15-G38),.91+.09*(G38-15))	ROUND(E38,2)*H38
39	0401	19.66	6	15	B39*(1-D39/100)		18.1	IF(G39<15,.91-.1*(15-G39),.91+.09*(G39-15))	ROUND(E39,2)*H39
40	"	19.3	6	12	B40*(1-D40/100)		17.3	IF(G40<15,.91-.1*(15-G40),.91+.09*(G40-15))	ROUND(E40,2)*H40
41	"	19.4	7	15	B41*(1-D41/100)	136	17.7	IF(G41<15,.91-.1*(15-G41),.91+.09*(G41-15))	ROUND(E41,2)*H41
42	"	19.3	6	17	B42*(1-D42/100)		17.5	IF(G42<15,.91-.1*(15-G42),.91+.09*(G42-15))	ROUND(E42,2)*H42
43	"	19.1	6	13	B43*(1-D43/100)		17.9	IF(G43<15,.91-.1*(15-G43),.91+.09*(G43-15))	ROUND(E43,2)*H43
44	"	15.04	9	18	B44*(1-D44/100)		17.8	IF(G44<15,.91-.1*(15-G44),.91+.09*(G44-15))	ROUND(E44,2)*H44
45	"	19.1	7	12	B45*(1-D45/100)	50	18.1	IF(G45<15,.91-.1*(15-G45),.91+.09*(G45-15))	ROUND(E45,2)*H45
46	"	19.36	8	16	B46*(1-D46/100)	133	18.0	IF(G46<15,.91-.1*(15-G46),.91+.09*(G46-15))	ROUND(E46,2)*H46
47	"	19.08	6	19	B47*(1-D47/100)		17.1	IF(G47<15,.91-.1*(15-G47),.91+.09*(G47-15))	ROUND(E47,2)*H47
48	"	18.84	7	20	B48*(1-D48/100)		17.6	IF(G48<15,.91-.1*(15-G48),.91+.09*(G48-15))	ROUND(E48,2)*H48
49	"	18.76	7	12	B49*(1-D49/100)		17.5	IF(G49<15,.91-.1*(15-G49),.91+.09*(G49-15))	ROUND(E49,2)*H49
50	"	11.44	6	11	B50*(1-D50/100)	140	17.6	IF(G50<15,.91-.1*(15-G50),.91+.09*(G50-15))	ROUND(E50,2)*H50
51					1				

Fig. 18.2 Formulas for beet invoice analysis spreadsheet (Cells A1:I51).

```
  | J || K || L || M || N || O || P || Q || R |
  |---------------------------------------------------------------------------------
 1|
 2|
 3|
 4| PREVIOUS CLEAN DELIVERIES TO DATE.........      3459.20 Tonnes
 5| PREVIOUS ADJUSTED DELIVERIES TO DATE......      4206.04 Tonnes
 6|
 7| PER       No. of Loads Delivered........                      COUNT(B37:B201)
 8| ACRE      Tops Tare :-                         Highest..       MAX(C37:C201)
 9| ----                                           Lowest..        MIN(C37:C201)
10| I10/2.471                                      Average..       AV(C37:C201)
11| I12/2.471 Total Tare :-                        Highest..       MAX(D37:D201)
12| -----                                          Lowest..        MIN(D37:D201)
13|                                                Average..       AV(D37:D201)
14| J10-J12   Sugar Content :-                     Highest..       MAX(G37:G201)
15|                                                Lowest..        MIN(G37:G201)
16| I16/2.471 Gross Weight Delivered (t) ...       Average..       AV(G37:G201)
17|           Gross Weight Delivered (t) ...                       SUM(B37:B201)
18| I18/2.471 Clean Weight Delivered (t) ...                       SUM(E37:E201)
19|           Total Adjusted Weight (t) ....                       SUM(I37:I201)
20| I20/2.471 Amino Nitrogen Maximum........                       MAX(F37:F201)
21|           Av. Income per Clean Tonne (£)                       SUM(R37:R201)/Q18
22| J18-J20   Total Net Income of Crop (£) .                       SUM(R37:R201)
23|
24| NEW CLEAN DELIVERIES TO DATE........>     O4+Q18 Tonnes
25| NEW ADJUSTED DELIVERIES TO DATE......     O5+Q19 Tonnes
26|
```

	N.F.U. Levy	6.56 p. / Tonne
27	R & E Levy	9 p. / Tonne
1.82		

! [GROWERS CREDITS] ! ! [GROWERS DEBITS] !								
! Beet	Trans	EDB! NFU	R E		! Total	Total	NET
! Value	Allow	LDB! Levy	Levy	Haulage!	! CREDITS	DEBITS	VALUE
! (£)	(£)	(£)! (£)	(£)	(£) !	! (£)	(£)	(£)
I37*J27	E37*J28	I37*O27/100			J37+K37+L37	M37+N37+O37	P37-Q37
I38*J27	E38*J28	I38*O27/100			J38+K38+L38	M38+N38+O38	P38-Q38
I39*J27	E39*J28	I39*O27/100			J39+K39+L39	M39+N39+O39	P39-Q39
I40*J27	E40*J28	I40*O27/100			J40+K40+L40	M40+N40+O40	P40-Q40
I41*J27	E41*J28	I41*O27/100			J41+K41+L41	M41+N41+O41	P41-Q41
I42*J27	E42*J28	I42*O27/100			J42+K42+L42	M42+N42+O42	P42-Q42
I43*J27	E43*J28	I43*O27/100			J43+K43+L43	M43+N43+O43	P43-Q43
I44*J27	E44*J28	I44*O27/100			J44+K44+L44	M44+N44+O44	P44-Q44
I45*J27	E45*J28	I45*O27/100			J45+K45+L45	M45+N45+O45	P45-Q45
I46*J27	E46*J28	I46*O27/100			J46+K46+L46	M46+N46+O46	P46-Q46
I47*J27	E47*J28	I47*O27/100			J47+K47+L47	M47+N47+O47	P47-Q47
I48*J27	E48*J28	I48*O27/100			J48+K48+L48	M48+N48+O48	P48-Q48
I49*J27	E49*J28	I49*O27/100			J49+K49+L49	M49+N49+O49	P49-Q49
I50*J27	E50*J28	I50*O27/100			J50+K50+L50	M50+N50+O50	P50-Q50

Fig. 18.3 Formulas for beet invoice analysis spreadsheet (Cells J1:R51).

Irrigation scheduling

Purpose: To provide day to day irrigation scheduling advice based on a water balance approach.

Author: Tim Hess

Spreadsheet Name: SCHEDULE

19.1 Introduction

This spreadsheet (Fig. 19.2) uses a field soil water balance to estimate the soil water content, and therefore the need for irrigation, on a day to day basis from local weather data, and can be used between 1 April and 30 September in any year. It is a simplified version of a method used to provide irrigation scheduling advice to farmers and growers in Eastern England (Hess & Mathieson, 1988).

It requires some background data on the crop characteristics and cover development rate. At the start of the season many of these may be unknown, in which case 'best estimates' should be entered, based on previous experience. As the season progresses however, these estimates may be updated with real values.

The irrigation plan contains information on the soil water deficit which can be allowed to develop before irrigation takes place. Maximum allowable deficits may be specified for up to three scheduling periods. In the example shown, a deficit of 30mm is allowed before the crop reaches 20% cover, then for a period of 6 weeks, the allowable deficit is reduced to 18mm, and then returned to 30mm for the remainder of the season. This would be a common strategy for the control of scab on potato crops. Typical maximum allowable deficits for UK crops are given in MAFF (1982).

19.2 Structure of the spreadsheet

The spreadsheet has four main sections (Fig. 19.1):

An area for the input of background data describing the site, crops, soil and irrigation plan (A1:F20),

Two look up tables generated from the background data to determine crop growth rate and irrigation plan for any date (I1:M11),

The daily scheduling form for input of weather data and output of scheduling advice (A26:F208),

A table of daily calculations between the input data and output (H26:O208).

A1 Background Input Data F20			I1 Look Up Tables M11	
A21 Date	B21 Daily Input Data	E21 Output	H21 Daily Derived Values	
A208	D208	F208		O208

Fig. 19.1 Structure of the SCHEDULE spreadsheet.

19.3 Background Input data

The input table (A1:F20) consists of four parts.

(a)   Site data

Input data	Location	Type
Farm name	B1	text
Field name	B2	text
Year	E1	value
Crop type	E2	text

(b)   Crop data

Input data	Locations	
	Day	Month
Planting date	B9	C9
Emergence date	B10	C10
Date of reaching 20% cover	B11	C11
Date of reaching full cover	B12	C12

Input data	Location
Planting depth (m)	C13
Maximum root depth (m)	C14

(c)   Irrigation Plan

Input data	Locations		
	Day	Month	MAD
Start of period 1	D10	E10	F10
Start of period 2	D11	E11	F11
Start of period 3	D12	E12	F12

For each of the scheduling periods the date of the start of the period is entered, followed by the maximum allowable soil water deficit (MAD). If irrigation is not to be considered in a particular period, a MAD can be entered that is greater than the available water capacity of the root zone (eg. 999). This will never be reached, and irrigation will not be advised.

(d)   Soils Data

Input data	Location
Total available water capacity (mm/m)	D19
Easily available water capacity (mm/m)	D20

Some information is required regarding the ability of the soil to store and release water. In this simplified model the soil is considered as a homogeneous unit, both vertically and spatially. The only information required therefore is the total available water capacity and the easily available water capacity. Total available water capaciity is the difference between the water content at field capacity (-0.05 bar potential) and at permanent wilting point (-15 bar potential). Easily available water capacity is the difference between the water content at field capacity and at the point at which plants start to incur stress, usually taken as the water content of -2 bar. Both are expressed as a depth of water (mm) per metre of soil.

19.4 Look-up tables

From the background input data, two look-up tables are generated.

(a)   Crop cover development rate (I7:J11)

The season is divided into five crop cover stages and a cover development rate is calculated for each. The date of the start of each period is calculated (as a day number) from the day and month numbers entered at B9:C12 and stored in I7:I11. The cover development rate (% cover per day) is calculated in the range (J7:J11).

Period	Location	Formula
1 April - Planting	J7	0
Planting - Emergence	J8	0
Emergence - 20% cover	J9	20 / (I10-I9)
20% cover - full cover	J10	80 / (I11-I10)
Full cover - 30 September	J11	0

(b)   Irrigation plan (L7:M10)

A similar procedure is used to generate a look up table for the irrigation plan with the start day numbers in L7:L10 and the maximum allowable deficit in M7:M10.

All the formulas used in the look-up tables are shown in Fig. 19.3.

19.5 Daily Scheduling

From row 26 onwards, each row is exactly the same in format and corresponds to a day in the irrigation season (April 1 to September 30). Column A contains the date. Column B contains the reference crop (grass) evapotranspiration for the day. This may be calculated on a daily basis from local meteorological data, or may be average data for the time of year obtained from published sources (eg. MAFF, 1976). The daily water inputs (rainfall and irrigation) are entered into columns C and D respectively, and the calculated soil water deficit is shown in column E. Column F contains the scheduling advice. If the soil water deficit exceeds the allowable deficit given in the irrigation plan, the word 'IRRIGATE' appears in the advice column, otherwise it is left blank.

Columns H to O contain values derived from the input data. They are used for working only and may be hidden if required. First the actual evapotranspiration is calculated from the reference crop evapotranspiration and crop cover, and then soil water deficit is calculated from a water balance.

19.5.1 Daily Input Data

For each day, the date (as a value), reference crop evapotranspiration, rainfall, and irrigation amounts (all in mm) are entered into columns A to D.

Rainfall and irrigation must be measured at the site under consideration. Ideally, rainfall should be measured in each field to be scheduled and irrigation applications should be measured with catch-cans.

19.5.2 Derived Daily Values

(a)   Crop cover

The crop cover percentage on each day is calculated from the previous day's cover plus the daily cover development rate (found by looking-up today's date in the look-up table).

ie. today's cover = yesterday's cover + cover rate

eg. H26 = H25 + VLOOKUP(A26, I7:J11, 1)

(b)   Root depth

The season is split into three periods for estimating the root depth. Prior to planting, the root depth is assumed to be equal to planting depth. This is simply to avoid division by zero errors in the calculation of Ks (see below). The root depth is then calculated using nested IF statements.

If date < planting date, root depth = planting depth

  otherwise, if date > full cover date, root depth = maximum root depth

  otherwise, root depth = function of time (See Borg & Grimes, 1986)

eg. I26 = IF(A26<I8, C13, IF(A26>I11, C14,
          C13 + (C14-C13)*(0.5+0.5 *SIN(3.03*((A26-I8)/(I11-I8))-1.47))))

(c)   Soil evaporation

The evaporation loss from bare soil is calculated as a function of the soil water deficit.

$Esoil = (1-(SWD_{i-1}/15))*ETo_i$
where
$Esoil$ = soil evaporation,
SWD_{i-1} = yesterday's soil water deficit,
ETo_i = today's reference crop evapotranspiration.

If yesterday's soil water deficit is greater than 15mm, the above formula will yield a negative number. A lower limit of zero can be set using the MAX function.

eg. J26 = MAX(0, (1-(E25/15)) * B26)

(d)   Potential crop evapotranspiration

Potential crop evapotranspiration (ETc) is dependent on crop cover and reference crop evapotranspiration (ETo) as shown below. The factor, Kc used when crop cover is in excess of 85% is crop dependent, but a value of 1.1 can be used for most field crops.

Crop cover %	ETc
0	0
1 - 85	ETo
>85	Kc * ETo

eg. K26 = IF(H26=0, 0, IF(H26<85, B26, 1.1*B26))

(e)   Restriction due to limiting deficit

When the soil water deficit of the root zone exceeds the easily available water capacity of the root zone, the actual crop ET falls below the potential. A soil factor, Ks, can be defined as follows:

If $SWD_{i-1} < EAWC*RD_i$, $Ks = 1$

otherwise, $Ks = 1 - (SWD_{i-1}/RD_{i-1} - EAWC)/(TAWC-EAWC)$

where
SWD_{i-1} = yesterday's soil water deficit (mm),
RD_{i-1} = yesterday's root depth (m),
EAWC = soil easily available water capacity (mm/m),
TAWC = soil total available water capacity (mm/m).

eg. L26 = IF(E25<D20*I25, 1, 1- (E25/I25-D20)/(D19-D20))

(f)   Actual crop evapotranspiration

Actual crop evapotranspiration depends upon the potential (ETc) and the restriction due to limiting deficits.

ETca = ETc * Ks

eg. M26 = K26*L26

(g)   Actual evapotranspiration

The actual evapotranspiration, from soil and crop, is calculated as the average of the soil evaporation and ETca, weighted by crop area.

ETa = (1-CC) * Esoil + CC * ETca

where
CC   = crop cover fraction,
Esoil = soil evaporation,
ETca = actual crop ET.

eg. N26 = J26*(1-H26/100) + M26*(H26/100)

(h)   Allowable soil water deficit

The allowable soil water deficit is derived from the look-up table of irrigation plan, according to the date.

eg. O26 = VLOOKUP(A26,L7:M10,1)

19.5.3 Daily Output

(a)   Soil water deficit

The day's soil water deficit is calculated from the water balance equation:

$SWD_i = SWD_{i-1}$ - $rain_i$ - $irrig_i$ + ETa_i

where
SWD_i = soil water deficit on day i,
SWD_{i-1} = soil water deficit on day i-1,
$rain_i$ = rainfall on day i,
$irrig_i$ = irrigation on day i,
ETa_i = actual evapotranspiration on day i.

As it is assumed that any excess water will drain off within one day, the soil water deficit cannot be negative, therefore a lower limit of zero is set using the MAX function.

eg. E26 = MAX(E25-C26-D26+N26, 0)

Each day's soil water deficit depends to some extent on the previous day's, therefore some arbitrary starting point must be assumed. It is common practice in the UK to assume that the soil is at field capacity (ie. SWD = 0) on 31 March.

(b)   Irrigation advice

If the soil water deficit is greater than the allowable deficit, then the word 'IRRIGATE' is written in the advice column, otherwise it is left blank.

eg. F26 =IF(E26>O26, "IRRIGATE", " ")

The amount of water to be applied at that time will depend on the farm circumstances, and in particular on the equipment capabilities. The soil water deficit on the day of irrigation represents the upper limit to the application amount. Any further application will result in runoff or drainage and will be a waste of water, labour, power and equipment. An amount less than the soil water deficit is quite acceptable, and will leave some storage capacity, such that if some rain falls soon after irrigation it can be stored in the soil and will not be lost to drainage.

References

Borg H and D W Grimes (1986) Depth development of roots with time. An empirical description. *Trans. ASAE* **29**:194-197.

Hess T M and I K Mathieson (1988) Irrigation scheduling services 4, Irrigation Management Services. *Irrig. News* **13**:25-32.

Ministry of Agriculture Fisheries and Food (1976), Technical Bulletin 35. *The agricultural climate of England and Wales*. HMSO, London.

Ministry of Agriculture Fisheries and Food (1982), Reference Book 138. *Irrigation*. HMSO, London.

	A	B	C	D	E	F	G	H
1	FARM	Tim		YEAR	1984			
2	FIELD	Big		CROP TYPE Potatoes				
3	==							
4								
5		CROP DATA			IRRIGATION PLAN			
6								
7		Day	Month		After	Irrigate at		
8	--------------------------------			Day	Month	Deficit (mm)		
9	Planting	12	4	----------------------------------				
10	Emergence	15	5	1	4	999		
11	20% cover	31	5	31	5	18		
12	Full cover	29	7	15	7	30		
13	Planting depth		.2 m					
14	Max root depth		.7 m					
15	==							
16								
17	SOILS DATA							
18								
19	Total AWC			140 mm/m				
20	Easily AWC			100 mm/m				
21	===							=========
22	Date	ETo	Rain	Irrig	Soil Water	Advice		Cove
23					Deficit			
24		mm	mm	mm	mm			%
25	===							=========
26	01-Apr-84	1.7	0	0	1.7			0
27	02-Apr-84	1.5	0	0	3.0			0
28	03-Apr-84	1.6	0	0	4.3			0
29	04-Apr-84	1.5	0	0	5.4			0
30	05-Apr-84	.4	2	0	3.6			0
31	06-Apr-84	.5	1.4	0	2.6			0
32	07-Apr-84	.7	0	0	3.2			0
33	08-Apr-84	.6	.1	0	3.6			0
34	09-Apr-84	.8	0	0	4.2			0
35	10-Apr-84	1.4	.3	0	4.9			0
36	11-Apr-84	.9	5	0	.5			0
37	12-Apr-84	1.9	.1	0	2.2			0
38	13-Apr-84	2.5	0	0	4.4			0
39	14-Apr-84	2.8	0	0	6.3			0
40	15-Apr-84	1.2	0	0	7.0			0
41	16-Apr-84	2	0	0	8.1			0
.....								
.....								
.....								
.....								
200	22-Sep-84	1.5	7.1	0	.0			100
201	23-Sep-84	1.2	4.8	0	.0			100
202	24-Sep-84	1.1	0	0	1.2			100
203	25-Sep-84	.6	0	0	1.9			100
204	26-Sep-84	1.1	0	0	3.1			100
205	27-Sep-84	.8	0	0	4.0			100
206	28-Sep-84	1.5	3.4	0	2.2			100
207	29-Sep-84	1.6	2.3	0	1.7			100
208	30-Sep-84	0	0	0	1.7			100

Fig. 19.2 Irrigation scheduling spreadsheet (Rows 1:41 and 200:208).

	I		J		K		L		M		N		O		P

1											
2	Lookup table 1.			Lookup table 2						
3	Cover development rate			Irrigation plan						
4										
5	Start date	%/day		Start date	MAD					
6	--------------------			--------------------						
7	31-Mar-84	.00		31-Mar-84	999					
8	12-Apr-84	.00		01-Apr-84	999					
9	15-May-84	1.25		31-May-84	18					
10	31-May-84	1.36		15-Jul-84	30					
11	29-Jul-84	.00								
12	===									

	r	Roots	Soil Evap	Potential Crop ET	Ks	Actual Crop ET	Actual ET	Allowable Deficit
22–24		m	mm	mm		mm	mm	mm
26		.20	1.70	.00	1.0	.00	1.7	999
27		.20	1.33	.00	1.0	.00	1.3	999
28		.20	1.28	.00	1.0	.00	1.3	999
29		.20	1.07	.00	1.0	.00	1.1	999
30		.20	.26	.00	1.0	.00	.3	999
31		.20	.38	.00	1.0	.00	.4	999
32		.20	.58	.00	1.0	.00	.6	999
33		.20	.47	.00	1.0	.00	.5	999
34		.20	.61	.00	1.0	.00	.6	999
35		.20	1.01	.00	1.0	.00	1.0	999
36		.20	.61	.00	1.0	.00	.6	999
37		.20	1.84	.00	1.0	.00	1.8	999
38		.20	2.13	.00	1.0	.00	2.1	999
39		.20	1.99	.00	1.0	.00	2.0	999
40		.20	.69	.00	1.0	.00	.7	999
41		.21	1.06	.00	1.0	.00	1.1	999
....								
....								
....								
....								
200		.70	1.50	1.65	1.0	1.65	1.7	30
201		.70	1.20	1.32	1.0	1.32	1.3	30
202		.70	1.10	1.21	1.0	1.21	1.2	30
203		.70	.55	.66	1.0	.66	.7	30
204		.70	.96	1.21	1.0	1.21	1.2	30
205		.70	.64	.88	1.0	.88	.9	30
206		.70	1.10	1.65	1.0	1.65	1.7	30
207		.70	1.36	1.76	1.0	1.76	1.8	30
208		.70	.00	.00	1.0	.00	.0	30

	I ||	J ||	K ||	L ||	M	
1	Lookup table 1.			Lookup table 2	
2	Cover development rate			Irrigation plan	
3					
4					
5	Start date	%/day		Start date	MAD
6	-------------	-----		-------------	---
7	DATE(3,31,E1)	0		DATE(3,31,E1)	999
8	DATE(C9,B9,E1)	0		DATE(E10,D10,E1)	F10
9	DATE(C10,B10,E1)	20/(I10-I9)		DATE(E11,D11,E1)	F11
10	DATE(C11,B11,E1)	80/(I11-I10)		DATE(E12,D12,E1)	F12
11	DATE(C12,B12,E1)	0			
12	=============	=====		=============	===

Fig. 19.3 Formulas used in cells I1:M12 of irrigation scheduling spreadsheet.

The Penman equation

Purpose: To calculate potential evapotranspiration from weather data.

Authors: Tim Hess and William Stephens

Spreadsheet Name: PENMAN

20.1 Introduction

Four weather variables control the rate of transfer of water from a crop to the atmosphere (evapotranspiration): solar radiation (sunshine), temperature, humidity and wind speed. Various equations have been proposed for calculating evapotranspiration based on some or all of these variables. One of the most accurate methods was developed by Penman (1948) to calculate the potential evapotranspiration from a short, green, well watered grass surface using readily available meteorological measurements. MAFF (1967) presented a method for the solution of the Penman equation, using lookup tables for the important derived parameters, however with the advent of PCs these parameters can be found more easily and accurately using the equations in a spreadsheet.

This spreadsheet calculates potential evapotranspiration, from measurements of daily mean air temperature, sunshine duration, relative humidity and daily wind run, using the Penman method. If measurements of solar radiation are available these may be used directly, but otherwise values are estimated from sunshine duration, latitude and time of year. The method can be used for any location, although the constants used in the radiation equation may need to be changed outside of the UK.

20.2 Structure of the spreadsheet

The spreadsheet (Fig 20.1) has three main sections:

An area for basic data input and display of the calculated answer (A1:F10).

An area where constants are either entered or calculated from the input data (A21:C31).

The calculations leading to the estimate of potential evapotranspiration (A33:C65).

20.3 Input data

The basic data required to calculate potential evapotranspiration relate to the site, the date and the weather.

Input data	Location	
Day	B4	
Month	B5	
Year	B6	
Latitude (degrees N)	B7	
Altitude (m)	B8	
Relative humidity (%)	E4	
Mean air temperature (°C)	E5	
Mean wind speed (km/d)	E6	
Sunshine duration (h)	E7	
Solar radiation $(MJ/m^2/d)$	E8	(optional value)

20.4 Constants

Some constants are required as input to the Penman calculations, in particular to describe the empirical relationship between sunshine duration and received solar radiation, R_s. The values of the two constants, a and b, used in the radiation equation given below are taken from MAFF (1967) and relate to the UK south of 54.5 °N. For other locations, different values may be more appropriate. Further experimentally determined constants are presented by Doorenbos and Pruitt (1977).

Constant	Location	Value
a	B23	0.16
b	B24	0.62

20.5 Derived values

Before calculations can take place certain values need to be derived from the basic input data and some conversion of units is required.

20.5.1 Latitude in radians

The value of the latitude given in degrees is converted to radians using the formula

$$L_r = \frac{2 \pi L_d}{360}$$

where L_r = latitude (radians)
L_d = latitude (degrees)

ie. B26 = 2 * PI * B7 / 360

20.5.2 Mean air pressure

The mean air pressure depends upon the altitude of the site and can be estimated from (Mason, 1978) by

$$p = 1013.25 \, (1 - 2.2569 \times 10^{-4} \, A)^{(1/0.190284)}$$

where p = air pressure (mbar)
$\quad\quad\quad A$ = altitude (m)

ie. B27 = 1013.25 * (1 - 0.000022569*B8)^(1/0.190284)

20.5.3 Day number

The date can be expressed as a day number (1 January = 1, etc.) by using the in-built date function and subtracting the value of the last day in December of the previous year from the value of the current date. This automatically takes account of leap years.

ie. B28 = DATE(B5,B4,B6) - DATE(12,31,B6 -1)

20.5.4 Temperature in Kelvin

The mean air temperature measured in degrees Celsius can be converted into Kelvin by adding 273.15

ie. B29 = E5 + 273.15

20.5.5 Latent heat of vaporisation

Although often simplified to a constant, the latent heat of vaporisation is a function of the mean air temperature and may be calculated from (Mason, 1978) by

$$L = 597.31 - 0.565 \, T$$

where L = latent heat of vaporisation (cal g^{-1})
$\quad\quad\quad T$ = mean air temperature (°C)

ie. B30 = 597.31 - 0.565*E5

This can be converted to $J \, g^{-1}$ using a conversion factor of 4.1868.

ie. B31 = B30 * 4.1868

20.6 Calculations

The potential evapotranspiration can be calculated from (Penman, 1948) by

$$E = \frac{H \, \delta/\gamma + Ea}{\delta/\gamma + 1}$$

where E = Potential evapotranspiration (mm d^{-1})
$\quad\quad\quad H$ = Energy term (mm d^{-1})
$\quad\quad\quad \delta$ = Rate of change of vapour pressure with temperature (mbar °C^{-1})
$\quad\quad\quad \gamma$ = Psychrometric constant (mbar °C^{-1})
$\quad\quad\quad Ea$ = Aerodynamic term (mm d^{-1})

The energy and aerodynamic terms are calculated separately (see Sections 20.6.1 and 20.6.2) and then combined in the above equation (Section 20.6.4). The methods used are those of MAFF (1967) with necessary modifications for units used, except where otherwise stated.

20.6.1 Energy term

If solar radiation has not been measured at the site, the shortwave radiation received at the surface is estimated from the sunshine duration, latitude and time of year (Smith, 1986).

20.6.1.1 Estimated solar radiation

The solar declination is calculated from the time of year.

$$SD = 0.4093 \, SIN(0.0172 \, J - 1.405)$$

where SD = Solar declination (radians)
J = Day number

ie. B35 = 0.4093 * SIN(0.0172*B28 - 1.405)

The day length is calculated from the solar declination and latitude. Two intermediary values, XX and YY are calculated (Smith, 1986).

$$XX = SIN(SD) \, SIN(L)$$

$$YY = COS(SD) \, COS(L)$$

$$Nr = ACOS(-XX / YY)$$

$$N = 7.6394 \, Nr + 0.1$$

where SD = solar declination
L = latitude (rad)
Nr = day length (rad)
N = day length (h)

ie.   B36 = SIN(B35) * SIN(B26)
B37 = COS(B35) * COS(B26)
B38 = ACOS(-B36/B37)
B41 = 7.6394 * B38 + 0.1

The solar distance correction is given by

$$SL = 1 -1 \, 0.01673 \, COS(0.017214 \, J)$$

where SL = solar distance correction
J = day number

ie. B39 = 1 - 0.01673 * COS(0.017214*B28)

and the extra-terrestrial shortwave radiation by

$$Ra = \frac{15.54 \, ((Nr * XX) + SIN(Nr) * YY)}{SL^2}$$

where Ra = extra-terrestrial shortwave radiation (mm d^{-1})
        Nr = day length (rad)
        XX = as above
        YY = as above
        SL = solar distance correction

ie. B40 = 15.54 * (B38 * B36 + SIN(B38) * B37) / B39^2

The shortwave radiation received at the surface depends upon the cloudiness and therefore the relative sunshine duration. It can be estimated from (Penman, 1948) as

Rs = Ra (a + b n/N)

where Rs = shortwave radiation received at the surface (mm d^{-1})
        Ra = extra-terrestrial shortwave radiation (mm d^{-1})
        n   = sunshine duration (h)
        N   = day length (h)
        a   = constant (see Section 20.4 above)
        b   = constant (see Section 20.4 above)

ie. B42 = B40 * (B23 + B24 * E7 / B41)

About 25% of the shortwave radiation received at the surface, is reflected back into the atmosphere, thus the net shortwave radiation is given by

RNs = 0.75 Rs

where RNs = net shortwave radiation (mm d^{-1})

ie. B43 = 0.75 * B42

20.6.1.2 Measured shortwave radiation

Alternatively if received shortwave radiation has been given, the net shortwave radiation can be calculated from

$$RNs = \frac{750\ Rs}{L}$$

where RNs = net shortwave radiation (mm d^{-1})
        Rs = measured shortwave radiation (MJ m^{-2} d^{-1})
        L   = latent heat of vaporisation (J g^{-1})

ie. B45 = 750 * E8 / B31

20.6.1.3 Shortwave radiation

If a value greater than zero has been entered for measured shortwave radiation, then this will be used in subseqent calculations, otherwise the value estimated from sunshine hours is used.

ie. B47 = IF(B45>0,B45,B43)

20.6.1.4 Vapour pressure

The vapour pressure is a measure of the humidity of the air and can be calculated from temperature and relative humidity. The saturation vapour pressure, that is the maximum amount of water the air can hold at a given temperature, may be calculated from (Tetens, 1937) by

$$ea = 6.108 \; e^{(17.27 \; T/(T+237.3))}$$

where ea = saturation vapour pressure (mbar)
      T = mean air temperature (°C)

ie. B49 = 6.108 * EXP(17.27 * E5 / (E5 + 237.3))

and the actual vapour pressure from

$$ed = ea \; RH/100$$

where ed = actual vapour pressure (mbar)
      ea = saturation vapour pressure (mbar)
      RH = relative humidity (%)

ie. B50 = B49 * E4 / 100

20.6.1.5 Longwave radiation

The net outgoing longwave radiation can be estimated from the air temperature, the vapour pressure and the cloudiness.

The effect of temperature is given by

$$f(T) = \sigma \; T^4$$

and

$$\sigma = \frac{1.171 \; 10^{-7}}{L} * 10$$

where σ = Steffan-Boltzman constant (mm K^{-4})
     L = latent heat of vaporisation (cal g^{-1})
     T = mean air temperature (K)

ie.   B52 = 0.000001171 / B30
        B53 = B52 * B29^4

The effect of humidity is given by

$$f(ed) = 0.47 - 0.075 \; \sqrt{(0.75 \; ed)}$$

where ed = actual vapour pressure (mbar)

ie. B54 = 0.47 - 0.075*SQRT(B50*0.75)

The effect of cloudiness is given by

$$f(n/N) = \; 0.17 + 0.83 \; n/N$$

where   n = sunshine duration (h)
        N = day length (h)

ie. B55 = 0.17 + 0.83 * E7 / B41

The net longwave radiation (mm) is the product of the above three terms

ie. RNl = f(T) f(ed) f(n/N)

ie. B56 = B53 * B54 * B55

20.6.1.6 Energy term

Finally the energy term to be used in the Penman equation is given by

H = RNs - RNl

where   H   = energy term (mm d^{-1})
        RNs = net shortwave radiation (mm d^{-1})
        RNl = net longwave radiation (mm d^{-1})

ie. B58 = B47 - B56

20.6.2 Aerodynamic term

The wind function is given by (Mason, 1978) as

f(U) = 0.26252156 (1 + 0.01 U/1.609334)

where   f(U)= wind function (mm mbar^{-1} d^{-1})
        U   = wind speed (km d^{-1})

ie. B60 = 0.26252156 * (1 + 0.01*E6/1.609334)

and the aerodynamic term to be used in the Penman equation by

Ea = f(U) (ea - ed)

where   f(U)= wind function (mm mbar^{-1} d^{-1})
        ed = actual vapour pressure (mbar)
        ea = saturation vapour pressure (mbar)

ie. B61 = B60 * (B49-B50)

20.6.3 Weighting factors

The two weighting factors, γ and δ, to be used in the Penman equation are both functions of air temperature. The rate of change of vapour pressure with temperature (δ) is given by (Tetens, 1937) as

$$\delta = \frac{4098 \ ea}{(T + 237.3)^2}$$

where δ = rate of change of vapour pressure with temperature (mbar °C^{-1})
        ea = vapour pressure (mbar)
        T   = mean air temperature (°C)

ie. B63 = 4098 * B49 / (E5 + 237.3)^2

The psychrometric constant is given by (Mason, 1978) as

$$\gamma = \frac{0.24 \, p}{0.62196 \, L}$$

where γ = psychrometric constant (mbar $°C^{-1}$)
      p = mean air pressure (mbar)
      L = latent heat of vaporisation (cal g^{-1})

ie. B64 = 0.24 * B27 / (0.62196 * B30)

The weighting factor is given by δ/γ.

ie. B65 = B63 / B64

20.6.4 Potential evapotranspiration

Potential evapotranspiration is calculated from the Penman formula (see above)

$$E = \frac{H \, \delta/\gamma + Ea}{\delta/\gamma + 1}$$

where E = Potential evapotranspiration (mm d^{-1})
      H = Energy term (mm d^{-1})
      δ = Rate of change of vapour pressure with temperature (mbar $°C^{-1}$)
      γ = Psychrometric constant (mbar $°C^{-1}$)
      Ea = Aerodynamic term (mm d^{-1})

ie. B10 = (B58 * B65 + B61) / (B65 + 1)

All the formulas used in the spreadsheet are shown in Fig. 20.2

References

Doorenbos, J. and Pruitt, W.O. (1977). *Crop water requirements* (revised). FAO Irrigation and Drainage Paper No. 24. FAO, Rome.

MAFF (1967). *Potential transpiration.* Ministry of Agriculture, Fisheries and Food, Tech. Bull. 16. HMSO, London.

Mason, D.J. (1978). Input parameters for combination equation. *MSc thesis.* Silsoe College, Silsoe, Bedford, UK. Unpublished.

Penman, H. L. (1948). Natural evaporation from open water, bare soil and grass. *Proceedings of the Royal Society, London, Series (A)* **193**:120-145.

Smith, M. (1986). Calculation procedures of modified Penman equation for computers and calculators. FAO, Rome. Unpublished.

Tetens, O. (1937). Über einiger meteorologische Begriffe. *Z. Geophys* **6**:297-309

```
            |  A    ||   B    ||    C    ||       D        ||  E   ||    F     |
 1   ============================================================================
 2   ET by Penman Method
 3   ============================================================================
 4   Day                 15          Relative Humidity      60  %
 5   Month                6          Mean Temperature       15  °C
 6   Year                91          Wind Speed            100  km/d
 7   Latitude            52 °N       Sunshine               10  h
 8   Altitude           100 m        Solar Radiation            MJ/m²/d
 9   ============================================================================
10   ET                 3.9 mm/d
11   ============================================================================
12
13
14
15
16
17
18
19
20
21   Constants
22   ============================================================================
23   Solar-a            .16          Constant
24   Solar-b            .62          Constant
25
26   Lr                 .91 rad      Latitude
27   p             1001.29 mbar      Pressure                       Mason, 1978
28   J              166.00           Day number
29   Tk             288.15 K         Mean temperature
30   Lambda         588.84 cal/g     Latent heat of vaporisation
31   Lambda_j      2465.33 J/g       Latent heat of vaporisation
32
33   Calculations
34   ============================================================================
35   SD                 .41 rad      Solar declination
36   XX                 .31          intermediate value
37   YY                 .57          intermediate value
38   Nr                2.15 rad      Day length
39   SL                1.02 rad      Solar distance correction
40   Ra               17.20 mm/d     Extraterrestrial radiation
41   NN               16.56 h        Day length                     Smith, 1986
42   Rs                9.20 mm/d     Shortwave radiation            Penman, 1948
43   Rns(N)            6.90 mm/d     Net shortwave radiation
44                                      from sunshine hours
45   Rns(S)             .00 mm/d     Net shortwave radiation
46                                      from solar radiation
47   RNS               6.90 mm/d     Value of Rns used in calculation
48
49   ea               17.05 mbar     Saturated vapour pressure      Tetens, 1937
50   ed               10.23 mbar     Actual vapour pressure
51
52   sigma       1.98867e-9 mm/K     Stefan-Boltzman constant
53   f(Tk)            13.71          Temperature function
54   f(ed)              .26          Vapour pressure function
55   f(n/N)             .67          Sunshine function
56   Rnl               2.41 mm/d     Longwave radiation             MAFF, 1967
57
58   H                 4.48 mm/d     Energy term
59
60   f(U)               .43          Wind function                  Mason, 1978
61   aeromm            2.90 mm/d     Aerodynamic term               MAFF, 1967
62
63   delta             1.10 mbar/°C  Slope of SVP curve             Tetens, 1937
64   gamma              .66 mbar/°C  Psychometric constant          Mason, 1978
65   del/gam           1.67          Weighting factor
```

Fig. 20.1 Penman equation spreadsheet.

```
        |   A    ||                   B                    ||   C   |
1     ===========================================================
2     ET by Penman Method
3     ===========================================================
4     Day        15
5     Month      6
6     Year       91
7     Latitude   22                                          °N
8     Altitude   100                                         m
9     ===========================================================
10    ET         (B58*B65+B61)/(B65+1)                       mm/d
11    ===========================================================
12
13
14
15
16
17
18
19
20
21    Constants
22    ===========================================================
23    Solar-a    .16
24    Solar-b    .62
25
26    Lr         2*PI*B7/360                                 rad
27    p          1013.25*(1-.000022569*B8)^(1/.190284)       mbar
28    J          DATE(B5,B4,B6)-DATE(12,31,B6-1)
29    Tk         E5+273.15                                   K
30    Lambda     597.31-.565*E5                              cal/g
31    Lambda_j   B30*4.1868                                  J/g
32
33    Calculations
34    ===========================================================
35    SD         .4093*SIN(.0172*B28-1.405)                  rad
36    XX         SIN(B35)*SIN(B26)
37    YY         COS(B35)*COS(B26)
38    Nr         ACOS(-B36/B37)                              rad
39    SL         1-.01673*COS(.017214*B28)                   rad
40    Ra         15.54*(B38*B36+SIN(B38)*B37)/B39^2          mm/d
41    NN         7.6394*B38+.1                               h
42    Rs         B40*(B23+B24*(E7/B41))                      mm/d
43    Rns(N)     .75*B42                                     mm/d
44
45    Rns(S)     750*E8/B31                                  mm/d
46
47    RNS        IF(B45>0,B45,B43)                           mm/d
48
49    ea         6.108*EXP(17.27*E5/(E5+237.3))              mbar
50    ed         B49*E4/100                                  mbar
51
52    sigma      .000001171/B30                              mm/K
53    f(Tk)      B52*B29^4
54    f(ed)      .47-.075*SQRT(B50*.75)
55    f(n/N)     .17+.83*E7/B41
56    Rnl        B53*B54*B55                                 mm/d
57
58    H          B47-B56                                     mm/d
59
60    f(U)       .26252156*(1+.01*E6/1.609334)
61    aeromm     B60*(B49-B50)                               mm/d
62
63    delta      4098*B49/(E5+237.3)^2                       mbar/°C
64    gamma      .24*B27/(.62196*B30)                        mbar/°C
65    del/gam    B63/B64
```

Fig. 20.2 Formulas for the Penman equation spreadsheet.

Machine performance analysis

Purpose: To help the farmer/adviser/student appreciate the effects of changes in the operating parameters when using or choosing farm equipment.

Author: Andrew Landers

Spreadsheet Name: WORKRATE

21.1 Introduction

The computer operator is able to demonstrate how the workrate of an implement will change when parameters such as width and filling time are altered, eg:

(a) A farmer may be considering changing from a 12 metre tramline system to an 18 metre tramline system. The effect of changing implement widths - drill, fertiliser spreader and crop sprayer can be clearly seen in the resulting work rates.

(b) An adviser can demonstrate that changing crop sprayer boom width will only increase output marginally, whereas altering the logistics - filling time in the field, will increase work rate considerably.

(c) A fertiliser representative may use the program to show the effect on work rate of using large half or one tonne big bags to speed up filling the hopper compared with traditional 50kg bags.

(d) A farm machinery representative may be trying to convince a farmer that an implement gives a certain output; both parties could use the program to double check their respective queries.

The spreadsheet is displayed at Fig. 21.1

21.2 Input data

The program user needs to enter the following:

	Location	
	Machine Model A	Machine Model B
(a) Technical specifications of the implements -		
implement width (m)	E9	F9
hopper or tank capacity (kg or litres)	E10	F10
(b) Operating parameters -		
forward speed (km/h)	E11	F11
application rate (kg/ha or l/ha)	E12	F12
time taken to transport the implement to the field (min)	E13	F13
time taken to fill hopper (min)	E14	F14
(c) The field efficiency (%)	E15	F15

21.3 Calculations

Fig. 21.2 shows all the formulas used to calculate the output values for MODEL A (column E). Corresponding formulas are used to calculate the output values for MODEL B (column F).

The basis of the entries in the cells in column E are as follows:

(a) Area covered per load (ha) = $\dfrac{\text{capacity (kg or l)}}{\text{application rate (kg/ha or l/ha)}}$

ie. E24 = E10 / E12

(b) Filling rate (kg/min or l/min) = $\dfrac{\text{capacity (kg or l)}}{\text{filling time (min)}}$

ie. E25 = E10 / E14

(c) Spot work rate (ha/h) = implement width (m) * forward speed (km/h) / 10

ie. E26 = E9 * E11 / 10

(d) Total time per load (min) = filling time (min) + 2 * transport time(min) +

$$\dfrac{6000 * \text{area covered by load (ha)}}{\text{spot workrate(ha/h) * field efficiency(\%)}}$$

ie. E28 = E14 + 2*E13 + (6000*E24)/(E26*E15)

(e) Overall work rate (ha/h) = $\dfrac{60 * \text{area covered per load (ha)}}{\text{total time per load (min)}}$

ie. E29 = 60 * E24 / E28

(f) Overall efficiency (%) = $\dfrac{100 * \text{overall work rate (ha/h)}}{\text{spot work rate (ha/h)}}$

ie. E30 = 100 * E29 / E26

(g) Application time per load (min) = $\dfrac{6000 * \text{area covered per load (ha)}}{\text{spot work rate} * \text{field efficiency (%)}}$

ie. E34 = 6000 * E24 / (E26*E15)

(h) Application time (%) = $\dfrac{100 * \text{application time per load (min)}}{\text{total time per load (min)}}$

ie. E35 = 100 * E34 / E28

(i) Filling time per load (min) = filling time (min)

ie. E36 = E14

(j) Filling time (%) = $\dfrac{100 * \text{filling time per load (min)}}{\text{total time per load (min)}}$

ie. E37 = 100 * E36 / E28

(k) Transport time per load (min) = 2 * transport time (min)

ie. E38 = 2 * E13

(l) Transport time (%) = $\dfrac{100 * \text{transport time per load (min)}}{\text{total time per load (min)}}$

ie. E39 = 100 * E38 / E28

21.4 Sources of data

Useful data regarding capacities, field efficiencies, etc. are obtainable from:

Bowers W (1981) *Fundamentals of Machine Operation - Machinery Management (2nd edition)*. John Deere Service Publications, Moline, Illinois, USA.

Hunt D R (1983) *Farm Power and Machinery Management (8th edition)*. Iowa State University Press.

Landers A J (1984) Labour and Machinery Planning. Unpublished MSc Thesis, Silsoe College, Cranfield Institute of Technology, Bedford

Scottish Agricultural Colleges (1989). *Farm Management Handbook (10th edition)*. Scottish Agricultural Colleges, Edinburgh.

Acknowledgement

The author wishes to acknowledge the assistance given in the development of this program by Mr. Peter Clarke, a student on the Rural Estate Management Course at the Royal Agricultural College, Cirencester, 1984-1987.

```
    |  A   ||  B   ||  C   ||  D   ||  E   ||  F   ||  G   |
1   ================================================================
2   WORKRATE - A spreadsheet to compare farm machinery outputs
3   A.J.Landers, Royal Agricultural College, Cirencester, Glos.
4   ================================================================
5
6   INPUT DATA                               MODEL    MODEL
7   ----------                                 A        B
8
9   Implement width (m)                        12       18
10  Capacity (kg or litres)                  1500     1500
11  Forward speed (km/h)                       10       10
12  Application rate (kg/ha or l/ha)          150      150
13  Transport time (min)                       20       20
14  Filling time (min)                          5        5
15  Field efficiency (%)                       75       75
16
17
18
19
20  ================================================================
21                                           MODEL    MODEL
22  OUTPUT                                     A        B
23  ------
24  Area covered per load (ha)               10.0     10.0
25  Filling rate (kg/min or l/min)          300.0    300.0
26  Spot work rate (ha/h)                    12.0     18.0
27
28  Total time per load (min)               111.7     89.4
29  Overall work rate (ha/h)                  5.4      6.7
30  Overall efficiency (%)                   44.8     37.3
31
32  COMPONENTS
33  ----------
34  Application time per load (min)          66.7     44.4
35  Application time (%)                     59.7     49.7
36  Filling time per load (min)               5.0      5.0
37  Filling time (%)                          4.5      5.6
38  Transport time per load (min)            40.0     40.0
39  Transport time (%)                       35.8     44.7
40  ================================================================
```

Fig. 21.1 Machine Performance Analysis Spreadsheet.

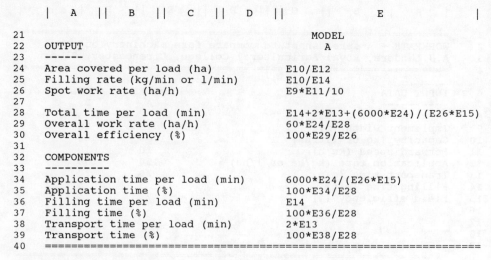

```
          |  A   ||   B   ||   C   ||   D   ||              E                |
21                                            MODEL
22    OUTPUT                                   A
23    ------
24    Area covered per load (ha)              E10/E12
25    Filling rate (kg/min or l/min)          E10/E14
26    Spot work rate (ha/h)                   E9*E11/10
27
28    Total time per load (min)               E14+2*E13+(6000*E24)/(E26*E15)
29    Overall work rate (ha/h)                60*E24/E28
30    Overall efficiency (%)                  100*E29/E26
31
32    COMPONENTS
33    ----------
34    Application time per load (min)         6000*E24/(E26*E15)
35    Application time (%)                    100*E34/E28
36    Filling time per load (min)             E14
37    Filling time (%)                        100*E36/E28
38    Transport time per load (min)           2*E13
39    Transport time (%)                      100*E38/E28
40    ==================================================================
```

Fig. 21.2 Formulas for Machine Performance Analysis Spreadsheet.

Livestock breeding and management calendar

Purpose: To produce a calendar for the breeding management of commercial livestock.

Author: Ioan Ap Dewi

Spreadsheet Name: BREEDCAL

22.1 Application

The spreadsheet, Figs. 22.1 and 22.2, produces a calendar for the breeding management of commercial livestock. It utilises the ability of spreadsheet programmes to manipulate dates. A calendar for up to six treatments or events at each of three production stages can be defined, namely, pre-mating, before-birth and after-birth. The user can specify one of three dates within the breeding cycle and all other required dates are then calculated. The spreadsheet prevents calculation if more than one date is specified.

22.2 Possible uses

The spreadsheet would be used to simplify the calculations required in the breeding management of livestock. Many hormonal, disease control and feeding treatments have to be given within specific periods before mating or parturition and many other operations have to be well-timed if performance targets are to be achieved. The user can define the timing of events in the periods before mating, before-birth and after-birth. A target date can then be specified for either the first pre-mating treatment, mating or birth. The calculations are essentially simple and are familiar to livestock producers but the spreadsheet allows them to be performed quickly and allows the effect of different timings on the breeding calendar to be examined.

22.3 Input data

(a) Basic information

E8 to E13	Days before mating for pre-mating treatments
E16 to E21	Days before birth for pre-birth treatments
E24 to E29	Days after birth for after-birth treatments
E31	Gestation length (days)

(b) Target dates:

The user may enter one of three target dates (pre-mating treatment 1, mating or birth) in columns D:F of rows 38:40. If more than one target date is entered "ERROR" will be displayed in cell E42 and the breeding/management calendar will not be produced.

22.4 Hidden cells

The contents of the hidden cells used in this spreadsheet (G38:H40 and E44) are shown in Fig. 22.3. There are three types:

(a) Cells G38:G40. These are used to test to see if a target date has been entered.

eg. G40 = IF(SUM(D40:F40)>0 , 1, 0)

If any numerical value has been entered in column D, E or F of rows 38 to 40 then the value stored in column G of that row will be 1, otherwise it will be zero.

These values are used in cell E42 to see if more than one target date has been entered. Thus

E42 = IF(SUM(G38:G40)>1 , ERROR, (" "))

ie. E42 is left blank if only one target date has been entered. If more than one has been entered the message "ERROR" appears.

(b) Cells H38:H40. These make use of the DATE function to generate a date for whichever of the target dates has been specified.

eg. H40 = DATE(E40, D40, F40)

These are subsequently used in the calculation of the breeding/management calendar.

(c) Cell E44. All the date calculations in the breeding/management calendar are based on the mating date. This is calculated in hidden cell E44, provided only one target date has been specified (ie. provided the ERROR message does not appear in cell E42).

Provided that this is so then one of three calculations is performed:

If pre-mating date 1 is specified (G38 equates to 1) then
Mating date = Pre-mating date 1 + days between pre-mating date 1 and mating.

ie. E44 = H38 + E8

If mating date is specified (G39 equates to 1) then mating date is used.

ie. E44 = H39

If birth date is specified (G40 equates to 1) then
Mating date = Birth date - gestation length

ie. E44 = H40 - E31

The full formula for cell E44 is given in Fig. 22.3.

22.5 Breeding/management calendar dates

All calendar dates (E49:E68) are calculated in relation to mating date (E44) as follows:

Pre-mating dates = Mating date - days before mating

eg. E49 = E44 - E8

Before-birth dates = Mating date + gestation length - days before birth

eg. E56 = E44 + E31 - E16

Birth date = Mating date + gestation length

E62 = E44 + E31.

After-birth dates = Mating date + gestation length + days after birth.

eg. E63 = E44 + E31 +E24

22.6 Example

In the example, for breeding ewes, three treatments have been defined. These represent a Progesterone Sponge at 16 days before tupping, an injection to induce lambing at 2 days pre-lambing and weaning at 56 days after lambing. A target lambing date of 1 January 1990 is specified. The programme converts the requirements into real dates and produces a calendar of events which also includes tupping (mating) and lambing (birth).

```
    |  A   ||   B   ||   C   ||   D   ||   E   ||   F   ||   G   |

1   ===================================================================
2   LIVESTOCK BREEDING AND MANAGEMENT CALENDAR          I. Ap Dewi
3   ===================================================================
4
5   1. Basic information
6   -----------------------
7                                    Days before mating
8   Pre-mating : treatment 1               16
9   Pre-mating : treatment 2                0
10  Pre-mating : treatment 3                0
11  Pre-mating : treatment 4                0
12  Pre-mating : treatment 5                0
13  Pre-mating : treatment 6                0
14
15                                   Days before birth
16  Before-birth : treatment 1             2
17  Before-birth : treatment 2             0
18  Before-birth : treatment 3             0
19  Before-birth : treatment 4             0
20  Before-birth : treatment 5             0
21  Before-birth : treatment 6             0
22
23                                   Days after birth
24  After-birth : treatment 1             56
25  After-birth : treatment 2              0
26  After-birth : treatment 3              0
27  After-birth : treatment 4              0
28  After-birth : treatment 5              0
29  After-birth : treatment 6              0
30
31  Gestation length (days)               145
32
33  2. Target date (Only one is allowed)
34  ---------------------------------------
35
36                                  Day    Month    Year
37  --------------------------      ------  ------  ------
38  Pre-mating treatment 1
39  Mating
40  Birth                            1       1       90
41  =================================================================
42
```

Fig. 22.1 Livestock breeding and management calendar spreadsheet (Cells A1:G42).

```
        |   A    ||   B    ||   C    ||   D    ||   E    ||   F    ||   G    |
43
44      3. Breeding/Management calendar
45      ----------------------------------
46
47
48
49      Pre-mating : treatment 1              24 Jul 89
50      Pre-mating : treatment 2
51      Pre-mating : treatment 3
52      Pre-mating : treatment 4
53      Pre-mating : treatment 5
54      Pre-mating : treatment 6
55      Mating date                            9 Aug 89
56      Before-birth : treatment 1            30 Dec 89
57      Before-birth : treatment 2
58      Before-birth : treatment 3
59      Before-birth : treatment 4
60      Before-birth : treatment 5
61      Before-birth : treatment 6
62      Birth date                             1 Jan 90
63      After-birth : treatment 1             26 Feb 90
64      After-birth : treatment 2
65      After-birth : treatment 3
66      After-birth : treatment 4
67      After-birth : treatment 5
68      After-birth : treatment 6
69      =================================================
```

Fig. 22.2 Livestock breeding and management calendar spreadsheet (Cells A43:G69).

```
      |   A   ||  B  ||  C  ||  D  ||  E  ||  F  ||  G  ||   H
33    2. Target date (Only one is allowed)
34    --------------------------------------
35
36                                Day   Month   Year
37                                ---   -----   ----
38    Pre-mating treatment 1                          IF(SUM(D38:F38)>0,1,0)  DATE(E38,D38,F38)
39    Mating                                          IF(SUM(D39:F39)>0,1,0)  DATE(E39,D39,F39)
40    Birth                        1      1      90   IF(SUM(D40:F40)>0,1,0)  DATE(E40,D40,F40)
41    ====================================
42                                IF(SUM(G38:G40)>1,ERROR,(" "))
43
44    3. Breeding/Management calendar    IF(ISERROR(E42),(" "),IF(G38=1,H38+E8,IF(G39=1,H39,IF(G40=1,H40-E31,(" ")))))
45    ----------------------------------
46
47
48
49    Pre-mating : treatment 1      IF(E44=(" "),E44,IF(E8=0,(" "),E44-E8))
50    Pre-mating : treatment 2      IF(E44=(" "),E44,IF(E9=0,(" "),E44-E9))
51    Pre-mating : treatment 3      IF(E44=(" "),E44,IF(E10=0,(" "),E44-E10))
52    Pre-mating : treatment 4      IF(E44=(" "),E44,IF(E11=0,(" "),E44-E11))
53    Pre-mating : treatment 5      IF(E44=(" "),E44,IF(E12=0,(" "),E44-E12))
54    Pre-mating : treatment 6      IF(E44=(" "),E44,IF(E13=0,(" "),E44-E13))
55    Mating date                   E44
56    Before-birth : treatment 1    IF(E44=(" "),E44,IF(E16=0,(" "),E44+E31-E16))
57    Before-birth : treatment 2    IF(E44=(" "),E44,IF(E17=0,(" "),E44+E31-E17))
58    Before-birth : treatment 3    IF(E44=(" "),E44,IF(E18=0,(" "),E44+E31-E18))
59    Before-birth : treatment 4    IF(E44=(" "),E44,IF(E19=0,(" "),E44+E31-E19))
60    Before-birth : treatment 5    IF(E44=(" "),E44,IF(E20=0,(" "),E44+E31-E20))
61    Before-birth : treatment 6    IF(E44=(" "),E44,IF(E21=0,(" "),E44+E31-E21))
62    Birth date                    IF(E44=(" "),E44,E44+E31)
63    After-birth : treatment 1     IF(E44=(" "),E44,IF(E24=0,(" "),E44+E31+E24))
64    After-birth : treatment 2     IF(E44=(" "),E44,IF(E25=0,(" "),E44+E31+E25))
65    After-birth : treatment 3     IF(E44=(" "),E44,IF(E26=0,(" "),E44+E31+E26))
66    After-birth : treatment 4     IF(E44=(" "),E44,IF(E27=0,(" "),E44+E31+E27))
67    After-birth : treatment 5     IF(E44=(" "),E44,IF(E28=0,(" "),E44+E31+E28))
68    After-birth : treatment 6     IF(E44=(" "),E44,IF(E29=0,(" "),E44+E31+E29))
69    ====================================
```

Fig. 22.3 Formulas used in the livestock breeding and management calendar spreadsheet.

Beef breed selection

Purpose: To compare the economics of producing beef from nine different sire breeds, either using discounted cashflows or on the basis of working capital requirements (net cashflows).

Authors: Alistair W. Stott and Dylan Gorvy

Spreadsheet Name: BEEFSIRE

23.1 Introduction

Production of beef from dairy-bred Friesian and beef breedxFriesian steers is common in the UK. Many different beef breeds are available which vary widely in price, feed requirements, growth rate and rate of maturity. It is therefore important for beef producers to select the sire breed which best meets their individual requirements. This spreadsheet application is primarily intended to assist producers with this choice by comparing nine breeds simultaneously on the basis of their expected discounted cashflows. With appropriate data the spreadsheet could also be used to compare up to nine different beef production systems which vary in terms of any combination of breed, growth rate, rate of maturity, carcass quality, feed costs and other variable costs.

Production and carcass information for the nine sire breeds involved (Aberdeen Angus, Charolais, Devon, Friesian, Hereford, Lincoln Red, Simmental, South Devon and Sussex) was obtained respectively from Southgate, Cook and Kempster (1982) and Kempster, Cook and Southgate (1982). This was combined with current financial information such as calf prices, feed prices, sale prices and interest rates obtained primarily from the Farm Management Handbook (Scottish Agricultural Colleges, 1988). As this information is subject to change and uncertainty it was important to be able to update it and perform sensitivity analysis to test the stability of breed choice to changing circumstances. Also the results and assumptions used in such an analysis require careful interpretation under particular business situations which cannot be prespecified. For this reason it was important that the methodology used was clear and flexible. All these criteria favoured a spreadsheet application.

23.2 Input Data

The layout of the entire spreadsheet is displayed in Fig. 23.1. The input data is displayed in Figs. 23.2 to 23.4. It is divided into six parts.

(a) Weight gains

The data in this and the next section is presented in eight 9x4 tables. The columns (B:J) of each table refer to the nine sire breeds. The rows of each table refer to the four growth periods from weaning to slaughter. There is an extra row for slaughter weight in Table 1 (Tables 1 to 15 referred to in this Chapter will be found in the spreadsheet - see Figs. 23.2 to 23.5).

Location

Weight gains by growth period (kg)	B29:J32
Final slaughter weight (kg)	B33:J33

Final slaughter weights for each breed can only be entered as an alternative to weight gains. If this option is chosen, a 1 should be entered in every other cell of Table 1.

(b) Feed requirements

The seven tables in this section refer to the seven possible ration constituents. There are two alternatives for this section dependent on data availability.

(i) If feed requirement is expressed as feed conversion efficiency (kg feed/kg grain or ha forage/kg gain) the feed requirements can be assumed to be the same for each sire breed (Southgate et. al. 1982). In this case there is no need to know the feed intake of each breed. Only the breed differences in weight gain for each growth period are required (Table 1). Default entries are made in this way with reference to a typical ration for 18 month beef production given in the Farm Management Handbook (Scottish Agricultural Colleges, 1988).

(ii) If the feed intakes of each breed are known, these can be entered directly. In this case only final slaughter weights should be given in Table 1.

Location

TABLE 2 Milk Substitute (kg or kg/kg gain)	B37:J40
TABLE 3 Calf Concentrate (kg or kg/kg gain)	B49:J52
TABLE 4 Hay (kg or kg/kg gain)	B57:J60
TABLE 5 Rearing Concentrate (kg or kg/kg gain)	B69:J72
TABLE 6 Barley (kg or kg/kg gain)	B77:J80
TABLE 7 Silage (Ha or Ha/kg gain)	B89:J92
TABLE 8 Grazing (Ha or Ha/kg gain)	B97:J100

(c) Other physical data (Table 9)

Location

Calf weight at start of period 1 (kg)	B108:J108
Slaughter age (days)	B109:J109
Killing out (%)	B110:J110
Carcass conformation group 1 (textual values)	B111:J111
Carcass conformation group 2 (textual values)	B112:J112
Number of animals	B113:J113

Breed differences in carcass conformation are expressed according to the EC beef classification scheme codes. Default values are from Kempster et al. (1982) who slaughtered at a fixed level of fatness in line with commercial practice. Limited control is given over the range of carcass conformation expected within each breed by providing two carcass conformation groups. The proportions expected in each group can be adjusted by entering the percentage of carcasses which fall into group 1 (J115).

Breed differences in demand for fixed resources can be expressed by entering the maximum number of animals that a particular business could carry in the last row of Table 9.

(d) Financial information differentiated by breed (£) (Table 10)

Location

Calf price	B128:J128
Veterinary costs by growth period	B132:J135
Other non-feed costs by growth period	B137:J140

(e) Other financial information (Table 11)

Location

Milk substitute price (£/tonne)	B147
Calf concentrate price (£/tonne)	B148
Hay price (£/tonne)	B149
Rearing concentrate price (£/tonne)	B150
Barley price (£/tonne)	B151
Grass silage production costs (£/Ha)	B154
Grazing costs (£/Ha)	B155
Discount rate (%)	J147
Overdraft interest rate (%)	J148
Opening bank balance (£)	J149
Carcass Value (p/kg DW) by conformation class: U+	J152
U-	J153
R	J154
O+	J155
O-	J156
Common Headage Premium (£)	J158
Maximum number of head entitled to Headage Premium	J159

The spreadsheet can either be used to compare different breeds using discounted cashflows (DCF) or on the basis of working capital requirements (net cashflows). If DCF then only the discount rate (J147) should be entered and both the overdraft interest rate (J148) and opening bank balance (J149) must be set to zero. If, alternatively, comparison is on the basis of working capital requirements then the discount rate must be set to zero and the other two values entered.

For details of the Common Headage Premium Scheme see Scanlan (1989).

(f) Duration of growth periods (Table 12)

Location

Duration of each growth period for each breed(months)	B167:J170

The default growth periods are for a typical 18 month beef production system. Period 1 is from birth to 3 months old. Period 2, the first winter from January to April. Period 3, grazing from May to September. Period 4 is the second winter period and is calculated from the slaughter age (B109:J109) less the sum of the three other periods.

23.3 Intermediate Calculations

Intermediate calculations (A181:J234) are performed in order to calculate feed costs, carcass value, headage premium and carcass weight. The results of the calculations are shown in Fig. 23.5. Formulas in this section are displayed in Fig. 23.6 for the Aberdeen Angus sire breed only (column B).

(a) Feed costs (£) (Tables 13 & 14)

Feed costs are calculated for every sire breed and each of the seven possible ration constituents within each growth period.

	Location
TABLE 13 Growth period 1	B186:J192
TABLE 13 Growth period 2	B194:J200
TABLE 14 Growth period 3	B206:J212
TABLE 14 Growth period 4	B214:J220

All feed costs are the product of feed intake per kg gain, feed cost (£/kg) and weight gain (kg). For example, the cost of milk substitute in period 1 for the Aberdeen Angus sire breed is given by:

B186 = B37 * (B147/1000) * B29

Notice that if feed intakes have been entered directly, weight gain (B29) will be unity and the same formula still applies.

(b) Carcass Value (pence/kg deadweight) (Table 15)

The carcass value of each sire breed is calculated separately for each conformation group. The average carcass value of the two quality groups is then calculated for subsequent use.

	Location
Carcass value group 1	B227:J227
Carcass value group 2	B228:J228
Mean carcass value	B230:J230

Carcass value is obtained by matching the carcass conformation class for each breed (Table 9) with the value of each class (Table 11). This is done using a hidden LOOKUP table in C152:D156. For example, the formula for carcass value group 1, Aberdeen Angus is:

B227 = VLOOKUP(B111,C152:D156,1)

and hence the mean carcass value for this breed is

B230 = B227*(J115/100) + B228*(J116/100)

The hidden look up table is necessary because the left hand column of a look up table must be in ascending order. The existing table of carcass values (I152:J156) does not have this property. The hidden lookup table is therefore:

	Column	
Row	**C**	**D**
152	("O+")	J155
153	("O-")	J156
154	("R")	J154
155	("U+")	J152
156	("U-")	J153

(c) Headage Premium (£) (Table 15)

The Common Headage Premium is paid on a maximum number of head (J159), so this calculation requires modification if the number of head (B113:J113) exceed this Fig. For example for the Aberdeen Angus sire breed

B232 = J158 * MIN(B113,J159)

(d) Carcass weight (kg) (Table 15)

This intermediate calculation is the product of slaughter weight and killing out percentage. If the slaughter weight was not included in Table 1, it must be calculated from the sum of calf weight and weight gain in each growth period. Using the same example breed :

B234 = (B110/100) * IF(B33=0, B108+SUM(B29:B32), B33)

23.4 Main Output

The main output consists of nine identical cashflow tables, one for each sire breed (Figs. 23.7 to 23.9), followed by a summary table of the net cashflow or discounted cashflow for every breed (Fig. 23.10 part (a)). The cashflow columns (L:O) represent the four growth periods. Row totals are calculated in column P. Only the formulas used in the calculation of period 1 of the first cashflow table (Aberdeen Angus) are described here and shown in Fig. 23.11. The calculations for other periods and breeds are similar.

(a) Discount factor

The present value of one pound (discount factor) received in year n with discount rate r is given by:

Discount Factor = $1/(1+r)^n$

For growth period 1 (L4) (hidden) this becomes:

L4 = 1 / (1+J147/100)^(L5/12)

(b) Output (£) = (number of animals * carcass value * carcass weight) + Headage Premium

Output is only received in period 4, but the appropriate formula is included in Fig. 23.11.

ie. O7 = (B113*B234*B230/100) + B232

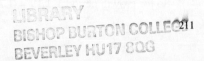

(c) Calf costs (£) (Period 1 only,) = Number of animals * calf price.

    ie. L9 = B113*B128

(d) Feed costs (£) (All periods, L10:O10)

    = Number of animals * the sum of all 7 feed constituents in the period.

    So for period 1, L10 = B113*SUM(B186:B192)

(e) Veterinary and medicine costs (£) (All periods, L11:O11)

    = Number of animals * vet costs for growth period

    So for period 1, L11 = B113*B132

(f) Other non-feed costs (£) (All periods, L12:O12)

    = Number of animals * other non-feed costs

    So for period 1, L12 = B113*B137

(g) Opening Balance (£) (All periods, L14:O14)

    is given by J149 in period 1, otherwise by the closing balance for the previous growth period plus any interest charges

    eg. for period 4, O14 = N15+N17

(h) Closing Balance (£) (All periods, L15:O15)

    = Opening balance + Output - Sum of all costs

    So for period 1, L15 = L14 + L7 - SUM(L9:L12)

(i) Interest (£) (All periods, L17:O17)

    This calculation is only undertaken if the discount factor is zero and the average of the opening and closing balance for the growth period is less than zero. If both these conditions hold then interest charge is given by:

    Average balance * Overdraft interest rate * Duration of growth period

    So for period 1, L17 = (L14+L15)/2 * (J148/1200) * L5

    The full formula including the associated conditional statements is shown in Fig. 23.11.

(j) Discounted Cashflow (£) (All periods, L19:O19)

    If the discount rate (J148) is zero, the text 'NCF' (net cashflow) appears in K19. Otherwise the text 'DCF' (discounted cashflow) appears.

    The DCF or NCF is given by:

    [Output - (Sum all costs - interest charge)] * discount factor

    So for growth period 1, L19 = (L7 - (SUM(L9:L12)-K17)) * L4

Notice that for NCF, L4 will be 1. For DCF, K17 will be 0.

Finally, the formulas used to produce the summary table showing total net cashflow or net present value (NPV) for each breed are shown in Fig. 23.10 part (b) and are self-explanatory.

23.5 The Spreadsheet in Use

The results section (Fig 23.10 part (a)) was designed to fit within a vertical split window. This allows changes to be made to the input data and the effects on NPV to be viewed simultaneously. Sensitivity analysis can be quickly conducted in this way.

This spreadsheet can assist with a variety of decisions commonly faced by beef producers. As well as calf sire choice these may include:

1. Maximum calf purchase prices for each breed.
2. Minimum sale values.
3. Value of carcass quality premia.
4. Matching animal numbers and breeds to resource constraints, for example maximum bank borrowing facilities.
5. Tolerance to bank interest rates.
6. Sensitivity to changes in variable costs, particularly ration constituents.
7. Experimenting with different growth rates and associated changes in feed requirements and ages at slaughter. This may be done before and during production in response to changes in markets, forage availability etc.

The emphasis of the spreadsheet is on maximum flexibility to modify the cashflow budgets according to business circumstances and data availability. Best results will be obtained by a process of trial, error and modification in the field. Default values are linked closely to performances under research conditions. Commercial situations may show considerably greater variation. Other problems associated with omissions and assumptions have been mentioned. However sensible use of the spreadsheet as part of a business planning and control system should lead to better decision making.

References

Kempster, A.J., Cook, G.L. and Southgate, J.R. (1982). A Comparison of the Progeny of British Friesian Dams and Different Sire Breeds in 16- and 24- Month Beef Production Systems. 2.Carcass Characteristics and Rate and Efficiency of Meat Gain. *Anim. Prod.* **34**:167-178.

Scanlan, (1989). Beef Policy Reforms. *Monthly Economic Survey 15(3):*3. March 1989. Scottish Agricultural Colleges.

Scottish Agricultural Colleges, (1988). *Farm Management Handbook 1988/89.*

Southgate, J.R., Cook, G.L. and Kempster, A.J. (1982). A Comparison of the Progeny of British Friesian Dams and Different Sire Breeds in 16- and 24- Month Beef Production Systems. 1. Live-Weight Gain and Efficiency of Food Utilization. *Anim. Prod.* **34**:155-166.

Acknowledgements

We are grateful to Dr.G. Simm and other colleagues at the Edinburgh School of Agriculture for help and advice with the concept and construction of this spreadsheet.

Row No.	<---------Columns A-J---------->|	<---------Columns K-P---------->
1 20	INTRODUCTORY SCREEN	CASHFLOW 1 ABERDEEN ANGUS
21 40	TABLE 1:Weight Gains TABLE 2:Feed Intake 1 (Milk Substitute)	CASHFLOW 2 CHAROLAIS

41
 	
60
	TABLE 3:Feed Intake 2
	    (Calf Concentrate)
	TABLE 4:Feed Intake 3
	    (Hay)
		CASHFLOW 3 DEVON

61
 	
80
	TABLE 5:Feed Intake 4
	    (Rearing Concentrate)
	TABLE 6:Feed Intake 5
	    (Barley)
		CASHFLOW 4 FRIESIAN

81
 	
100
	TABLE 7:Feed Intake 6
	    (Silage)
	TABLE 8:Feed Intake 7
	    (Grazing)
		CASHFLOW 5 HEREFORD

101 120	TABLE 9:Miscellaneous Physical Data	CASHFLOW 6 LINCOLN RED
121 140	TABLE 10:Financial Data 1	CASHFLOW 7 SIMMENTAL
141 160	TABLE 11:Financial Data 2	CASHFLOW 8 SOUTH DEVON
161 180	TABLE 12:Duration of Growth Periods	CASHFLOW 9 SUSSEX
181 200	TABLE 13:Feed Cost Calculation (Periods 1 & 2)	NET PRESENT VALUE RESULTS FOR EACH SIRE BREED
201 220	TABLE 14:Feed Cost Calculation (Periods 3 & 4)	
221 240	TABLE 15:Carcass Value Calc.	

Fig. 23.1 Layout of the beef breed selection spreadsheet.

	A	|| B ||	C ||	D ||	E ||	F ||	G ||	H ||	I ||	J	

1	Sire Breed Evaluation For October-Born 18 Month Dairy-Beef Production	
2	Using Discounted Cashflow Budgets	
3		
4	Alistair.W.Stott and Dylan Gorvy	
5	Edinburgh School of Agriculture, West Mains Road, Edinburgh. EH9 3JG	
6		
7	**** Page Right and Then Down for Discounted Cashflows by Breed (9)	
8	**** Page Down For 8 Pages of Input Data	
9		
10	KEY: CASHFLOW PERIODS*	SIRE BREEDS
11	PERIOD 1: Birth to 3 months	AA: Aberdeen Angus
12	PERIOD 2: 1st Winter January-April	C : Charolais
13	PERIOD 3: Grazing May-September	D : Devon
14	PERIOD 4: 2nd Winter October-Slaughter	F : Friesian
15		H : Hereford
16	*The Duration of these time periods can be	L : Lincoln Red
17	adjusted. See input TABLE 12	S : Simmental
18		SD: South Devon
19		SU: Sussex
20		
21	Sire Breed Evaluation For 18 Month Beef Production	
22		
23	DATA INPUT SCREEN 1 - PHYSICAL DATA	
24	------------------------------------	

			AA	C	D	F	H	L	S	SD	SU
25	Sire Breeds:								TABLE 1		
26			AA	C	D	F	H	L	S	SD	SU
27	Weight Gains (kg)										
28	By Cashflow Period										
29		PERIOD 1:	42	40	40	40	37	38	35	40	41
30		PERIOD 2:	77	90	81	80	78	77	86	83	83
31		PERIOD 3:	161	190	167	179	172	176	187	178	172
32		PERIOD 4:	60	142	65	107	77	101	132	111	77
33	* FINAL SLAUGHTER WT:		0	0	0	0	0	0	0	0	0
34			*-Only enter if period gains set to 1 (see text)								
35	Feed Intakes (kg* or kg/kg gain)										
36	By Cashflow Period								TABLE 2		
37	Milk	PERIOD 1:	.20	.20	.20	.20	.20	.20	.20	.20	.20
38	Substitute	PERIOD 2:	0	0	0	0	0	0	0	0	0
39		PERIOD 3:	0	0	0	0	0	0	0	0	0
40		PERIOD 4:	0	0	0	0	0	0	0	0	0

41	Sire Breed Evaluation For 18 Month Beef Production	
42		
43	DATA INPUT SCREEN 2 - PHYSICAL DATA	
44	------------------------------------	

			AA	C	D	F	H	L	S	SD	SU
45	Sire Breeds:								TABLE 3		
46			AA	C	D	F	H	L	S	SD	SU
47	Feed Intakes (kg* or kg/kg)										
48	By Cashflow Period										
49	Calf	PERIOD 1:	2.31	2.31	2.31	2.31	2.31	2.31	2.31	2.31	2.31
50	Concentrate	PERIOD 2:	0	0	0	0	0	0	0	0	0
51		PERIOD 3:	0	0	0	0	0	0	0	0	0
52		PERIOD 4:	0	0	0	0	0	0	0	0	0
53											
54											
55											
56									TABLE 4		
57	Hay	PERIOD 1:	.54	.54	.54	.54	.54	.54	.54	.54	.54
58		PERIOD 2:	0	0	0	0	0	0	0	0	0
59		PERIOD 3:	0	0	0	0	0	0	0	0	0
60		PERIOD 4:	0	0	0	0	0	0	0	0	0

Fig. 23.2 Input data for the beef breed selection spreadsheet (Cells A1:J60).

```
        |        A        || B || C|| D|| E || F || G || H || I || J |

 61        Sire Breed Evaluation For October-Born 18 Month Dairy-Beef Production
 62
 63                        DATA INPUT SCREEN 3 - PHYSICAL DATA
 64                        -------------------------------------
 65                  Sire Breeds:                              TABLE 5
 66                  AA      C       D       F       H       L       S      SD      SU
 67   Feed Intakes (kg* or kg/kg)
 68   By Cashflow Period
 69    Rearing    PERIOD 1:    0       0       0       0       0       0       0       0       0
 70   Concentrate PERIOD 2: 2.90    2.90    2.90    2.90    2.90    2.90    2.90    2.90    2.90
 71               PERIOD 3:    0       0       0       0       0       0       0       0       0
 72               PERIOD 4:    0       0       0       0       0       0       0       0       0
 73
 74
 75
 76                                                             TABLE 6
 77    Barley     PERIOD 1:    0       0       0       0       0       0       0       0       0
 78               PERIOD 2:    0       0       0       0       0       0       0       0       0
 79               PERIOD 3:  .40     .40     .40     .40     .40     .40     .40     .40     .40
 80               PERIOD 4: 3.31    3.31    3.31    3.31    3.31    3.31    3.31    3.31    3.31
 81        Sire Breed Evaluation For October-Born 18 Month Dairy-Beef Production
 82
 83                        DATA INPUT SCREEN 4 - PHYSICAL DATA
 84                        -------------------------------------
 85                  Sire Breeds:                              TABLE 7
 86                  AA      C       D       F       H       L       S      SD      SU
 87   Feed Intakes (Ha* or Ha/kg Gain)
 88   By Cashflow Period
 89    Silage     PERIOD 1:    0       0       0       0       0       0       0       0       0
 90               PERIOD 2: .0004   .0004   .0004   .0004   .0004   .0004   .0004   .0004   .0004
 91               PERIOD 3:    0       0       0       0       0       0       0       0       0
 92               PERIOD 4: .0009   .0009   .0009   .0009   .0009   .0009   .0009   .0009   .0009
 93
 94
 95
 96                                                             TABLE 8
 97    Grazing    PERIOD 1:    0       0       0       0       0       0       0       0       0
 98               PERIOD 2:    0       0       0       0       0       0       0       0       0
 99               PERIOD 3: .001    .001    .001    .001    .001    .001    .001    .001    .001
100               PERIOD 4:    0       0       0       0       0       0       0       0       0
101        Sire Breed Evaluation For October-Born 18 Month Dairy-Beef Production
102
103                        DATA INPUT SCREEN 5 - PHYSICAL DATA
104                        -------------------------------------
105                  Sire Breeds:                              TABLE 9
106                  AA      C       D       F       H       L       S      SD      SU
107   Other Physical Data
108   Calf Weight (kg)      36      59      44      45      52      50      61      55      46
109   Slaughter Age (days) 438     523     440     500     453     486     506     491     460
110   Killing Out (%)       49      52      49      50      49      51      50      50      50
111   Carcass Conform. 1*    R      U-       R       R       R       R      U-       R       R
112   Carcass Conform. 2*    R      U-      O+      O+       R       R      U-       R       R
113   Number of Animals      1       1       1       1       1       1       1       1       1
114
115   *EEC Beef Carcass Classification Scheme:      *Percent in quality     1:     50
116                                                                          2:     50
117   (Good) U+, U-, R, O+, O- (Poor)   Enter as Textual Values
118                                     For example ("R") for R
119
120   See Input Screen 7 for Associated Prices
```

Fig. 23.3 Input data for the beef breed selection spreadsheet (Cells A61:J120).

```
  |        A       || B || C || D || E || F || G || H || I || J |
```

121   Sire Breed Evaluation For October-Born 18 Month Dairy-Beef Production
122
123   DATA INPUT SCREEN 6 - FINANCIAL INFORMATION
124   --
125   Sire Breeds: TABLE 10
126   AA   C   D   F   H   L   S   SD   SU
127 Gross Output Data
128 Calf Price (£)   120   140   125   140   140   135   139   125   125
129
130 Variable Costs (£)
131 By Cashflow Period
132 Vet &   PERIOD 1:   3   3   3   3   3   3   3   3   3
133 Medicine   PERIOD 2:   3   3   3   3   3   3   3   3   3
134   PERIOD 3:   3   3   3   3   3   3   3   3   3
135   PERIOD 4:   3   3   3   3   3   3   3   3   3
136
137 Other   PERIOD 1:   0   0   0   0   0   0   0   0   0
138 Non-Feed   PERIOD 2:   0   0   0   0   0   0   0   0   0
139 Expenses   PERIOD 3:   0   0   0   0   0   0   0   0   0
140   PERIOD 4:   22   22   22   22   22   22   22   22   22
141   Sire Breed Evaluation For October-Born 18 Month Dairy-Beef Production
142
143   DATA INPUT SCREEN 7 - FINANCIAL INFORMATION
144   --
145   TABLE 11
146 Feed Costs (£/tonne)
147 Milk Substitute   860   Discount Rate (%)   8
148 Calf Concentrate   190   Overdraft Interest Rate (%)*   0
149 Hay   60   Opening Bank Balance*   0
150 Rearing Concentrate   150
151 Barley   100   Carcass Value (p/kg DW)
152   by Conformation Class: U+   190.0
153 Feed Costs (£/Ha)   U-   189.4
154 Grass Silage   130   R   188.4
155 Grazing   110   O+   186.4
156   O-   182.2
157 *NOTE: Interest rate and opening
158   bank balance must both be   Common Headage Premium (£)   28
159   set to 0 when discounting   Maximum Head for Premium   90
160
161   Sire Breed Evaluation For October-Born 18 Month Dairy-Beef Production
162
163   DATA INPUT SCREEN 8 - DURATION OF GROWTH PERIODS
164   --
165   Sire Breeds: TABLE 12
166   AA   C   D   F   H   L   S   SD   SU
167 PERIOD 1:   2.6   2.6   2.6   2.6   2.6   2.6   2.6   2.6   2.6
168 PERIOD 2:   3.0   3.0   3.0   3.0   3.0   3.0   3.0   3.0   3.0
169 PERIOD 3:   6.1   6.1   6.1   6.1   6.1   6.1   6.1   6.1   6.1
170 PERIOD 4:   2.7   5.6   2.8   4.8   3.2   4.3   5.0   4.5   3.5
171
172   If PERIOD 4 durations are incorrect check
173   slaughter ages in row 109
174
175
176
177
178
179
180 *****************************END OF DATA INPUT*****************************
```

**Fig. 23.4** Input data for the beef breed selection spreadsheet (Cells A121:J180).
```

	A	B	C	D	E	F	G	H	I	J
181	Sire Breed Evaluation For 18 Month Beef Production									
182										
183	SCREEN 9 INTERMEDIATE CALCULATIONS									
184	FOOD COSTS (£)	------------------------------------							TABLE 13	
185	PERIOD 1	AA	C	D	F	H	L	S	SD	SU
186	Milk Substitute	7	7	7	7	6	7	6	7	7
187	Calf Concentrate	18	18	18	18	16	17	15	18	18
188	Hay	1	1	1	1	1	1	1	1	1
189	Rearing Concentrate	0	0	0	0	0	0	0	0	0
190	Barley	0	0	0	0	0	0	0	0	0
191	Silage	0	0	0	0	0	0	0	0	0
192	Grazing	0	0	0	0	0	0	0	0	0
193	PERIOD 2									
194	Milk Substitute	0	0	0	0	0	0	0	0	0
195	Calf Concentrate	0	0	0	0	0	0	0	0	0
196	Hay	0	0	0	0	0	0	0	0	0
197	Rearing Concentrate	33	39	35	35	34	33	37	36	36
198	Barley	0	0	0	0	0	0	0	0	0
199	Silage	4	5	4	4	4	4	4	4	4
200	Grazing	0	0	0	0	0	0	0	0	0
201	Sire Breed Evaluation For 18 Month Beef Production									
202										
203	SCREEN 10 - INTERMEDIATE CALCULATIONS									
204	FOOD COSTS (£)	------------------------------------							TABLE 14	
205	PERIOD 3	AA	C	D	F	H	L	S	SD	SU
206	Milk Substitute	0	0	0	0	0	0	0	0	0
207	Calf Concentrate	0	0	0	0	0	0	0	0	0
208	Hay	0	0	0	0	0	0	0	0	0
209	Rearing Concentrate	0	0	0	0	0	0	0	0	0
210	Barley	6	8	7	7	7	7	7	7	7
211	Silage	0	0	0	0	0	0	0	0	0
212	Grazing	18	21	18	20	19	19	21	20	19
213	PERIOD 4									
214	Milk Substitute	0	0	0	0	0	0	0	0	0
215	Calf Concentrate	0	0	0	0	0	0	0	0	0
216	Hay	0	0	0	0	0	0	0	0	0
217	Rearing Concentrate	0	0	0	0	0	0	0	0	0
218	Barley	20	47	22	35	25	33	44	37	25
219	Silage	7	17	8	13	9	12	15	13	9
220	Grazing	0	0	0	0	0	0	0	0	0
221	Sire Breed Evaluation For 18 Month Beef Production									
222										
223	SCREEN 11 - INTERMEDIATE CALCULATIONS									
224	------------------------------------								TABLE 15	
225	Carcass Value (p/kg DW)									
226		AA	C	D	F	H	L	S	SD	SU
227	Carcass Value Group 1	188	189	188	188	188	188	189	188	188
228	Carcass Value Group 2	188	189	186	186	188	188	189	188	188
229										
230	Mean Carcass Value	188	189	187	187	188	188	189	188	188
231										
232	EC Headage Premium(£)	28	28	28	28	28	28	28	28	28
233										
234	Carcass Wt (kg)	182	268	193	224	204	223	253	234	208
235										
236										
237										
238										
239										
240										

Fig. 23.5 Intermediate calculations in the beef selection spreadsheet (Cells A181:J240).

	A	|| B ||	C ||	D ||	E ||	F ||	G ||	H ||	I ||	J	

```
181              Sire Breed Evaluation For 18 Month Beef Production
182
183                    SCREEN 9 INTERMEDIATE CALCULATIONS
184  FOOD COSTS (£)    ------------------------------------      TABLE 13
185  PERIOD 1                  AA
186  Milk Substitute   B37*(B147/1000)*B29
187  Calf Concentrate  B49*(B148/1000)*B29
188  Hay               B57*(B149/1000)*B29
189  Rearing Concentrate B69*(B150/1000)*B29
190  Barley            B77*(B151/1000)*B29
191  Silage            B89*B154*B29
192  Grazing           B97*B155*B29
193  PERIOD 2
194  Milk Substitute   B38*(B147/1000)*B30
195  Calf Concentrate  B50*(B148/1000)*B30
196  Hay               B58*(B149/1000)*B30
197  Rearing Concentrate B70*(B150/1000)*B30
198  Barley            B78*(B151/1000)*B30
199  Silage            B90*B154*B30
200  Grazing           B98*B155*B30
201              Sire Breed Evaluation For 18 Month Beef Production
202
203                    SCREEN 10 - INTERMEDIATE CALCULATIONS
204  FOOD COSTS (£)    -------------------------------------     TABLE 14
205  PERIOD 3                  AA
206  Milk Substitute   B39*(B147/1000)*B31
207  Calf Concentrate  B51*(B148/1000)*B31
208  Hay               B59*(B149/1000)*B31
209  Rearing Concentrate B71*(B150/1000)*B31
210  Barley            B79*(B151/1000)*B31
211  Silage            B91*B154*B31
212  Grazing           B99*B155*B31
213  PERIOD 4
214  Milk Substitute   B40*(B147/1000)*B32
215  Calf Concentrate  B52*(B148/1000)*B32
216  Hay               B60*(B149/1000)*B32
217  Rearing Concentrate B72*(B150/1000)*B32
218  Barley            B80*(B151/1000)*B32
219  Silage            B92*B154*B32
220  Grazing           B100*B155*B32
221              Sire Breed Evaluation For 18 Month Beef Production
222
223                    SCREEN 11 - INTERMEDIATE CALCULATIONS
224                    -------------------------------------     TABLE 15
225  Carcass Value (p/kg DW)
226                           AA
227  Carcass Value Group 1 VLOOKUP(B111,C152:D156,1)
228  Carcass Value Group 2 VLOOKUP(B112,C152:D156,1)
229
230  Mean Carcass Value    B227*(J115/100) + B228*(J116/100)
231
232  EC Headage Premium(£) J158*MIN(B113,J159)
233
234  Carcass Wt (kg)       (B110/100)*IF(B33=0,B108+SUM(B29:B32),B33)
235
236
237
238
239
240
```

Fig. 23.6 Formulas for intermediate calculations (Column B only) for beef breed selection spreadsheet.

	K	L	M	N	O	P
1	Sire Breed Evaluation For 18 Month Beef Production					CASHFLOW
2						1
3	*** Aberdeen Angus ***	Period: 1	2	3	4	
4						TOTAL
5	Period Duration (Months)	2.6	3.0	6.1	2.7	14
6	-------					
7	OUTPUT (Sale Value & Headage Prem.)				372	372
8	-------					
9	Calf Cost	120				120
10	Feed Costs	27	37	24	27	115
11	Veterinary and Medicine Costs	3	3	3	3	12
12	Other Non-Feed Costs	0	0	0	22	22
13	-------					
14	OPENING BALANCE	0	-150	-190	-218	0
15	CLOSING BALANCE	-150	-190	-218	103	103
16	-------					
17	INTEREST (0 when discounting)	0	0	0	0	0
18	-------					
19	DCF:	-148	-39	-25	292	80
20	-------					
21	Sire Breed Evaluation For 18 Month Beef Production					CASHFLOW
22						2
23	*** Charolais ***	Period: 1	2	3	4	
24						TOTAL
25	Period Duration (Months)	2.6	3.0	6.1	5.6	17
26	-------					
27	OUTPUT (Sale Value)				537	537
28	-------					
29	Calf Cost	140				140
30	Feed Costs	26	44	29	64	162
31	Veterinary and Medicine Costs	3	3	3	3	12
32	Other Non-Feed Costs	0	0	0	22	22
33	-------					
34	OPENING BALANCE	0	-169	-215	-247	0
35	CLOSING BALANCE	-169	-215	-247	201	201
36	-------					
37	INTEREST (0 when discounting)	0	0	0	0	0
38	-------					
39	DCF:	-166	-45	-29	401	161
40	-------					
41	Sire Breed Evaluation For 18 Month Beef Production					CASHFLOW
42						3
43	*** Devon ***	Period: 1	2	3	4	
44						TOTAL
45	Period Duration (Months)	2.6	3.0	6.1	2.8	15
46	-------					
47	OUTPUT (Sale Value)				389	389
48	-------					
49	Calf Cost	125				125
50	Feed Costs	26	39	25	29	119
51	Veterinary and Medicine Costs	3	3	3	3	12
52	Other Non-Feed Costs	0	0	0	22	22
53	-------					
54	OPENING BALANCE	0	-154	-196	-224	0
55	CLOSING BALANCE	-154	-196	-224	111	111
56	-------					
57	INTEREST (0 when discounting)	0	0	0	0	0
58	-------					
59	DCF:	-151	-41	-26	305	87
60	-------					

Fig. 23.7 Beef breed selection spreadsheet (Cells K1:P60).

```
    |              K          ||  L   ||   M   ||   N   ||   O   ||   P   |

61              Sire Breed Evaluation For 18 Month Beef Production   CASHFLOW
62                                                                          4
63   *** Friesian ***            Period: 1       2       3       4
64                                                                     TOTAL
65   Period Duration (Months)       2.6     3.0     6.1     4.8        17
66   -----------------------------------------------------------------------
67   OUTPUT (Sale Value)                                     448        448
68   -----------------------------------------------------------------------
69   Calf Cost                      140                                 140
70   Feed Costs                      26      39      27      48         139
71   Veterinary and Medicine Costs    3       3       3       3          12
72   Other Non-Feed Costs             0       0       0      22          22
73   -----------------------------------------------------------------------
74   OPENING BALANCE                  0    -169    -211    -240           0
75   CLOSING BALANCE               -169    -211    -240     134         134
76   -----------------------------------------------------------------------
77   INTEREST (0 when discounting)    0       0       0       0           0
78   -----------------------------------------------------------------------
79   DCF:                                  -166     -40     -28    337   103
80   -----------------------------------------------------------------------
81              Sire Breed Evaluation For 18 Month Beef Production   CASHFLOW
82                                                                          5
83   *** Hereford ***             Period: 1       2       3       4
84                                                                     TOTAL
85   Period Duration (Months)       2.6     3.0     6.1     3.2        15
86   -----------------------------------------------------------------------
87   OUTPUT (Sale Value)                                     413        413
88   -----------------------------------------------------------------------
89   Calf Cost                      140                                 140
90   Feed Costs                      24      38      26      34         122
91   Veterinary and Medicine Costs    3       3       3       3          12
92   Other Non-Feed Costs             0       0       0      22          22
93   -----------------------------------------------------------------------
94   OPENING BALANCE                  0    -167    -208    -237           0
95   CLOSING BALANCE               -167    -208    -237     117         117
96   -----------------------------------------------------------------------
97   INTEREST (0 when discounting)    0       0       0       0           0
98   -----------------------------------------------------------------------
99   DCF:                          -164     -39     -27     321          91
100  -----------------------------------------------------------------------
101             Sire Breed Evaluation For 18 Month Beef Production   CASHFLOW
102                                                                         6
103  *** Lincoln Red ***          Period: 1       2       3       4
104                                                                    TOTAL
105  Period Duration (Months)       2.6     3.0     6.1     4.3        16
106  -----------------------------------------------------------------------
107  OUTPUT (Sale Value)                                     449        449
108  -----------------------------------------------------------------------
109  Calf Cost                      135                                 135
110  Feed Costs                      24      37      26      45         134
111  Veterinary and Medicine Costs    3       3       3       3          12
112  Other Non-Feed Costs             0       0       0      22          22
113  -----------------------------------------------------------------------
114  OPENING BALANCE                  0    -162    -203    -232           0
115  CLOSING BALANCE               -162    -203    -232     146         146
116  -----------------------------------------------------------------------
117  INTEREST (0 when discounting)    0       0       0       0           0
118  -----------------------------------------------------------------------
119  DCF:                          -160     -39     -27     342         116
120  -----------------------------------------------------------------------
```

Fig. 23.8 Beef breed selection spreadsheet (Cells K61:P120).

	K	L	M	N	O	P
121	Sire Breed Evaluation For 18 Month Beef Production					CASHFLOW
122						7
123	*** Simmental ***	Period: 1	2	3	4	
124						TOTAL
125	Period Duration (Months)	2.6	3.0	6.1	5.0	17
126	-----	-----	-----	-----	-----	-----
127	OUTPUT (Sale Value)				507	507
128	-----	-----	-----	-----	-----	-----
129	Calf Cost	139				139
130	Feed Costs	23	42	28	59	151
131	Veterinary and Medicine Costs	3	3	3	3	12
132	Other Non-Feed Costs	0	0	0	22	22
133	-----	-----	-----	-----	-----	-----
134	OPENING BALANCE	0	-165	-209	-240	0
135	CLOSING BALANCE	-165	-209	-240	182	182
136	-----	-----	-----	-----	-----	-----
137	INTEREST (0 when discounting)	0	0	0	0	0
138	-----	-----	-----	-----	-----	-----
139	DCF:	-162	-43	-29	380	146
140	-----	-----	-----	-----	-----	-----
141	Sire Breed Evaluation For 18 Month Beef Production					CASHFLOW
142						8
143	*** South Devon ***	Period: 1	2	3	4	
144						TOTAL
145	Period Duration (Months)	2.6	3.0	6.1	4.5	16
146	-----	-----	-----	-----	-----	-----
147	OUTPUT (Sale Value)				469	469
148	-----	-----	-----	-----	-----	-----
149	Calf Cost	125				125
150	Feed Costs	26	40	27	50	142
151	Veterinary and Medicine Costs	3	3	3	3	12
152	Other Non-Feed Costs	0	0	0	22	22
153	-----	-----	-----	-----	-----	-----
154	OPENING BALANCE	0	-154	-197	-227	0
155	CLOSING BALANCE	-154	-197	-227	168	168
156	-----	-----	-----	-----	-----	-----
157	INTEREST (0 when discounting)	0	0	0	0	0
158	-----	-----	-----	-----	-----	-----
159	DCF:	-151	-42	-28	356	135
160	-----	-----	-----	-----	-----	-----
161	Sire Breed Evaluation For 18 Month Beef Production					CASHFLOW
162						9
163	*** Sussex ***	Period: 1	2	3	4	
164						TOTAL
165	Period Duration (Months)	2.6	3.0	6.1	3.5	15
166	-----	-----	-----	-----	-----	-----
167	OUTPUT (Sale Value)				421	421
168	-----	-----	-----	-----	-----	-----
169	Calf Cost	125				125
170	Feed Costs	26	40	26	34	127
171	Veterinary and Medicine Costs	3	3	3	3	12
172	Other Non-Feed Costs	0	0	0	22	22
173	-----	-----	-----	-----	-----	-----
174	OPENING BALANCE	0	-154	-198	-227	0
175	CLOSING BALANCE	-154	-198	-227	135	135
176	-----	-----	-----	-----	-----	-----
177	INTEREST (0 when discounting)	0	0	0	0	0
178	-----	-----	-----	-----	-----	-----
179	DCF:	-152	-42	-27	328	107
180	-----	-----	-----	-----	-----	-----

Fig. 23.9 Beef breed selection spreadsheet (Cells K121:P180).

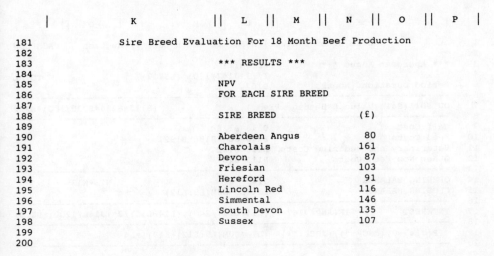

	K	L	M	N	O	P
181		Sire Breed Evaluation For 18 Month Beef Production				
182						
183		*** RESULTS ***				
184						
185		NPV				
186		FOR EACH SIRE BREED				
187						
188		SIRE BREED			(£)	
189						
190		Aberdeen Angus			80	
191		Charolais			161	
192		Devon			87	
193		Friesian			103	
194		Hereford			91	
195		Lincoln Red			116	
196		Simmental			146	
197		South Devon			135	
198		Sussex			107	
199						
200						

Fig. 23.10 Part (a) Beef breed selection spreadsheet summary table (Cells K181:P200).

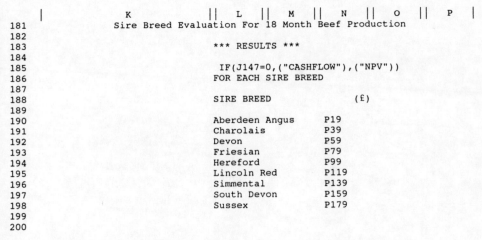

	K	L	M	N	O	P
181		Sire Breed Evaluation For 18 Month Beef Production				
182						
183		*** RESULTS ***				
184						
185		IF(J147=0,("CASHFLOW"),("NPV"))				
186		FOR EACH SIRE BREED				
187						
188		SIRE BREED			(£)	
189						
190		Aberdeen Angus		P19		
191		Charolais		P39		
192		Devon		P59		
193		Friesian		P79		
194		Hereford		P99		
195		Lincoln Red		P119		
196		Simmental		P139		
197		South Devon		P159		
198		Sussex		P179		
199						
200						

Fig. 23.10 Part (b) Formulas used in beef breed selection spreadsheet summary table (Cells K181:P200).

	K		L		M		N		O		P
1			Sire Breed Evaluation For 18 Month Beef Production								CASHFLOW
2											1
3	*** Aberdeen Angus ***		Period: 1		2		3		4		
4			1/(1+J147/100)^(L5/12)								TOTAL
5	Period Duration (Months)		B167								
6	---
7	OUTPUT (Sale Value & Headage Prem.)						(B113*B234*B230/100)+B232				
8	---
9	Calf Cost		B113*B128								
10	Feed Costs		B113*SUM(B186:B192)								
11	Veterinary and Medicine Costs		B113*B132								
12	Other Non-Feed Costs		B113*B137								
13	---
14	OPENING BALANCE		J149				N15+N17				
15	CLOSING BALANCE		L14+L7-SUM(L9:L12)								
16	---
17	INTEREST		IF(AND(J147=0,(L14+L15)/2<0),(L14+L15)/2*(J148/1200)*L5,0)								
18	---
19	IF(J147=0,("NCF:"),("DCF:"))		(L7-(SUM(L9:L12)-K17))*L4								
20	---

Fig. 23.11 Formulas used in beef breed selection spreadsheet
(Column L and Cells 07, 014 and K19 only).

Suckler herd embryo transfer model

Purpose: To evaluate the economic, physical and genetic results of using embryo transfer within a commercial suckler herd.

Author: Ioan Ap Dewi

Spreadsheet Name: SHEM

Editors' Note

As this is a large spreadsheet (748 rows), no attempt is made to explain the calculations involved in it. What follows is a description of the contents of the spreadsheet along with a complete printout. It has been included in order to demonstrate what we consider to be an important example of the use of spreadsheets.

24.1 Possible uses

Embryo collection and transfer is becoming increasingly important as a way of improving the quality of animals in both dairy and suckler herds. There are commercial companies and organisations that now offer an "embryo transfer" service to farmers. Although embryo collection and transfer has benefits, it is important to evaluate the economics of its use within suckler herds since there are costs involved, both in embryo collection and transfer and in the preparation and feeding of recipients. The spreadsheet allows the user to evaluate the impact of embryo transfer in physical, genetic and economic terms.

24.2 Application

The user specifies the number of cows in the herd and the number to be used as embryo donors. The user can also provide details of mortality, culling and embryo transfer success rates. The spreadsheet contains standard values for production costs and output targets which can be modified by the user to meet specific requirements. The spreadsheet generates a detailed herd structure and calculates an economic summary over a ten year period. The example (Figures 1 to 4) explores the use of embryo transfer in an upland spring calving herd of 50 cows. Five cows are used as embryo donors at 5 years of age.

24.3 Speadsheet structure

The spreadsheet is divided into thirteen sections or modules as described below. The modules are arranged seqentially in relation to row numbers to allow the large spreadsheet to be modified easily. The cell references for each module are given in parentheses.

Module 1 [A1:H53]: Basic information

Module 1 has three sections where basic information about the herd are entered, including cow numbers, number used as embryo donors, mortality rates, cows per bull and embryo collection and transfer targets (Fig. 24.1).

Module 2 [A54:H86]: Herd structure

This module defines the structure of the herd in relation to mature cow and bull numbers, numbers of replacements from embryo transfer and natural mating, recipients required, numbers of beef calves sold and number of culls. These are allocated to either a spring or autumn calving period (Fig. 24.2).

Module 3 [A87:F123]: Forage costs

Fertiliser, seed and other forage variable costs are defined in terms of quantity applied and cost per unit of application. The module calculates forage variable costs per hectare for lowland grazing and upland grazing and calculates, using entered yield data, a cost per tonne (fresh material) for silage. The forage costs are used in subsequent modules to calculate animal feeding and grazing costs (Fig. 24.3).

Module 4 [A124:H280]: Heifer rearing

Heifer rearing costs can be specified in relation to feeding, bedding, veterinary and forage costs. The module is divided into several periods from birth to weaning of first calf. Not all of these periods are used in calculating total heifer rearing costs subject to the basic information provided in Module 1 regarding weaning ages of calf and age at first calving (Figs. 24.4 to 24.6).

Module 5 [A281:G335]: Bull rearing

Replacement bull rearing costs can be specified in relation to feeding, bedding, veterinary and forage costs as described in Module 4 (Fig. 24.7).

Module 6 [A336:G427]: Beef finishing

Beef finishing costs are calculated for autumn and spring born bull and heifer calves sold at 18 months of age. Variable costs can be calculated for several production stages (Figs. 24.8 and 24.9).

Module 7 [A428:G462]: Mature cow - annual costs

Output and annual variable costs for mature cows, including calf rearing to weaning, are calculated for spring and autumn calving cows (Fig. 24.10).

Module 8 [A463:G483]: Mature bull - annual costs

Annual variable costs for mature bulls are specified in terms of feeding, veterinary, bedding and grazing costs (Fig. 24.10).

Module 9 [A484:G545]: Recipients

Purchase and sale prices for recipients are entered by the user for several production stages.

Total recipient costs are calculated for those where embryo transfer is unsuccessful and for recipients kept until their calf is weaned (Fig. 24.11).

Module 10 [A546:E554]: Embryo collection and transfer costs

Embryo transfer costs are specified in relation to costs of embryo collection, transfer, recipient preparation and artificial insemination costs (Fig. 24.12).

Module 11 [A555:J611]: Genetic progress

This module estimates genetic progress and requires the entry of several assumptions regarding selected characteristics. The user must also enter values, obtained from standard tables, related to the proportion of animals retained as replacements (Figs. 24.12 and 24.13).

Module 12 [A611:E634]: Fixed costs and additional income

Ten items of fixed costs can be included in this Module. Two items of additional income and a closing valuation for the scheme can also be included. All items can be named and the names and values are carried forward to Module 13 (Fig. 24.13).

Module 13 [A635:Q748]: Financial summary

Module 13 produces a financial summary for the scheme over a ten year period. In Section A [A635:Q692] of this module the user enters the distribution of items of expenditure and income during the ten year period. For each item, in each year of the budget, the user specifies the proportion of the cost or income to be used. A value of 0 would exclude items from the cash flow calculations for each year in which 0 occurred. Similarly a value of 1 would cause items to be included at their full amount. In Section B [A693:Q748] a cash flow budget is calculated using calculated costs, income and numbers of animals derived in Modules 1 to 12 and their annual distribution as indicated in Section A. The budget calculates total income and expenditure and the cumulative surplus (Figs. 24.14 and 24.15).

24.4 Assumptions

1. Purebred suckler cows are not used as recipients. The number of recipients required is calculated and it is assumed that these will be purchased in addition to the number of purebred cows specified.

2. Purebred cows and heifers are used as embryo donors after their calves are weaned. It is assumed that only one calf will be reared by the donor in the following two years. The calf will be born in the opposite calving period to the one in which the cow is initially included. Financially, the donor will be treated as a cow belonging to the opposite calving period for two years.

    For financial calculations mature cow numbers are adjusted to take into account the numbers of mature donors:

    Spring calving = Spring calvers - (2*Spring Donors) + (2*Autumn Donors)

    Autumn calving = Autumn calvers - (2*Autumn Donors) + (2*Spring Donors)

3. If purebred heifers calve at 2.5 years then:

    In Spring calving herds the heifers calve for the first time in the Autumn and then in the Spring at 4 years of age.

227

In Autumn calving herds the heifers calve for the first time in the Spring and then in the Autumn at 4 years of age.

4. Culling age - it is assumed that a calf is produced in the year of culling.

5. If a heifer is used as an embryo donor then it is assumed that the heifer will be used after its first calving and that this has no effect on subsequent calving pattern in a 2.5 year old calving heifer which will calve again at 4 years. For a 2 year old heifer, using it as an embryo donor causes it to calve again at 4 years old.

6. The current model assumes that embryos are collected in late-Summer/early-Autumn and that recipients will be purchased in order to be available at this time.

7. It is assumed that all calves, not retained as replacements, are finished on an 18-month beef system. However, the model can be modified to handle sale of progeny as stores or the use of alternative finishing systems.

```
  |  A   ||  B   ||  C   ||  D   ||  E   ||  F   ||  G   ||  H   |
1  -----------------------------------------------------------------------
2  SUCKLER HERD EMBRYO TRANSFER MODEL (SHEM) V 2.0   I. Ap Dewi  March 1990
3  -----------------------------------------------------------------------
4  MODULE 1: BASIC INFORMATION
5
6  1. Cow Numbers
7                                                        Calving Period
8                                                       Spring    Autumn
9  Total Number of Cows (exc. replacement heifers)      50.00      .00
10 Average Culling Age of Cows (Years)                             7.00
11 Calving Age of Purebred Heifers (0=2yrs:1=2.5yrs)               .00
12
13 Embryo Donors in age groups
14 -----------------------------------------------------------------------
15 Age            2.00     3.00     4.00     5.00     6.00     7.00
16             -----------------------------------------------------------
17 Spring                                    5.00
18 Autumn
19 -----------------------------------------------------------------------
20 Age
21             -----------------------------------------------------------
22 Spring
23 Autumn
24 -----------------------------------------------------------------------
25
26                                                    Spring    Autumn
27 Total number of mature (>1 calving) donors          5.00      .00
28 Total number of heifer donors                        .00      .00
29
30 2. Herd Structure
31
32 Natural Calf Mortality (%)                                    2.00
33 Mature Cow, Bull and Heifer Mortality (%)                     1.00
34 Cows per Bull - Natural Service                              25.00
35 Number of years bulls used for mating - Natural Service       3.00
36 Bulls age at first mating - Natural Service (years)           2.00
37 Proportion of replacements from ET calves                     1.00
38
39 3. Embryo Collection and Transfer
40
41 Number of flushes per donor/annum                             2.00
42 Number of transferrable embryos per flush                     3.00
43 Transferrble Embryos Produced per Donor                       6.00
44 Embryos Transferred per Donor                                 6.00
45 Embryos per recipient                                         1.00
46 Calves Born per Embryo Transferred                             .50
47 Embryo transfer Calf mortality (%)                            2.00
48 Weaning Age of Calves Born to Recipients (0=1 month:1=6 months) 1.00
49 Donors per Bull                                               5.00
50 Donors inseminated by AI (No=0:Yes=1)                          .00
51 Number of years bulls used for mating - ET                    3.00
52 Bulls age at first mating - ET (years)                        2.00
53 -----------------------------------------------------------------------
```

Fig. 24.1 Module 1 of suckler herd embryo transfer model.

	A		B		C		D		E		F		G		H	

		Calving Period	
54	MODULE 2: HERD STRUCTURE		
55			
56		Calving	Period
57		Spring	Autumn
58	Number of Mature Cows Calving Naturally (>1 Calving)	44.55	.00
59	Mature Cow Embryo Donors	4.95	.00
60	Heifer Embryo Donors	.00	.00
61	Heifer Replacements Required	8.42	.00
62	Embryos Produced	29.70	.00
63	Recipients Required	30.00	.00
64	E.T. Calves Weaned at 1 month	n/c	n/c
65	E.T. Calves Weaned at 6 months	14.70	.00
66	Recipients Sold at 18 months	14.85	.00
67	Recipients Sold After Weaning	14.85	.00
68	Natural Calves Reared from Mature Cow/Donors/Heifers	51.91	2.43
69	Natural Heifer Replacements Produced	25.95	1.21
70	Natural Bull Replacements Produced	25.95	1.21
71	Bull Replacements Required	1.57	.00
72	E.T. Heifer Replacements Produced	7.35	.00
73	E.T. Heifer Replacements Retained	7.35	.00
74	E.T. Bull Replacements Produced	7.35	.00
75	E.T. Bull Replacements Retained	1.57	.00
76	Natural Heifer Replacements Retained	1.07	.00
77	Natural Bull Replacements Retained	.00	.00
78	18 Month Beef Sucklers - Steers	25.95	1.21
79	18 Month Beef Sucklers - Heifers	24.89	1.21
80	18 Month Beef E.T. - Steers	5.78	.00
81	18 Month Beef E.T. - Heifers	.00	.00
82	Cull Cows	8.25	.00
83	Cull Bulls	1.55	.00
84	Adjusted Mature Cow Numbers	40.00	10.00
85	Adjusted Mature Bull Numbers	3.14	.00
86	--		

Fig. 24.2 Module 2 of suckler herd embryo transfer model.

	A	B	C	D	E	F
87	MODULE 3: FORAGE COSTS					
88						
89	1. Silage					
90						
91			Quantity	Price	Cost	Total
92			/ha	£/unit	£	£/ha
93	Nitrogen		300.00	.33	99.00	
94	P		50.00	.50	25.00	
95	K		50.00	.20	10.00	
96	Seed		2.00	1.50	3.00	
97	Other		1.00	10.00	10.00	147.00
98						
99	Fresh yield (t/ha)				30.00	
100	Cost/tonne (£)				4.90	
101						
102	2. Lowland Grazing					
103						
104			Quantity	Price	Cost	Total
105			/ha	£/unit	£	£/ha
106	Nitrogen		200.00	.33	66.00	
107	P		40.00	.50	20.00	
108	K		40.00	.20	8.00	
109	Seed		2.00	1.50	3.00	
110	Other		1.00	10.00	10.00	107.00
111						
112	3. Upland Grazing					
113						
114			Quantity	Price	Cost	Total
115			/ha	£/unit	£	£/ha
116	Nitrogen		.00	.33	.00	
117	P		10.00	.50	5.00	
118	K		10.00	.20	2.00	
119	Seed		1.00	1.50	1.50	
120	Other		1.00	10.00	10.00	18.50
121						
122						
123	--					

Fig. 24.3 Module 3 of suckler herd embryo transfer model.

	A	B	C	D	E	F	G	H
124	MODULE 4: HEIFER REARING							
125								
126	1. 1-3 Months		Days=	90.00				
127								
128			Quantity	Quantity	Value	Cost	Total	
129			/day(kg)	(kg)	£/tonne	£/head	£/head	
130	Concentrates		1.50	135.00	180.00	24.30		
131	Milk Substitute		.28	25.20	850.00	21.42		
132	Straw		1.00	90.00	40.00	3.60		
133	Vet & Med.					3.00		
134	Hay		.25	22.50	80.00	1.80		
135	Silage		1.00	90.00	4.90	.44	54.56	
136								
137	2. 3-6 Months		Days=	90.00				
138								
139	(a) Autumn born							
140								
141			Quantity	Quantity	Value	Cost	Total	
142			/day(kg)	(kg)	£/tonne	£/head	£/head	
143	Concentrates		2.00	180.00	150.00	27.00		
144	Straw		1.00	90.00	40.00	3.60		
145	Vet & Med.					1.00		
146	Hay		.00	.00	80.00	.00		
147	Silage		4.00	360.00	4.90	1.76	33.36	
148								
149	(b) Spring born							
150								
151			Quantity	Quantity	Value	Cost	Total	
152			/day(kg)	(kg)	£/tonne	£/head	£/head	
153	Concentrates		1.00	90.00	150.00	13.50		
154	Vet & Med.					1.00		
155								
156	Lowland grazing (ha)			.25	107.00	6.60	21.10	
157								
158								
159	3. 6 Months to 1 month post-calving							
160								
161	(a) Autumn born							
162								
163			Quantity	Quantity	Value	Cost	Total	
164			/day(kg)	(kg)	£/tonne	£/head	£/head	
165	SUMMER	Days=	60.00					
166	Concentrates		1.00	60.00	150.00	9.00		
167	Vet & Med.					1.00		
168	Lowland grazing (ha)			.25	107.00	4.40		
169	Upland grazing (ha)			.00	18.50	.00	14.40	
170								
171	WINTER	Days=	180.00					
172	Concentrates		1.00	180.00	150.00	27.00		
173	Straw		4.00	720.00	40.00	28.80		
174	Vet & Med.					5.00		
175	Hay		.00	.00	80.00	.00		
176	Silage		10.00	1800.00	4.90	8.82		
177	Lowland Grazing (ha)			.00	107.00	.00	69.62	

Fig. 24.4 Module 4 (Cells A124:H177) of suckler herd embryo transfer model.

	A	B	C	D	E	F	G	H
178								
179	SUMMER	Days= 180.00						
180	Concentrates		.50	90.00	150.00	13.50		
181	Vet & Med.					1.00		
182	Lowland grazing (ha)			.25	107.00	13.19		
183	Upland grazing (ha)			.00	18.50	.00	27.69	
184								
185	!! Calving at 2.5 yrs only							
186	WINTER	Days= 180.00						
187	Concentrates		2.00	360.00	150.00	54.00		
188	Straw		.10	18.00	40.00	.72		
189	Vet & Med.					2.00		
190	Hay			.00	80.00	.00		
191	Silage		4.00	720.00	4.90	3.53		
192	Lowland Grazing (ha)			.50	107.00	26.38	86.63	
193								
194	(b) Spring born							
195								
196			Quantity	Quantity	Value	Cost	Total	
197			/day(kg)	(kg)	£/tonne	£/head	£/head	
198	WINTER	Days= 180.00						
199	Concentrates		.50	90.00	150.00	13.50		
200	Straw		.10	18.00	40.00	.72		
201	Vet & Med.					1.00		
202	Hay			.00	.00	80.00	.00	
203	Silage		1.00	180.00	4.90	.88		
204	Lowland Grazing (ha)			.50	107.00	26.38	42.49	
205								
206	SUMMER	Days= 60.00						
207	Concentrates		.20	12.00	150.00	1.80		
208	Vet & Med.					1.00		
209	Upland grazing (ha)			.50	18.50	1.52	4.32	
210								
211	WINTER	Days= 180.00						
212	Concentrates		.50	90.00	150.00	13.50		
213	Straw		.10	18.00	40.00	.72		
214	Vet & Med.					1.00		
215	Hay			.00	.00	80.00	.00	
216	Silage		1.00	180.00	4.90	.88		
217	Lowland Grazing (ha)			.50	107.00	26.38	42.49	
218								
219	!! Calving at 2.5 yrs only							
220	SUMMER	Days= 60.00						
221	Concentrates		.10	6.00	150.00	.90		
222	Vet & Med.					1.50		
223	Lowland grazing (ha)			.00	107.00	.00		
224	Upland grazing (ha)			.50	18.50	1.52	3.92	
225								
226	4. 1 month to 6 months post calving							
227								

Fig. 24.5 Module 4 (Cells A178:H227) of suckler herd embryo transfer model.

	A	B	C	D	E	F	G	H
228	(a) Calf autumn born			Days=	150.00			
229								
230			Quantity	Quantity	Value	Cost	Total	
231			/day(kg)	(kg)	£/tonne	£/head	£/head	
232	Concentrates		1.00	150.00	150.00	22.50		
233	Straw		.10	15.00	40.00	.60		
234	Vet & Med.					1.50		
235	Hay			.00	80.00	.00		
236	Silage		12.00	1800.00	4.90	8.82		
237	Lowland Grazing (ha)			.25	107.00	10.99	44.41	
238								
239	(b) Calf spring born			Days=	150.00			
240								
241			Quantity	Quantity	Value	Cost	Total	
242			/day(kg)	(kg)	£/tonne	£/head	£/head	
243	Concentrates		.10	15.00	150.00	2.25		
244	Vet & Med.					1.00		
245	Upland grazing (ha)			.50	18.50	3.80	7.05	
246								
247	5. Weaning to transfer to mature cow							
248								
249	Autumn born heifer			Days=	90.00			
250								
251			Quantity	Quantity	Value	Cost	Total	
252			/day(kg)	(kg)	£/tonne	£/head	£/head	
253	Concentrates		1.00	90.00	150.00	13.50		
254	Straw		.10	9.00	40.00	.36		
255	Vet & Med.					2.00		
256	Hay			.00	80.00	.00		
257	Silage		12.00	1080.00	4.90	5.29		
258	Upland grazing (ha)			.00	18.50	.00		
259	Lowland Grazing (ha)			.25	107.00	6.60	27.75	
260								
261	Spring born heifer			Days=	90.00			
262								
263			Quantity	Quantity	Value	Cost	Total	
264			/day(kg)	(kg)	£/tonne	£/head	£/head	
265	Concentrates		1.00	90.00	150.00	13.50		
266	Straw		.10	9.00	40.00	.36		
267	Vet & Med.					2.00		
268	Hay			.00	80.00	.00		
269	Silage		12.00	1080.00	4.90	5.29		
270	Upland grazing (ha)			.00	18.50	.00		
271	Lowland Grazing (ha)			.25	107.00	6.60	27.75	
272								
273	TOTAL HEIFER REARING COSTS							
274								
275								Spring	Autumn
276	Natural Heifer						124.09	183.87
277	ET born Heifer						124.09	183.87
278								
279								
280	---							

Fig. 24.6 Module 4 (Cells A228:H280) of suckler herd embryo transfer model.

```
        |   A   ||   B   ||   C   ||   D   ||   E   ||   F   ||   G   |
281   MODULE 5: BULL REARING
282
283   1. 1-3 Months           Days= 90.00
284
285                       Quantity Quantity    Value      Cost     Total
286                       /day(kg)     (kg)   £/tonne    £/head    £/head
287   Concentrates            1.50   135.00    180.00     24.30
288   Milk Substitute          .28    25.20    850.00     21.42
289   Straw                   1.00    90.00     40.00      3.60
290   Vet & Med.                                           3.00
291   Hay                      .25    22.50     80.00      1.80
292   Silage                  1.00    90.00      4.90       .44     54.56
293
294   2. 3-6 Months           Days= 90.00
295
296                       Quantity Quantity    Value      Cost     Total
297                       /day(kg)     (kg)   £/tonne    £/head    £/head
298   Concentrates            4.00   360.00    150.00     54.00
299   Straw                   1.00    90.00     40.00      3.60
300   Vet & Med.                                           1.00
301   Hay                              .00     80.00       .00
302   Silage                  4.00   360.00      4.90      1.76     60.36
303
304   3. Performance Test (6-13 Months)
305
306                           Days= 200.00
307
308                       Quantity Quantity    Value      Cost     Total
309                       /day(kg)     (kg)   £/tonne    £/head    £/head
310   Concentrates            5.00  1000.00    150.00    150.00
311   Straw                   1.00   200.00     40.00      8.00
312   Vet & Med.                                           1.00
313   Hay                      .00     .00     80.00       .00
314   Silage                  6.00  1200.00      4.90      5.88    164.88
315
316   4. End of test to mating
317
318                           Days= 200.00
319
320                       Quantity Quantity    Value      Cost     Total
321                       /day(kg)     (kg)   £/tonne    £/head    £/head
322   Concentrates            5.00  1000.00    150.00    150.00
323   Straw                   1.00   200.00     40.00      8.00
324   Vet & Med.                                           1.00
325   Hay                      .00     .00     80.00       .00
326   Silage                  6.00  1200.00      4.90      5.88
327   Lowland grazing (ha)             .00    107.00       .00    164.88
328
329   TOTAL BULL REARING COSTS
330
331
332   Natural Bull                                                 329.76
333   ET born Bull                                                 329.76
334
335   -------------------------------------------------------------------
```

Fig. 24.7 Module 5 of suckler herd embryo transfer model.

235

```
        |  A   ||   B   ||   C   ||   D   ||   E   ||   F   ||   G   |
```

336 MODULE 6: BEEF FINISHING
337
338 1. Calves from suckler herd and recipients
339
340 OUTPUT
341
342 Sale Spring born calf at 18 months-Steer   500.00
343 Sale Spring born calf at 18 months-Heifer   400.00
344 Sale Autumn born calf at 18 months-Steer   500.00
345 Sale Autumn born calf at 18 months-Heifer   400.00
346
347 VARIABLE COSTS
348
349 (a) Spring Born
350
351 Final winter   Days= 180.00
352

353 STEER	Quantity	Quantity	Value	Cost	Total
354	/day(kg)	(kg)	£/tonne	£/head	£/head
355 Concentrates	2.00	360.00	150.00	54.00	
356 Straw	1.00	180.00	40.00	7.20	
357 Vet & Med.				1.00	
358 Hay	.00	.00	80.00	.00	
359 Silage	4.00	720.00	4.90	3.53	
360 Lowland grazing (ha)		.00	107.00	.00	65.73

361

362 HEIFER	Quantity	Quantity	Value	Cost	Total
363	/day(kg)	(kg)	£/tonne	£/head	£/head
364 Concentrates	1.50	270.00	150.00	40.50	
365 Straw	1.00	180.00	40.00	7.20	
366 Vet & Med.				1.00	
367 Hay	.00	.00	80.00	.00	
368 Silage	4.00	720.00	4.90	3.53	
369 Lowland grazing (ha)		.00	107.00	.00	52.23

370
371 (b) Autumn Born
372
373 STEER
374
375 Winter   Days= 180.00
376

377	Quantity	Quantity	Value	Cost	Total
378	/day(kg)	(kg)	£/tonne	£/head	£/head
379 Concentrates	4.00	720.00	150.00	108.00	
380 Straw	1.00	180.00	40.00	7.20	
381 Vet & Med.				1.00	
382 Hay	.00	.00	80.00	.00	
383 Silage	6.00	1080.00	4.90	5.29	
384 Lowland grazing (ha)		.00	107.00	.00	121.49
```

**Fig. 24.8**  Module 6 (Cells A336:H384) of suckler herd embryo transfer model.
```

	A	B	C	D	E	F	G
385							
386	Summer		Days=	90.00			
387							
388		Quantity	Quantity	Value	Cost	Total
389		/day(kg)	(kg)	£/tonne	£/head	£/head
390	Concentrates		.00	.00	150.00	.00	
391	Vet & Med.					.00	
392	Lowland grazing (ha)			.00	107.00	.00	.00
393							
394	HEIFER						
395							
396	Winter		Days=	180.00			
397							
398		Quantity	Quantity	Value	Cost	Total
399		/day(kg)	(kg)	£/tonne	£/head	£/head
400	Concentrates		2.00	360.00	150.00	54.00	
401	Straw		1.00	180.00	40.00	7.20	
402	Vet & Med.					1.00	
403	Hay		.00	.00	80.00	.00	
404	Silage		10.00	1800.00	4.90	8.82	
405	Lowland grazing (ha)			.00	107.00	.00	71.02
406							
407	Summer		Days=	90.00			
408							
409		Quantity	Quantity	Value	Cost	Total
410		/day(kg)	(kg)	£/tonne	£/head	£/head
411	Concentrates		.00	.00	150.00	.00	
412	Vet & Med.					.00	
413	Lowland grazing (ha)			.00	107.00	.00	.00
414							
415	TOTAL BEEF PRODUCTION COSTS						
416							
417	BORN TO COWS IN SUCKLER HERD						
418	Sale Spring born calf at 18 months-Steer						65.73
419	Sale Spring born calf at 18 months-Heifer						52.23
420	Sale Autumn born calf at 18 months-Steer						121.49
421	Sale Autumn born calf at 18 months-Heifer						71.02
422	BORN TO RECIPIENTS						
423	Sale Spring born calf at 18 months-Steer						65.73
424	Sale Spring born calf at 18 months-Heifer						52.23
425	Sale Autumn born calf at 18 months-Steer						121.49
426	Sale Autumn born calf at 18 months-Heifer						71.02
427	--

Fig. 24.9 Module 6 (Cells A385:H427) of suckler herd embryo transfer model.

	A	B	C	D	E	F	G

```
428  MODULE 7: MATURE COW - ANNUAL COSTS (INCLUDING CALF TO WEANING)
429
430  OUTPUT
431
432  Suckler cow premium                                    47.43
433  Compensatory allowance                                 54.50
434  Cull cows                                             500.00
435
436  VARIABLE COSTS
437
438  (a) Spring Calving
439                            Quantity    Value     Cost    Total
440                               (kg)   £/tonne   £/head   £/head
441
442  Concentrates (1)           150.00   200.00    30.00
443  Concentrates (2)           100.00   150.00    15.00
444  Straw                      200.00    40.00     8.00
445  Vet & Med.                                     5.00
446  Hay                           .00    80.00      .00
447  Silage                    1000.00     4.90     4.90
448  Upland grazing (ha)          1.00    18.50    18.50
449  Lowland grazing (ha)         .10    107.00    10.70    92.10
450
451  (a) Autumn Calving
452
453  Concentrates (1)           300.00   200.00    60.00
454  Concentrates (2)           180.00   150.00    27.00
455  Straw                      400.00    40.00    16.00
456  Vet & Med.                                     5.00
457  Hay                           .00    80.00      .00
458  Silage                    1000.00     4.90     4.90
459  Upland grazing (ha)          1.00    18.50    18.50
460  Lowland grazing (ha)         .10    107.00    10.70   142.10
461
462  -------------------------------------------------------------
463  MODULE 8: MATURE BULL - ANNUAL COSTS
464
465  OUTPUT
466
467  Cull                                                  900.00
468
469  VARIABLE COSTS
470
471                            Quantity    Value     Cost    Total
472                               (kg)   £/tonne   £/head   £/head
473
474  Concentrates (1)             .00    200.00      .00
475  Concentrates (2)          1000.00   150.00   150.00
476  Straw                      400.00    40.00    16.00
477  Vet & Med.                                     5.00
478  Hay                           .00    80.00      .00
479  Silage                    1000.00     4.90     4.90
480  Upland grazing (ha)          .00    18.50      .00
481  Lowland grazing (ha)         .20    107.00    21.40   197.30
482
483  -------------------------------------------------------------
```

Fig. 24.10 Modules 7 and 8 of suckler herd embryo transfer model.

```
    |  A   ||   B   ||   C   ||   D   ||   E   ||   F   ||   G   |

484  MODULE 9: RECIPIENTS
485
486  OUTPUT
487
488
489  Sale Value at 18 months (Failed)              500.00
490  Sale Value after weaning (Calved)             600.00
491  Purchase price at 12 months                   400.00
492
493  VARIABLE COSTS
494
495  (a) Purchase to sale of barren recipients (May)
496
497                      Days= 240.00
498
499            Quantity Quantity    Value      Cost     Total
500            /day(kg)     (kg)  £/tonne    £/head    £/head
501  Concentrates   2.00   480.00   150.00     72.00
502  Straw           .50   120.00    40.00      4.80
503  Vet & Med.                                 1.00
504  Hay             .00      .00    80.00       .00
505  Silage         8.00  1920.00     4.90      9.41
506  Lowland grazing (ha)      .10   107.00      7.04     94.24
507
508  (b) May to Calving (November)
509
510                      Days= 210.00
511
512            Quantity Quantity    Value      Cost     Total
513            /day(kg)     (kg)  £/tonne    £/head    £/head
514  Concentrates    .50   105.00   150.00     15.75
515  Vet & Med.                                 1.00
516  Lowland grazing (ha)      .25   107.00     15.39     32.14
517
518  (c) Calving to Sale (March)
519
520                      Days= 180.00
521
522            Quantity Quantity    Value      Cost     Total
523            /day(kg)     (kg)  £/tonne    £/head    £/head
524  Concentrates   3.00   540.00   150.00     81.00
525  Straw          1.00   180.00    40.00      7.20
526  Vet & Med.                                 1.00
527  Hay             .00      .00    80.00       .00
528  Silage        10.00  1800.00     4.90      8.82
529  Lowland grazing (ha)      .00   107.00       .00     98.02
530
531  (d) March to Sale (Late Summer)
532
533                      Days= 180.00
534
535            Quantity Quantity    Value      Cost     Total
536            /day(kg)     (kg)  £/tonne    £/head    £/head
537  Concentrates   1.00   180.00   150.00     27.00
538  Vet & Med.                                 1.00
539  Lowland grazing (ha)      .50   107.00     26.38     54.38
540
541
542  Total recipient variable costs - Failed              94.24
543  Total recipient variable costs - Calved             278.79
544
545  ----------------------------------------------------------------
```

Fig. 24.11 Module 9 of suckler herd embryo transfer model.

```
         |  A   ||   B   ||   C   ||   D   ||   E   ||   F   ||   G   ||   H   |

546   MODULE 10: MOET COSTS
547
548   Preparation of recipients            6.00
549   Embryo collection/flush             80.00
550   Embryo transfer/recipient           20.00
551   Maintenance of facilities         1000.00
552   Semen collection/bull/annum         50.00
553   Insemination cost                   10.00
554   --------------------------------------------------------------------
555   MODULE 11: GENETIC PROGRESS      Trait phenotypic average      220.00
556
557   1. Natural Mating
558
559                                        Bulls  Heifers
560   Natural replacements available       27.17    27.17
561   Natural replacments to be retained     .00     1.00
562
563   Selection Pathway (S=1:D=2:O=3)        231      231
564
565   Numbers selected
566   On sire record                           0        0
567   On dam record                            0        1
568   On own record                            0        0
569
570
571   2. Embryo Transfer
572
573                                        Bulls  Heifers
574   ET replacements available                7        7
575   ET replacements to be retained           2        7
576
577   Selection Pathway (S=1:D=2:O=3)        231      231
578
579   Numbers selected
580   On sire record                           0        0
581   On dam record                            0        7
582   On own record                            0        0
583
584
585
```

Fig. 24.12 Modules 10 and 11 (Cells A555 to H585) of suckler herd embryo transfer model.

Fig. 24.13 appears on pp. 242−3

	A	B	C	D	E	F	G	H	I	J	L
587	Pathway of gene transmission				Prop.	i	h2	sp	ih2sp		L
588					Selected						
590	NATURAL MATING										
592	Bull to Bull (1)				.00				.00		
593	Bull to Bull (2)				.00				.00		
594	Bull to Cow				.00				.00		2.50
595	Cow to Bull				.00	2.154			.00		4.50
596	Cow to Cow (1)				.04				.00		
597	Cow to Cow (2)				.00				.00		
599	MOET							Average Donor Age			
601	Bull to Bull (1)				.00		.20	33.00	.00		5.00
602	Bull to Bull (2)				.00		.20	33.00	.00		
603	Bull to Cow				.00		.20	33.00	.00		3.00
604	Cow to Bull				.00		.20	33.00	.00		
605	Cow to Cow (1)				.95	.109	.20	33.00	.72		7.00
606	Cow to Cow (2)				.00		.20	33.00	.00		
609	Annual rate of progress (%)								.72	17.00	
610									.02		

612	MODULE 12: FIXED COSTS AND ADDITIONAL INCOME		
613			
614	ADDITIONAL INCOME		Amount
615			
616	1.		
617	2.		
618	3.		
619			
620	FIXED COSTS		Cost
621			
622	1.	Labour	2940.00
623	2.	Power and Machinery	1680.00
624	3.	Rent	3600.00
625	4.	General Overheads	2100.00
626	5.		
627	6.		
628	7.		
629	8.		
630	9.		
631	10.		
632			
633			

Fig. 24.13 Module 11 (Cells A586 to J611) and 12 of suckler herd embryo transfer model.

	A	B	C	D	E	F	G	H
634	---
635	MODULE 13: FINANCIAL SUMMARY				Interest rate (%)		14.00	Year
636								
637	SECTION A: SETUP BUDGET							1.00
638	---
639	INCOME							
640						.00		
641						.00		
642	Comp. Allowances & Subs.			50.00	@	101.93		1.00
643	Cull Purebred Cows			8.25	@	500.00		1.00
644	Cull Purebred Bulls			1.55	@	900.00		1.00
645	18 Month Beef							
646	Recipients: Males-Spring			5.78	@	500.00		
647	Males-Autumn			.00	@	500.00		
648	Recipients: Heifers-Spring			.00	@	400.00		
649	Heifers-Autumn			.00	@	400.00		
650	Sucklers : Males-Spring			25.95	@	500.00		1.00
651	Males-Autumn			1.21	@	500.00		1.00
652	Sucklers : Heifers-Spring			24.89	@	400.00		1.00
653	Heifers-Autumn			1.21	@	400.00		1.00
654	Failed recipients			14.85	@	500.00		1.00
655	Calved recipients			14.85	@	600.00		
656								
657	EXPENDITURE							
658	Recipients (purchase)			30.00	@	400.00		1.00
659	FEEDING COSTS							
660	Recipients (Calved)			14.85	@	278.79		.28
661	Recipients (Failed)			14.85	@	94.24		.50
662	Heifer rearing:							
663	Recipients: Heifers-Spring			7.35	@	124.09		
664	Heifers-Autumn			.00	@	183.87		
665	Sucklers : Heifers-Spring			1.07	@	124.09		
666	Heifers-Autumn			.00	@	183.87		
667	Bull Rearing - From ET			1.57	@	329.76		
668	Bull Rearing - Natural			.00	@	329.76		
669	Beef Rearing:							
670	Recipients: Males-Spring			5.78	@	65.73		
671	Males-Autumn			.00	@	121.49		
672	Recipients: Heifers-Spring			.00	@	52.23		
673	Heifers-Autumn			.00	@	71.02		
674	Sucklers : Males-Spring			25.95	@	65.73		1.00
675	Males-Autumn			1.21	@	121.49		1.00
676	Sucklers : Heifers-Spring			24.89	@	52.23		1.00
677	Heifers-Autumn			1.21	@	71.02		1.00
678	Embryo Transfer							1.00
679	A.I.							1.00
680								
681	FIXED COSTS							
682	Labour			2940.00				.50
683	Power and Machinery			1680.00				.50
684	Rent			3600.00				.50
685	General Overheads			2100.00				.50
686				.00				.00
687				.00				.00
688				.00				.00
689				.00				.00
690				.00				.00
691				.00				.00
692								

Fig. 24.14 Module 13 (Cells A634:Q692) of suckler herd embryo transfer model.

I	J	K	L	M	N	O	P	Q
2.00	3.00	4.00	5.00	6.00	7.00	8.00	9.00	10.00
1.00	1.00	1.00	1.00	1.00	1.00	1.00	1.00	1.00
1.00	1.00	1.00	1.00	1.00	1.00	1.00	1.00	1.00
1.00	1.00	1.00	1.00	1.00	1.00	1.00	1.00	1.00
	1.00	1.00	1.00	1.00	1.00	1.00	1.00	1.00
	1.00	1.00	1.00	1.00	1.00	1.00	1.00	1.00
	1.00	1.00	1.00	1.00	1.00	1.00	1.00	1.00
	1.00	1.00	1.00	1.00	1.00	1.00	1.00	1.00
1.00	1.00	1.00	1.00	1.00	1.00	1.00	1.00	1.00
1.00	1.00	1.00	1.00	1.00	1.00	1.00	1.00	1.00
1.00	1.00	1.00	1.00	1.00	1.00	1.00	1.00	1.00
1.00	1.00	1.00	1.00	1.00	1.00	1.00	1.00	1.00
1.00	1.00	1.00	1.00	1.00	1.00	1.00	1.00	1.00
	1.00	1.00	1.00	1.00	1.00	1.00	1.00	1.00
1.00	1.00	1.00	1.00	1.00	1.00	1.00	1.00	1.00
.54	1.00	1.00	1.00	1.00	1.00	1.00	1.00	1.00
1.00	1.00	1.00	1.00	1.00	1.00	1.00	1.00	1.00
.11	.33	1.00	1.00	1.00	1.00	1.00	1.00	1.00
.11	.33	1.00	1.00	1.00	1.00	1.00	1.00	1.00
.11	.33	1.00	1.00	1.00	1.00	1.00	1.00	1.00
.11	.33	1.00	1.00	1.00	1.00	1.00	1.00	1.00
.18	.82	1.00	1.00	1.00	1.00	1.00	1.00	1.00
.18	.82	1.00	1.00	1.00	1.00	1.00	1.00	1.00
.33	.67	1.00	1.00	1.00	1.00	1.00	1.00	1.00
.33.	.67	1.00	1.00	1.00	1.00	1.00	1.00	1.00
.28	.72	1.00	1.00	1.00	1.00	1.00	1.00	1.00
.28	.72	1.00	1.00	1.00	1.00	1.00	1.00	1.00
1.00	1.00	1.00	1.00	1.00	1.00	1.00	1.00	1.00
1.00	1.00	1.00	1.00	1.00	1.00	1.00	1.00	1.00
1.00	1.00	1.00	1.00	1.00	1.00	1.00	1.00	1.00
1.00	1.00	1.00	1.00	1.00	1.00	1.00	1.00	1.00
1.00	1.00	1.00	1.00	1.00	1.00	1.00	1.00	1.00
1.00	1.00	1.00	1.00	1.00	1.00	1.00	1.00	1.00
1.00	1.00	1.00	1.00	1.00	1.00	1.00	1.00	1.00
1.00	1.00	1.00	1.00	1.00	1.00	1.00	1.00	1.00
1.00	1.00	1.00	1.00	1.00	1.00	1.00	1.00	1.00
1.00	1.00	1.00	1.00	1.00	1.00	1.00	1.00	1.00
.00	.00	.00	.00	.00	.00	.00	.00	.00
.00	.00	.00	.00	.00	.00	.00	.00	.00
.00	.00	.00	.00	.00	.00	.00	.00	.00
.00	.00	.00	.00	.00	.00	.00	.00	.00
.00	.00	.00	.00	.00	.00	.00	.00	.00
.00	.00	.00	.00	.00	.00	.00	.00	.00

```
        |  A   ||   B   ||   C   ||   D   ||   E   ||   F   ||   G   ||   H   |

693   SECTION B: FINANCIAL SUMMARY
694   ----------------------------------------------------------------------------
695   Year                                                                  1.00
696   ----------------------------------------------------------------------------
697   INCOME
698
699
700   Compensatory Allowances        50.00   @        101.93                 5097
701   Cull Purebred Cows              8.25   @        500.00                 4125
702   Cull Purebred Bulls             1.55   @        900.00                 1397
703   18 Month Beef
704   From Recipients - Males         5.78   @        500.00 *(1)
705   From Recipients - Heifers        .00   @    nc          *(1)
706   From Sucklers - Males          27.17   @        404.46 *(1)          13583
707   From Sucklers - Heifers        26.10   @        400.00 *(1)          10440
708   Failed recipients              14.85   @        500.00                 7425
709   Calved recipients              14.85   @        600.00
710                                                                     ---------
711   Total income                                                        42067
712
713   EXPENDITURE
714   Recipients (purchase)          30.00   @        400.00               12000
715   Feeding costs        Recipients (Calved)                             1159
716                        Recipients (Failed)                              700
717                        Heifer rearing
718                        Bull Rearing
719                        BEEF REARING
720                        From Recipients - Males
721                        From Recipients - Heifers
722                        From Sucklers - Males                            1853
723                        From Sucklers - Heifers                          1386
724
725   Embryo Transfer                                                       1792
726   A.I.                                                                     0
727
728   FIXED COSTS
729   Labour                                                                1470
730   Power and Machinery                                                    840
731   Rent                                                                  1800
732   General Overheads                                                     1050
733
734
735
736
737
738
739
740   INTEREST CHARGES
741                                                                     ---------
742   Total expenditure                                                   24050
743   ----------------------------------------------------------------------------
744   Surplus/(Deficit)                                                   18017
745   Closing Valuation
746   Cumulative Surplus/(Deficit)                                        18017
747   ----------------------------------------------------------------------------
748   *(1) Weighted average price for spring and autumn born calves.
```

Fig. 24.15 Module 13 (Cells A693:Q748) of suckler herd embryo transfer model.

I	J	K	L	M	N	O	P	Q
2.00	3.00	4.00	5.00	6.00	7.00	8.00	9.00	10.00
5097	5097	5097	5097	5097	5097	5097	5097	5097
4125	4125	4125	4125	4125	4125	4125	4125	4125
1397	1397	1397	1397	1397	1397	1397	1397	1397
	2891	2891	2891	2891	2891	2891	2891	2891
	0	0	0	0	0	0	0	0
13583	13583	13583	13583	13583	13583	13583	13583	13583
10440	10440	10440	10440	10440	10440	10440	10440	10440
7425	7425	7425	7425	7425	7425	7425	7425	7425
	8910	8910	8910	8910	8910	8910	8910	8910
42067	53868	53868	53868	53868	53868	53868	53868	53868
12000	12000	12000	12000	12000	12000	12000	12000	12000
2236	4140	4140	4140	4140	4140	4140	4140	4140
1400	1400	1400	1400	1400	1400	1400	1400	1400
115	345	1045	1045	1045	1045	1045	1045	1045
93	424	517	517	517	517	517	517	517
125	255	380	380	380	380	380	380	380
0	0	0	0	0	0	0	0	0
1853	1853	1853	1853	1853	1853	1853	1853	1853
1386	1386	1386	1386	1386	1386	1386	1386	1386
1792	1792	1792	1792	1792	1792	1792	1792	1792
0	0	0	0	0	0	0	0	0
2940	2940	2940	2940	2940	2940	2940	2940	2940
1680	1680	1680	1680	1680	1680	1680	1680	1680
3600	3600	3600	3600	3600	3600	3600	3600	3600
2100	2100	2100	2100	2100	2100	2100	2100	2100
0	0	0	0	0	0	0	0	0
31320	33914	34832	34832	34832	34832	34832	34832	34832
10747	19954	19035	19035	19035	19035	19035	19035	19035
								0
28764	48718	67754	86789	105825	124860	143895	162931	181966

Dairy cow ration formulation

Purpose: To formulate a daily food ration for a dairy cow on the basis of nutritional requirements and feed availability.

Authors: Nicolas Lampkin and Nigel Chapman

Spreadsheet Name: COWFEED

25.1 Introduction

The spreadsheet (Fig. 25.1) allows the estimation of a daily feed ration based upon specified feed requirements (metabolisable energy and digestible crude protein), dry matter intake capacity and feed availability.

Although not a least cost ration formulation program, the spreadsheet does allow rapid comparison of costs between different options allowing the decision maker to approach a least cost situation.

The procedure for developing a ration to meet the energy requirements and assessing dry matter intake capacity of the dairy cow is explained in detail in MAFF Reference Book 433 (HMSO, 1984). Feed requirements are broken down into those necessary for maintenance, milk production, pregnancy and for liveweight change. The relationships are explained below.

Digestible Crude Protein (DCP) requirements are based on data tables contained in Castle & Watkins (1979) and Nelson (1979). It should be noted that the DCP approach to meeting the protein requirement of ruminant livestock is being replaced by approaches which also take account of non-protein nitrogen which can be utilised by rumen microorganisms. These approaches, described in Orskov (1987) and Agricultural Research Council (1984), involve the estimation of undegradeable dietary protein (UDP) and rumen degradeable protein (RDP). However, standard data tables are not yet readily available for this approach to be adopted here.

The standard data are obtained from MAFF Reference Book 433 (HMSO, 1984), although this has to some extent been superceded by revised tables in MAFF (1986).

Other important nutritional factors, such as crude fibre and minerals, have not been included here but can readily be incorporated into the spreadsheet. Standard data are available from the sources indicated above.

25.2 The standard data set

The standard data set has been obtained from MAFF Reference Book 433 (HMSO, 1984) and the same code numbers have been used. It is entered in cells A64:F179 with the value 9999 entered in cell A180, and a space character entered as a Supercalc textual value ,(" "), in cells B180 and C180, to indicate the end of the data. This data is shown in Figs. 25.2 and 25.3. Own feed analyses can be entered if desired in the standard data table at codes 950-954 and 1350-1353. (Note that adjustments need to be made to manufacturers stated protein content to give a correct digestible crude protein value). Care should be taken to ensure that rows are not inserted outside the range specified in the VLOOKUP formulas (see Section 25.4.2).

25.3 Input data

25.3.1 Initial data input (F7:F13)

Data input is required as follows:

Data item	Location
Initial liveweight (kg)	F7
Average daily liveweight change (kg)	F8
Milk yield (kg/day)	F9
Butter fat content(g/kg)	F10
Solids not fat (g/kg)	F11
Days since calving	F12
Days pregnant	F13

25.3.2 Daily feed availability data (A37:E41)

Three items of data are required for the available feeds, viz.

Data item	Location
Feed code number - this refers to the code number used in the standard data	A37:A41
Quantity of feed (kg FW)	D37:D41
Cost of feed (£/t)	E37:E41

Space has been allowed for up to 5 feeds, but this can be extended if necessary. If less than 5 feeds are available then code number 9999 should be entered in column A.

25.4 Calculations

25.4.1 Daily feed requirements and dry matter intake capacity (A17:H29)

Formulas are required to estimate dry matter intake capacity (DMI) and metabolisable energy (ME) and digestible crude protein (DCP) requirements. The DMI capacity represents the maximum level of dry matter an animal could consume daily. The ME and DCP requirements are the levels needed to satisfy maintenance, milk production, pregnancy and liveweight change.

25.4.1.1 Maintenance (F23:H23)

To meet maintenance requirements, the following relationships apply:

DMI (kg DM) = 0.025*ILW (for mid-late lactation cows)
or
DMI = 0.025*ILW - 2.5   (for first 6 weeks of lactation)

(It should be noted that certain breeds such as Jersey cows have higher dry matter intake capacities than these figures would imply, especially in early lactation - for further details see Brigstocke et al.,(1982)).

ME (MJ) = $0.58*ILW^{0.73}$

DCP (g) = 90 + 0.4*ILW

where ILW is initial liveweight in kg

These formulas are entered in cells E23, F23 and G23 as follows:

F23 = IF(F12<42, .025*F7 - 2.5, .025*F7)
G23 = .58 * F7^.73
H23 = 90 + .4*F7

25.4.1.2 Milk production (F24:H24)

The equations used to calculate milk production requirements are:

DMI = 0.1*MY

ME = 1.694 * (0.0386*BF + 0.0205*SNF - 0.236)

DCP = MY * (8 + 1.23*BF)

where BF is butterfat (in g/kg),
SNF is solids not fat (in g/kg) and
MY is milk yield (in kg).

For further details see MAFF Reference Book 433, (HMSO, 1984)

These are entered in cells E24, F24 and G24 as follows:

F24 = .1 * F9
G24 = 1.694 * (.0386*F10 + .0205*F11 - .236)
H24 = F9 * (8 + 1.23*F10)

25.4.1.3 Pregnancy (G25:H25)

The equations used to calculate the requirements during pregnancy are:

ME = $1.13*e^{0.0106\,t}$
where t = number of days pregnant

DCP = 270g DCP per day for last 2 months before calving

For further details see MAFF Reference Book 433 (HMSO, 1984)

These are entered in cells F25 and G25 as follows:

G25 = 1.13 * EXP(.0106*F13)
H25 = IF(F13>210, 270, 0)

It has been suggested that dry matter intake declines in late pregancy, but no reliable data has been published in the sources examined to allow an equation to be included here.

25.4.1.4 Liveweight change (G26)

There is only an equation here for metabolisable energy:

ME = -28 MJ/kg liveweight loss
or
ME = +34 MJ/kg liveweight gain

For further details see MAFF Reference Book 433 (HMSO, 1984)

This is entered in cell G26 as:

G26 = IF(F8>0, F8*34, F8*28)

25.4.1.5 Totals

The formula for total DMI capacity is entered as:

F28 = SUM(F23:F26)

and then copied to cells G28 and H28.

25.4.2 *Daily Feed Availability (A32:I44)*

The code for feeds selected are entered in A37:A41. These codes are then used to VLOOKUP the standard data in A64:F180. The quantity of feed is entered in D37:D41, with the unit cost per tonne in E37:E41. Dry matter (DM), metabolisable energy (ME) and digestible crude protein (DCP) are then calculated in columns F to H from the standard data. The total cost per kg is calculated in column I.

The formulas for row 37 are as follows:

Description Part 1	B37 = VLOOKUP(A37,A64:F180,1)
Description Part 2	C37 = VLOOKUP(A37,A64:F180,2)
DM content (kg)	F37 = VLOOKUP(A37,A64:F180,3) * D37/1000
ME (MJ)	G37 = VLOOKUP(A37,A64:F180,4) * F37
DCP (G)	H37 = VLOOKUP(A37,A64:F180,5) * F37
Total cost (£)	I37 = D37*E37/1000

These can be copied down to rows 38 to 41 for the other feeds selected and the columns totalled in row 43 using

D43 = SUM(D37:D41)

which can then be copied across to cells F43:I43.

25.4.3 Daily Feed Balance (A48:G52)

The feed balances are calculated in cells F50:F52, these being the differences between the capacity/requirements in F28, G28 and H28 and the utilisation/availability in F43, G43 and H43, ie.

Dry Matter Capacity Available	F50 = F28-F43
Net ME Requirement	F51 = G28-G43
Net DCP Requirement	F52 = H28-H43

The DM capacity available (F50) indicates whether the DM content of the feed exceeds or is less than the DM intake capacity. The DM content should always be less than or equal to the maximum DM intake capacity, as the latter is the maximum amount of DM that is physically capable of being consumed.

The net ME and DCP requirements are likewise the differences between the ME and DCP required and available. A negative value indicates that the specified ration more than meets the requirements.

All the formulas used in the spreadsheet are displayed in Fig. 25.4.

References

Agricultural Research Council (1984). *The Nutrient Requirements of Ruminant Livestock, Supplement No. 1.* Commonwealth Agricultural Bureaux.

Brigstocke, T.D.A., Lindeman, M.A., Cuthbert, N.H., Wilson, P.N. and Cole J.P.L. (1982). A note on the dry matter intakes of Jersey cows. *Animal Production* **35**: 285-7.

Castle, M. E. & Watkins, P. (1979). *Modern Milk Production.* Faber.

HMSO, (1984). MAFF Reference Book 433, *Energy Allowances and Feeding Systems for Ruminants.*

MAFF (1986). *Feed Composition.* Chalcombe Publications.

Nelson, R. H. (1979). *An Introduction to Feeding Farm Livestock.* Pergamon.

Orskov, R. (1987). *The Feeding of Ruminants.* Chalcombe Publications.

```
         |  A  ||    B    ||  C   ||   D  ||   E   ||   F   ||   G   ||   H  ||   I  |
1    COWFEED - RATION FORMULATION FOR DAIRY COWS        Version 1.0 (2/09/1991)
2    Nicolas Lampkin & Nigel Chapman            UCW Aberystwyth
3    ************************************************************************
4
5    INITIAL DATA INPUT                                 Enter
6                                                       data:
7          Initial liveweight (kg)                       600
8          Av. daily liveweight change (kg)               .5
9          Milk yield (kg/day)                            25
10         Butter fat (g/kg)                              48
11         Solids not fat (g/kg)                          87
12         Days since calving                            330
13         Days pregnant                                 270
14
15   ************************************************************************
16
17   DAILY FEED REQUIREMENTS AND                         Dry
18   DRY MATTER INTAKE CAPACITY                         Matter  Metabo- Digestible
19                                                      Intake  lisable  Crude
20                                                     Capacity  Energy  Protein
21                                                     (kg DM)  (MJ ME)  (g DCP)
22                                                   ------------------------------
23                       Maintenance                   15.00    61.87     330
24                       Milk production                2.50     5.76    1676
25                       Pregnancy                       --     19.77     270
26                       Liveweight change               --     17.00      --
27                                                   ------------------------------
28                       TOTAL                         17.50   104.40    2276
29                                                   ==============================
30   ************************************************************************
31
32   DAILY FEED AVAILABILITY
33                                      Enter   Enter     DM
34   Enter                             Qnty    Cost  Content     ME     DCP    Total
35     Code    Description            (kgFW)   (£/t)   (kg)     (MJ)    (g)  Cost(£)
36   ----------------------------------------------------------------------------
37      804  Silage,grass highD       40.00   50.00    8.00    74.40  856.00    2.00
38     1205  Oats                      2.00  110.00    1.72    19.78  144.48     .22
39     1209  Beans,field spring        6.00  180.00    5.16    66.05 1279.68    1.08
40     9999                             .00     .00     .00      .00     .00     .00
41     9999                             .00     .00     .00      .00     .00     .00
42                                   ---------------------------------------------
43                                   48.00           14.88   160.23 2280.16    3.30
44                                   =============================================
45
46   ************************************************************************
47
48   DAILY FEED BALANCE
49
50         Dry Matter Capacity Available            2.62 kg
51         Net ME Requirement                     -55.83 MJ
52         Net DCP Requirement                     -4.16 g
53
54   ************************************************************************
55
56
```

Fig. 25.1 Dairy cow ration spreadsheet (Cells A1:I56).

```
            | A ||     B    ||   C   ||   D  ||   E  ||   F   |

57    STANDARD DATA
58    Data obtained from MAFF Reference Book 433 (HMSO 1984)
59    Energy allowance and feeding systems for ruminants
60    -------------------------------------------------
61                              DM (g   ME (MJ   DCP (g
62       No. Product Descript.  /kg FW） /kg DM)  /kg DM)
63    -------------------------------------------------
64       101 ArtichokeJerusalem   200    13.2      50
65       102 Carrots              130    12.8      62
66       104 Mangels,whiteflesh   110    12.5      64
67       105 Mangels, intermed.   120    12.4      58
68       106 Mangels, yellow      130    12.4      54
69       107 Mangels, long red    130    12.6      54
70       109 Potatoes             210    12.5      47
71       110 Sugar beet           230    13.7      35
72       111 Swede turnips        120    12.8      91
73       112 Turnip                90    11.2      73
74       201 Artichoke leaves     320     8.8      65
75       202 Carrot leaves        180     7.9     123
76       204 Mangel leaves        110      9      146
77       206 Sugar beet tops      160     9.9      88
78       207 Turnip leaves        120     9.2     130
79       301 Cabbage drumhead     110    10.4     100
80       302 Cabbage open-leaf    150    10.8     115
81       304 Kale 1000 head       160    11.1     106
82       305 Kale marrow          140     11      123
83       308 Mustard              150      9      126
84       309 Rape                 140     9.5     144
85       405 ForageRye inflower   230     9.5      88
86       501 Grass (pasture)      200    12.1     225
87       502 Grass (3-wk intrv)   200    12.1     185
88       503 Grass (monthintrv)   200    11.2     130
89       504 Grass (extensive)    200     10      124
90       505 Grass (winter)       200     9.7     101
91       507 Ryegrass,perennial   250     8.4      72
92       508 Ryegrass,Italian     250     8.7      84
93       509 Sorghum              200      8       60
94       510 Timothy in flower    250     8.5      52
95       601 Alsike               150     8.8     141
96       602 Crimson Clover       190     9.5     114
97       603 RedClover BgnFlowr   190    10.2     132
98       604 WhtClover BgnFlowr   190      9      152
99       605 Beans begin flower   150     9.2     154
100      606 Kidney vetch         180     8.7      77
101      607 Lucerne EarlyFlowr   240     8.2     130
102      608 Lucerne in bud       220     9.4     164
103      609 Lucerne before bud   150    10.2     213
104      610 Peas begin flowerg   170     8.5     140
105      611 SainfoinEarlyFlowr   230    10.3     143
106      612(Sainfoin FullFlowr   250     8.4     116
107      613 Trefoil              200      9      121
108      614 Vetches in flower    180     8.6     123
109      802 Silage,red clover    220     8.8     135
110      803 Silage,grs v.highD   200    10.2     116
111      804 Silage,grass highD   200     9.3     107
112      805 Silage,grass mod.D   200     8.8     102
113      806 Silage,grass low D   200     7.6      98
114      807 Silage,lucerne       250     8.5     113
115      808 Silage,maize         210    10.8      70
116      825 Silage,arable        270     9.6      82
117      904 Hay,RedClover good   850     8.9     103
118      905 Hay,RedClover poor   850     7.8      67
```

Fig. 25.2 Standard data for dairy cow ration spreadsheet (Cells A57:F118).

	A	B	C	D	E	F
119	907	Hay,grass v.high D		850	10.1	90
120	908	Hay,grass high D		850	9	58
121	909	Hay,grass mod. D		850	8.4	39
122	910	Hay,grass low D		850	7.5	45
123	911	Hay,grass v.low D		850	7	38
124	912	Hay,Lucerne Bef.Fl		850	8.3	143
125	913	Hay,Lucerne HalfFl		850	8.2	166
126	914	Hay,Lucerne FullFl		850	7.7	116
127	919	Hay,Rye Bef.Flower		850	9.5	85
128	920	Hay,SainfoinBef.Fl		850	9.2	129
129	921	Hay,Sainfoin in Fl		850	9	115
130	950	Silage 1 own anal.				
131	952	Silage 2 own anal.				
132	953	Hay 1 own analysis				
133	954	Hay 2 own analysis				
134	1101	Barley straw		860	7.3	9
135	1103	Bean straw		860	7.4	26
136	1106	Maize straw		850	7.3	20
137	1107	Oat straw		860	6.7	10
138	1109	Pea straw		860	6.5	50
139	1111	Rye straw		860	6.2	7
140	1114	Tare or vetch		860	6.3	48
141	1115	Wheat straw		860	5.6	1
142	1201	Barley		860	13.7	82
143	1202	Sorghum		860	13.4	87
144	1203	Maize		860	14.2	78
145	1204	Millet		860	11.3	92
146	1205	Oats		860	11.5	84
147	1207	Rye		860	14	110
148	1208	Wheat		860	14	105
149	1209	Beans,field spring		860	12.8	248
150	1210	Beans,field winter		860	12.8	209
151	1216	Peas		860	13.4	225
152	1217	Vetches		860	13.6	264
153	1237	Lucerne seed meal		880	14.1	316
154	1308	Cotton Cake Egypt.		900	8.7	203
155	1309	Cotton C. decort.		900	12.3	393
156	1310	Cotton C. semidec.		900	11.4	366
157	1311	Groundnut decort.		900	12.9	449
158	1312	Groundnut undecort		900	11.4	310
159	1332	Soya bean		900	13.3	454
160	1350	Comp. 1 Manuf.anal				
161	1351	Comp. 2 Manuf.anal				
162	1352	Comp. 3 Manuf.anal				
163	1353	Comp. 4 Manuf.anal				
164	1402	Fish meal		900	11.1	631
165	1409	Whole milk		128	20.2	250
166	1410	Buttermilk		92	15.7	368
167	1411	Milk separated		94	14.1	350
168	1414	Milk whey		66	14.5	91
169	1504	Brewers GrainFresh		220	10	149
170	1505	Brewers GrainEnsil		280	10	149
171	1506	Brewers GrainDried		900	10.3	145
172	1523	Maize, flaked		900	15	106
173	1528	Maize, gluten		900	13.5	223
174	1529	Maize, gluten		900	14.2	339
175	1550	Sugar Beet pressed		180	12.7	66
176	1551	Sugar Beet dried		900	12.7	59
177	1552	Sugar Beet molass.		900	12.2	61
178	1553	Sugar Beet		750	12.9	16
179	1556	Wheat middlings		880	10.1	126
180	9999					

Fig. 25.3 Standard data for dairy cow ration spreadsheet (Cells A119:F180).

Fig. 25.4 appears on pp. 258–9

A ||	B	||	C	|| D || E ||	F	

```
DAILY FEED REQUIREMENTS AND                                      Dry
DRY MATTER INTAKE CAPACITY                                     Matter
                                                              Intake
                                                            Capacity
                                                             (kg DM)
                                               ---------------------------------
                  Maintenance                  IF(F12<42,.025*F7-2.5,.025*F7)
                  Milk production              .1*F9
                  Pregnancy                               --
                  Liveweight change                       --
                                               ---------------------------------
                  TOTAL                        SUM(F23:F26)
                                               =================================
```

```
*******************************************************************************

DAILY FEED AVAILABILITY
                                       Enter   Enter                    DM
Enter                                   Qnty    Cost               Content
Code      Description                  (kgFW)   (£/t)                 (kg)
------------------------------------------------------------------------------
 804  VLU(A37,A64:E180,1) VLU(A37,A64:E180,2) 40    50   VLU(A37,A64:F180,3)*D37/1000
1205  VLU(A38,A64:E180,1) VLU(A38,A64:E180,2)  2   110   VLU(A38,A64:F180,3)*D38/1000
1209  VLU(A39,A64:E180,1) VLU(A39,A64:E180,2)  6   180   VLU(A39,A64:F180,3)*D39/1000
9999  VLU(A40,A64:E180,1) VLU(A40,A64:E180,2)  0     0   VLU(A40,A64:F180,3)*D40/1000
9999  VLU(A41,A64:E180,1) VLU(A41,A64:E180,2)  0     0   VLU(A41,A64:F180,3)*D41/1000
                                        ---------------------------------------
                                       SUM(D37:D41)      SUM(F37:F41)
                                       ========================================
```

```
*******************************************************************************

DAILY FEED BALANCE

      Dry Matter Capacity Available              F28-F43
      Net ME Requirement                         G28-G43
      Net DCP Requirement                        H28-H43

*******************************************************************************
```

Fig. 25.4 Formulas used in the dairy cow ration formulation spreadsheet. (Row numbers are shown between columns F and G)   (VLU=VLOOKUP)

```
       |              G               ||             H           ||     I     |
17
18                  Metabo-                    Digestible
19                  lisable                       Crude
20                   Energy                       Protein
21                  (MJ ME)                      (g DCP)
22     ----------------------------------------------------------------------
23      .58*F7^.73                      90+.4*F7
24      1.694*(.0386*F10+.0205*F11-.236) F9*(8+1.23*F10)
25      1.13*EXP(.0106*F13)             IF(F13>210,270,0)
26      IF(F8>0,F8*34,F8*28)            --
27     ----------------------------------------------------------------------
28      SUM(G23:G26)                    SUM(H23:H26)
29     ======================================================================
30     **********************************************************************
31
32
33
34                   ME                          DCP                  Total
35                  (MJ)                          (g)                Cost(£)
36     ----------------------------------------------------------------------
37      VLU(A37,A64:F180,4)*F37         VLU(A37,A64:F180,5)*F37  D37*E37/1000
38      VLU(A38,A64:F180,4)*F38         VLU(A38,A64:F180,5)*F38  D38*E38/1000
39      VLU(A39,A64:F180,4)*F39         VLU(A39,A64:F180,5)*F39  D39*E39/1000
40      VLU(A40,A64:F180,4)*F40         VLU(A40,A64:F180,5)*F40  D40*E40/1000
41      VLU(A41,A64:F180,4)*F41         VLU(A41,A64:F180,5)*F41  D41*E41/1000
42     ----------------------------------------------------------------------
43      SUM(G37:G41)                    SUM(H37:H41)             SUM(I37:I41)
44     ======================================================================
45
46     **********************************************************************
47
48
49
50      kg
51      MJ
52      g
53
54     **********************************************************************
```

are shown between columns F and G)   (VLU=VLOOKUP)